The Baltimore Catechism

The Doctrines of the Catholic Church – Lessons on God, His Commandments, Christ, Sin, Confession and Prayer – the 1891 Edition

By Third Council of Baltimore

Published by Pantianos Classics

ISBN-13: 978-1-78987-356-6

First published in 1891

Contents

Part One

Lesson First: On the End of Man

1. Q. Who made the world?
A. God made the world.
2. Q. Who is God?
A. God is the Creator of heaven and earth, and of all things.
3. Q. What is man?
A. Man is a creature composed of body and soul, and made to the image and likeness of God.
6. Q. Why did God make you?
A. God made me to know Him, to love Him, and to serve Him in this world, and to be happy with Him for ever in heaven.
9. Q. What must we do to save our souls?
A. To save our souls, we must worship God by faith, hope, and charity; that is, we must believe in Him, hope in
Him, and love Him with all our heart.
10. Q. How shall we know the things which we are to believe?
A. We shall know the things which we are to believe from the Catholic Church, through which God speaks to us.
11. Q. Where shall we find the chief truths which the Church teaches?
A. We shall find the chief truths which the Church teaches in the Apostles' Creed.
12. Q. Say the Apostles' Creed.

Lesson Second: On God and His Perfections

13. Q. What is God?
A. God is a spirit infinitely perfect.
14. Q. Had God a beginning
A. God had no beginning; He always was and He always will be.
15. Q. Where is God?
A. God is everywhere.
16. Q. If God is everywhere, why do we not see Him?
A. We do not see God, because He is a pure spirit and cannot be seen with bodily eyes.
17. Q. Does God see us?
A. God sees us and watches over us.

18. Q. Does God know all things?

A. God knows all things, even our most secret thoughts, words, and actions.

19. Q. Can God do all things?

A. God can do all things, and nothing is hard or impossible to Him.

20. Q. Is God just, holy, and merciful?

A. God is all just, all holy, all merciful, as He is infinitely perfect.

Lesson Third: On the Unity and Trinity of God

21. Q. Is there but one God?

A. Yes; there is but one God.

22. Q. Why can there be but one God?

A. There can be but one God, because God, being supreme and infinite, cannot have an equal.

23. Q. How many Persons are there in God?

A. In God there are three Divine Persons, really distinct, and equal in all things-the Father, the Son, and the Holy Ghost.

24. Q. Is the Father God?

A. The Father is God and the first Person of the Blessed Trinity.

25. Q. Is the Son God?

A. The Son is God and the second Person of the Blessed Trinity.

26. Q. Is the Holy Ghost God?

A. The Holy Ghost is God and the third Person of the Blessed Trinity.

27. Q. What is the Blessed Trinity?

A. The Blessed Trinity is one God in three Divine Persons.

29. Q. Are the three Divine Persons one and the same God?

A. The three Divine Persons are one and the same God, having one and the same Divine nature.

Lesson Fourth: On the Angels and Our First Parents

34. Q. Which are the chief creatures of God?

A. The chief creatures of God are men and angels.

35. Q. What are angels?

A. Angels are bodiless spirits created to adore and enjoy God in heaven.

39. Q. Who were the first man and woman?

A. The first man and woman were Adam and Eve.

40. Q. Were Adam and Eve innocent and holy when they came from the hand of God?

A. Adam and Eve were innocent and holy when they came from the hand of God.

43. Q. Did Adam and Eve remain faithful to God?

A. Adam and Eve did not remain faithful to God; but broke His command by eating the forbidden fruit.

44. Q. What befell Adam and Eve on account of their sin?

A. Adam and Eve on account of their sin lost innocence and holiness, and were doomed to misery and death.

45. Q. What evil befell us through the disobedience of our first parents?

A. Through the disobedience of our first parents we all inherit their sin and punishment, as we should have shared in their happiness if they had remained faithful.

47. Q. What is the sin called which we inherit from our first parents?

A. The sin which we inherit from our first parents is called original sin.

50. Q. Was any one ever preserved from original sin?

A. The Blessed Virgin Mary, through the merit of her Divine Son, was preserved free from the guilt of original sin, and this privilege is called her Immaculate Conception.

Lesson Fifth: On Sin and Its Kinds

51. Q. Is original sin the only kind of sin?

A. Original sin is not the only kind of sin; there is another kind of sin, which we commit ourselves, called actual sin.

52. Q. What is actual sin?

A. Actual sin is any willful thought, word, deed or omission contrary to the law of God.

53. Q. How many kinds of actual sin are there?

A. There are two kinds of actual sin-mortal and venial.

54. Q. What is mortal sin?

A. Mortal sin is a grievous offense against the law of God.

57. Q. What is venial sin?

A. Venial sin is a slight offense against the law of God in matters of less importance; or in matters of great importance it is an offence committed with out sufficient reflection or full consent of the will.

59. Q. Which are the chief sources of sin?

A. The chief sources of sin are seven: Pride, Covetousness, Lust, Anger, Gluttony, Envy, and Sloth; and they are commonly called capital sins.

Lesson Sixth: On the Incarnation and Redemption

60. Q. Did God abandon man after he fell into sin?

A. God did not abandon man after he fell into sin, but promised him a Redeemer, who was to satisfy for man's sin and reopen to him the gates of heaven.

61. Q. Who is the Redeemer?
A. Our Blessed Lord and Saviour Jesus Christ is the Redeemer of mankind.

62. Q. What do you believe of Jesus Christ?
A. I believe that Jesus Christ is the Son of God, the second Person of the Blessed Trinity, true God and true man.

69. Q. What do you mean by the Incarnation?
A. By the Incarnation I mean that the Son of God was made man.

70. Q. How was the Son of God made man?
A. The Son of God was conceived and made man by the power of the Holy Ghost, in the womb of the Blessed Virgin Mary.

74. Q. On what day was the Son of God conceived and made man?
A. The Son of God was conceived and made man on Annunciation day-the day on which the angel Gabriel announced to the Blessed Virgin Mary that she was to be the Mother of God.

75. Q. On what day was Christ born?
A. Christ was born on Christmas day in a stable at Bethlehem, over nineteen hundred years ago.

Lesson Seventh: On Our Lord's Passion, Death, Resurrection, And Ascension

78. Q. What did Jesus Christ Suffer?
A. Jesus Christ suffered a bloody sweat, a cruel scourging, was crowned with thorns, and was crucified.

79. Q. On what clay did Christ die?
A. Christ died on Good Friday.

83. Q. Why did Christ suffer and die?
A. Christ suffered and died for our sins

89. Q. On what day did Christ rise from the dead?
A. Christ rose from the dead, glorious and immortal, on Easter Sunday, the third day after His death.

91. Q. After Christ had remained forty days on earth, whither did He go?
A. After forty days Christ ascended into heaven, and the day on which He ascended into heaven is called Ascension day.

Lesson Eighth: On the Holy Ghost and His Descent Upon the Apostles

- De-scent', the act of coming down.
- En-a'ble, to make able.
- En-light'en, to make them understand better.
- Pen'te-cost, the fiftieth day after Easter.
- Preach, declare publicly, spread by word of mouth.
- Sanc'ti-fy, to make holy.
- Strength'en, make strong.
- Whit'sun-day, white Sunday.

94. Q. Who is the Holy Ghost?
A. The Holy Ghost is the third Person of the Blessed Trinity.

97. Q. On what day did the Holy Ghost come down upon the Apostles?
A. The Holy Ghost came down upon the Apostles ten days after the Ascension of our Lord; and the day on which He came down upon the Apostles is called Whitsunday, or Pentecost.

99. Q. Who sent the Holy Ghost upon the Apostles?
A. Our Lord Jesus Christ sent the Holy Ghost upon the Apostles.

100. Q. Why did Christ send the Holy Ghost?
A. Christ sent the Holy Ghost to sanctify His Church, to enlighten and strengthen the Apostles, and to enable them to preach the Gospel.

Part Two

Lesson First: On the End of Man

1. Q. Who made the world?
A. God made the world.

2. Q. Who is God?
A. God is the Creator of heaven and earth, and of all things.

3. Q. What is man?
A. Man is a creature composed of body and soul, and made to the image and likeness of God.

4. Q. Is this likeness in the body or in the soul?
A. This likeness is chiefly in the soul.

5. Q. How is the soul like to God?
A. The soul is like God because it is a spirit that will never die, and has understanding and free will.

6. Q. Why did God make you?
A. God made me to know Him, to love Him, and to serve Him in this world, and to be happy with Him forever in the next.

7. Q. Of which must we take more care, our soul or our body?
A. We must take more care of our soul than of our body.

8. Q. Why must we take more care of our soul than of our body?
A. We must take more care of our soul than of our body, because in losing our soul we lose God and everlasting happiness.

9. Q. What must we do to save our souls?
A. To save our souls we must worship God by faith, hope, and charity; that is, we must believe in Him, hope in Him, and love Him with all our heart.

10. Q. How shall we know the things which we are to believe?
A. We shall know the things which we are to believe from the Catholic Church, through which God speaks to us.

11. Q. Where shall we find the chief truths which the Church teaches?
A. We shall find the chief truths which the Church teaches in the Apostles' Creed.

12. Q. Say the Apostles' Creed.
A. I believe in God, the Father Almighty, Creator of heaven and earth; and in Jesus Christ, His only Son, our Lord; who was conceived by the Holy Ghost, born of the Virgin Mary, suffered under Pontius Pilate, was crucified; died, and was buried. He descended into hell: the third day He arose again from the dead: He ascended into heaven, and sitteth at the right hand of God, the Father Almighty; from thence He shall come to judge the living and the dead. I believe in the Holy Ghost, the Holy Catholic Church, the communion of

Saints, the forgiveness of sins, the resurrection of the body, and the life ever-lasting. Amen.

Lesson Second: On God and His Perfections

13. Q. What is God?
A. God is a spirit infinitely perfect.
14. Q. Had God a beginning
A. God had no beginning; He always was and He always will be.
15. Q. Where is God?
A. God is everywhere.
16. Q. If God is everywhere, why do we not see Him?
A. We do not see God, because He is a pure spirit and cannot be seen with bodily eyes.
17. Q. Does God see us?
A. God sees us and watches over us.
18. Q. Does God know all things?
A. God knows all things, even our most secret thoughts, words, and actions.
19. Q. Can God do all things?
A. God can do all things, and nothing is hard or impossible to Him.
20. Q. Is God just, holy, and merciful?
A. God is all just, all holy, all merciful, as He is infinitely perfect.

Lesson Third: On the Unity and Trinity of God

21. Q. Is there but one God?
A. Yes; there is but one God.
22. Q. Why can there be but one God?
A. There can be but one God, because God, being supreme and infinite, cannot have an equal.
23. Q. How many Persons are there in God?
A. In God there are three Divine Persons, really distinct, and equal in all things-the Father, the Son, and the Holy Ghost.
24. Q. Is the Father God?
A. The Father is God and the first Person of the Blessed Trinity.
25. Q. Is the Son God?
A. The Son is God and the second Person of the Blessed Trinity.
26. Q. Is the Holy Ghost God?
A. The Holy Ghost is God and the third Person of the Blessed Trinity.
27. Q. What do you mean by the Blessed Trinity?
A. By the Blessed Trinity I mean one God in three Divine Persons.
28. Q. Are the three Divine Persons equal in all things?
A. The three Divine Persons are equal in all things.

29. Q. Are the three Divine Persons one and the same God?

A. The three Divine Persons are one and the same God, having one and the same Divine nature and substance.

30. Q. Can we fully understand how the three Divine Persons are one and the same God?

A. We cannot fully understand how the three Divine Persons are one and the same God, because this is a mystery.

31. Q. What is a mystery?

A. A mystery is a truth which we cannot fully understand.

Lesson Fourth: On Creation

32. Q. Who created heaven and earth, and all things?

A. God created heaven and earth, and all things.

33. Q. How did God create heaven and earth?

A. God created heaven and earth from nothing by His word only; that is, by a single act of His all-powerful will.

34. Q. Which are the chief creatures of God?

A. The chief creatures of God are angels and men.

33. Q. What are angels?

A. Angels are pure spirits without a body, created to adore and enjoy God in heaven.

36. Q. Were the angels created for any other purpose?

A. The angels were also created to assist before the throne of God and to minister unto Him; they have often been sent as messengers from God to man; and are also appointed our guardians.

37. Q. Were the angels, as God created them, good and happy?

A. The angels, as God created them, were good and happy.

38. Q. Did all the angels remain good and happy?

A. All the angels did not remain good and happy; many of them sinned and were cast into hell, and these are called devils or bad angels.

Lesson Fifth: On Our First Parents and the Fall

39. Q. Who were the first man and woman?

A. The first man and woman were Adam and Eve.

40. Q. Were Adam and Eve innocent and holy when they came from the hand of God?

A. Adam and Eve were innocent and holy when they came from the hand of God.

41. Q. Did God give any command to Adam and Eve?

A. To try their obedience God commanded Adam and Eve not to eat of a certain fruit which grew in the garden of Paradise.

42. Q. Which were the chief blessings intended for Adam and Eve had they remained faithful to God?

A. The chief blessings intended for Adam and Eve, had they remained faithful to God, were a constant state of happiness in this life and everlasting glory in the next.

43. Q. Did Adam and Eve remain faithful to God?

A. Adam and Eve did not remain faithful to God; but broke His command by eating the forbidden fruit.

44. Q. What befell Adam and Eve on account of their sin?

A. Adam and Eve, on account of their sin, lost innocence and holiness, and were doomed to sickness and death.

45. Q. What evil befell us on account of the disobedience of our first parents?

A. On account of the disobedience of our first parents, we all share in their sin and punishment, as we should have shared in their happiness if they had remained faithful.

46. Q. What other effects followed from the sin of our first parents?

A. Our nature was corrupted by the sin of our first parents, which darkened our understanding, weakened our will, and left in us a strong inclination to evil.

47. Q. What is the sin called which we inherit from our first parents?

A. The sin which we inherit from our first parents is called original sin.

48. Q. Why is this sin called original?

A. This sin is called original because it comes down to us from our first parents, and we are brought into the world with its guilt on our soul.

49. Q. Does this corruption of our nature remain in us after original sin is forgiven?

A. This corruption of our nature and other punishments remain in us after original sin is forgiven.

50. Q. Was any one ever preserved from original sin?

A. The Blessed Virgin Mary, through the merits of her Divine Son, was preserved free from the guilt of original sin, and this privilege is called her Immaculate Conception.

Lesson Sixth: On Sin and Its Kinds

51. Q. Is original sin the only kind of sin?

A. Original sin is not the only kind of sin; there is another kind of sin, which we commit ourselves, called actual sin.

52. Q. What is actual sin?

A. Actual sin is any willful thought, word, deed, or omission contrary to the law of God.

53. Q. How many kinds of actual sin are there?

A. There are two kinds of actual sin-mortal and venial.

54. Q. What is mortal sin?

A. Mortal sin is a grievous offense against the law of God.

55. Q. Why is this sin called mortal?

A. This sin is called mortal because it deprives us of spiritual life, which is sanctifying grace, and brings everlasting death and damnation on the soul.

56. Q. How many things are necessary to make a sin mortal?

A. To make a sin mortal three things are necessary: a grievous matter, sufficient reflection, and full consent of the will.

57. Q. What is venial sin?

A. Venial sin is a slight offense against the law of God in matters of less importance, or in matters of great importance it is an offense committed without sufficient reflection or full consent of the will.

58. Q. Which are the effects of venial sin?

A. The effects of venial sin are the lessening of the love of God in our heart, the making us less worthy of His help, and the weakening of the power to resist mortal sin.

59. Q. Which are the chief sources of sin?

A. The chief sources of sin are seven: Pride, Covetousness, Lust, Anger, Gluttony, Envy, and Sloth; and they are commonly called capital sins.

Lesson Seventh: On the Incarnation and Redemption

60. Q. Did God abandon man after he fell into sin?

A. God did not abandon man after he fell into sin, but promised him a Redeemer, who was to satisfy for man's sin and reopen to him the gates of heaven.

61. Q. Who is the Redeemer?

A. Our Blessed Lord and Saviour Jesus Christ is the Redeemer of mankind.

62. Q. What do you believe of Jesus Christ?

A. I believe that Jesus Christ is the Son of God, the second Person of the Blessed Trinity, true God and true man.

63. Q. Why is Jesus Christ true God?

A. Jesus Christ is true God because He is the true and only Son of God the Father.

64. Q. Why is Jesus Christ true man?

A. Jesus Christ is true man because He is the Son of the Blessed Virgin Mary and has a body and soul like ours.

65. Q. How many natures are there in Jesus Christ?

A. In Jesus Christ there are two natures, the nature of God and the nature of man.

66. Q. Is Jesus Christ more than one person?

A. No, Jesus Christ is but one Divine Person.

67. Q. Was Jesus Christ always God?

A. Jesus Christ was always God, as He is the second Person of the Blessed Trinity, equal to His Father from all eternity.

68. Q. Was Jesus Christ always man?

A. Jesus Christ was not always man, but became man at the time of His Incarnation.

69. Q. What do you mean by the Incarnation?

A. By the Incarnation I mean that the Son of God was made man.

70. Q. How was the Son of God made man?

A. The Son of God was conceived and made man by the power of the Holy Ghost, in the womb of the Blessed Virgin Mary.

71. Q. Is the Blessed Virgin Mary truly the Mother of God?

A. The Blessed Virgin Mary is truly the Mother of God, because the same Divine Person who is the Son of God is also the Son of the Blessed Virgin Mary.

72. Q. Did the Son of God become man immediately after the sin of our first parents?

A. The Son of God did not become man immediately after the sin of our first parents, but was promised to them as a Redeemer.

73. Q. How could they be saved who lived before the Son of God became man?

A. They who lived before the Son of God became man could be saved by believing in a Redeemer to come, and by keeping the commandments.

74. Q. On what day was the Son of God conceived and made man?

A. The Son of God was conceived and made man on Annunciation day-the day on which the Angel Gabriel announced to the Blessed Virgin Mary that she was to be the Mother of God.

75. Q. On what day was Christ born?

A. Christ was born on Christmas day in a stable at Bethlehem, over nineteen hundred years ago.

76. Q. How long did Christ live on earth?

A. Christ lived on earth about thirty-three years, and led a most holy life in poverty and suffering.

77. Q. Why did Christ live so long on earth?

A. Christ lived so long on earth to show us the way to heaven by His teachings and example.

Lesson Eighth: On Our Lord's Passion, Death, Resurrection, and Ascension

78. Q. What did Jesus Christ suffer?

A. Jesus Christ suffered a bloody sweat, a cruel scourging, was crowned with thorns, and was crucified.

79. Q. On what day did Christ die?

A. Christ died on Good Friday.

80. Q. Why do you call that day "good" on which Christ died so sorrowful a death?

A. We call that day "good" on which Christ died because by His death He showed His great love for man, and purchased for him every blessing.

81. Q. Where did Christ die?

A. Christ died on Mount Calvary.

82. Q. How did Christ die?

A. Christ was nailed to the Cross and died on it between two thieves.

83. Q. Why did Christ suffer and die?

A. Christ suffered and died for our sins.

84. Q. What lessons do we learn from the sufferings and death of Christ?

A. From the sufferings and death of Christ we learn the great evil of sin, the hatred God bears to it, and the necessity of satisfying for it.

85. Q. Where did Christ's soul go after His death?

A. After Christ's death His soul descended into hell.

86. Q. Did Christ's soul descend into the hell of the damned?

A. The hell into which Christ's soul descended was not the hell of the damned, but a place or state of rest called Limbo, where the souls of the just were waiting for Him.

87. Q. Why did Christ descend into Limbo?

A. Christ descended into Limbo to preach to the **souls** who were in prison- that is, to announce to them the joyful tidings of their redemption.

88. Q. Where was Christ's body while His soul was in Limbo?

A. While Christ's soul was in Limbo His body was in the holy sepulchre.

89. Q. On what day did Christ rise from the dead?

A. Christ rose from the dead, glorious and immortal, on Easter Sunday, the third day after His death.

90. Q. How long did Christ stay on earth after His resurrection?

A. Christ stayed on earth forty days after His resurrection to show that He was truly risen from the dead, and to instruct His Apostles.

91. Q. After Christ had remained forty days on earth whither did He go?

A. After forty days Christ ascended into heaven, and the day on which He ascended into heaven is called Ascension day.

92. Q. Where is Christ in heaven?

A. In heaven Christ sits at the right hand of God the Father Almighty.

93. Q. What do you mean by saying that Christ sits at the right hand Of God?

A. When I say that Christ sits at the right hand of God I mean that Christ as God is equal to His Father in all things, and that as man He is in the highest place in heaven next to God.

Lesson Ninth: On the Holy Ghost and His Descent Upon the Apostles

94. Q. Who is the Holy Ghost?
A. The Holy Ghost is the third Person of the Blessed Trinity.

95. Q. From whom does the Holy Ghost proceed?
A. The Holy Ghost proceeds from the Father and the Son.

96. Q. Is the Holy Ghost equal to the Father and the Son?
A. The Holy Ghost is equal to the Father and the Son, being the same Lord and God as They are.

97. Q. On what day did the Holy Ghost come down upon the Apostles?
A. The Holy Ghost came down upon the Apostles ten days after the Ascension of our Lord; and the day on which He came down upon the Apostles is called Whitsunday, or Pentecost.

98. Q. How did the Holy Ghost come down upon the Apostles?
A. The Holy Ghost came down upon the Apostles in the form of tongues of fire.

99. Q. Who sent the Holy Ghost upon the Apostles?
A. Our Lord Jesus Christ sent the Holy Ghost upon the Apostles.

100. Q. Why did Christ send the Holy Ghost?
A. Christ sent the Holy Ghost to sanctify His Church, to enlighten and strengthen the Apostles, and to enable them to preach the Gospel.

101. Q. Will the Holy Ghost abide with the Church forever?
A. The Holy Ghost will abide with the Church forever, and guide it in the way of holiness and truth.

Lesson Tenth: On the Effects of the Redemption

102. Q. Which are the chief effects of the Redemption?
A. The chief effects of the Redemption are two: The satisfaction of God's justice by Christ's sufferings and death, and the gaining of grace for men.

103. Q. What do you mean by grace?
A. By grace I mean a supernatural gift of God bestowed on us, through the merits of Jesus Christ, for our salvation.

104. Q. How many kinds of grace are there?
A. There are two kinds of grace, sanctifying grace and actual grace.

105. Q. What is sanctifying grace?
A. Sanctifying grace is that grace which makes the soul holy and pleasing to God.

106. Q. What do you call those graces or gifts of God by which we believe in Him, hope in Him, and love Him?
A. Those graces or gifts of God by which we believe in Him, and hope in Him, and love Him, are called the Divine virtues of Faith, Hope, and Charity.

107. Q. What is Faith?

A. Faith is a Divine virtue by which we firmly believe the truths which God has revealed.

108. Q. What is Hope?

A. Hope is a Divine virtue by which we firmly trust that God will give us eternal life and the means to obtain it.

109. Q. What is Charity?

A. Charity is a Divine virtue by which we love God above all things for His own sake, and our neighbor as ourselves for the love of God.

110. Q. What is actual grace?

A. Actual grace is that help of God which enlightens our mind and moves our will to shun evil and do good.

111. Q. Is grace necessary to salvation?

A. Grace is necessary to salvation, because without grace we can do nothing to merit heaven.

112. Q. Can we resist the grace of God?

A. We can and unfortunately often do resist the grace of God.

113. Q. What is the grace of perseverance?

A. The grace of perseverance is a particular gift of God which enables us to continue in the state of grace till death.

Lesson Eleventh: On the Church

114. Q. Which are the means instituted by our Lord to enable men at all times to share in the fruits of the Redemption?

A. The means instituted by our Lord to enable men at all times to share in the fruits of His Redemption are the Church and the Sacraments.

115. Q. What is the Church?

A. The Church is the congregation of all those who profess the faith of Christ, partake of the same Sacraments, and are governed by their lawful pastors under one visible head.

116. Q. Who is the invisible Head of the Church?

A. Jesus Christ is the invisible Head of the Church.

117. Q. Who is the visible Head of the Church?

A. Our Holy Father the Pope, the Bishop of Rome, is the Vicar of Christ on earth and the visible Head of the Church.

118. Q. Why is the Pope, the Bishop of Rome, the visible Head of the Church?

A. The Pope, the Bishop of Rome, is the visible Head of the Church because lie is the successor of St. Peter, whom Christ made the chief of the Apostles and the visible Head of the Church.

119. Q. Who are the successors of the other Apostles?

A. The successors of the other Apostles are the bishops of the Holy Catholic Church.

120. Q. Why did Christ found the Church?

A. Christ founded the Church to teach, govern, sanctify, and save all men.

121. Q. Are all bound to belong to the Church?

A. All are bound to belong to the Church, and he who knows the Church to be the true Church and remains out of it cannot be saved.

Lesson Twelfth: On the Attributes and Marks of the Church

122. Q. Which are the attributes of the Church?

A. The attributes of the Church are three: authority infallibility, and indefectibility.

123. Q. What do you mean by the authority of the Church?

A. By the authority of the Church I mean the right and power which the Pope and the bishops, as the successors of the Apostles, have to teach and to govern the faithful.

124. Q. What do you mean by the infallibility of the Church?

A. By the infallibility of the Church I mean that the Church cannot err when it teaches a doctrine of faith or morals.

125. Q. When does the Church teach infallibly?

A. The Church teaches infallibly when it speaks through the Pope and the bishops, united in general council, or through the Pope alone when he proclaims to all the faithful a doctrine of faith or morals.

126. Q. What o you mean by the indefectibility of the Church?

A. By the indefectibility of the Church I mean that the Church, as Christ founded it, will last till the end of time.

127. Q. In whom are these attributes found in their fullness?

A. These attributes are found in their fullness in the Pope, the visible Head of the Church, whose infallible authority to teach bishops, priests, and people in matters of faith or morals will last till the end of the world.

128. Q. Has the Church any marks by which it may be known?

A. The Church has four marks by which it may be known: it is One; it is Holy; it is Catholic; it is Apostolic.

129. Q. How is the Church One?

A. The Church is One because all its members agree in one faith, are all in one communion, and are all under one Head.

130. Q. How is the Church Holy?

A. The Church is Holy because its founder, Jesus Christ, is holy; because it teaches a holy doctrine; invites all to a holy life; and because of the eminent holiness of so many thousands of its children.

131. Q. How is the Church Catholic or universal?

A. The Church is Catholic or universal because it subsists in all ages, teaches all nations, and maintains all truth.

132. Q. How is the Church Apostolic?

A. The Church is Apostolic because it was founded by Christ on His Apostles, and is governed by their lawful successors, and because it has never ceased, and never will cease, to teach their doctrine.

133. Q. In which Church are these attributes and marks found?

A. These attributes and marks are found in the Holy Roman Catholic Church alone.

134. Q. From whom does the Church derive its undying life and infallible authority?

A. The Church derives its undying life and infallible authority from the Holy Ghost, the spirit of truth, who abides with it forever.

135. Q. By whom is the Church made and kept One, Holy, and Catholic?

A. The Church is made and kept One, Holy, and Catholic by the Holy Ghost, the spirit of love and holiness, who unites and sanctifies its members throughout the world.

Lesson Thirteenth: On the Sacraments in General

136. Q. What is a Sacrament?

A. A Sacrament is an outward sign instituted by Christ to give grace.

137. Q. How many Sacraments are there?

A. There are seven Sacraments: Baptism, Confirmation, Holy Eucharist, Penance, Extreme Unction, Holy Orders, and Matrimony.

138. Q. Whence have the Sacraments the power of giving grace?

A. The Sacraments have the power of giving grace from the merits of Jesus Christ.

139. Q. What grace do the Sacraments give?

A. Some of the Sacraments give sanctifying grace, and others *increase* it in our souls.

140. Q. Which are the Sacraments that give sanctifying grace?

A. The Sacraments that give sanctifying grace are Baptism and Penance; and they are called Sacraments of the dead.

141. Q. Why are Baptism and Penance called Sacraments of the dead?

A. Baptism and Penance are called Sacraments of the dead, because they take away sin, which is the death of the soul, and give grace, which is its life.

142. Q. Which are the Sacraments that increase sanctifying grace in our soul?

A. The Sacraments that increase sanctifying grace in our soul are: Confirmation, Holy Eucharist, Extreme Unction, Holy Orders, and Matrimony; and they are called Sacraments of the living.

143. Q. Why are Confirmation, Holy Eucharist, Extreme Unction, Holy Orders, and Matrimony called Sacraments of the living?

A. Confirmation, Holy Eucharist, Extreme Unction, Holy Orders, and Matrimony are called Sacraments of the living, because those who receive them worthily are already living the life of grace.

144. Q. What sin does he commit who receives the Sacraments of the living in mortal sin?

A. He who receives the Sacraments of the living in mortal sin commits a sacrilege, which is a great sin, because it is an abuse of a sacred thing.

145. Q. Besides sanctifying grace do the Sacraments give any other grace?

A. Besides sanctifying grace the Sacraments give another grace, called sacramental.

146. Q. What is sacramental grace?

A. Sacramental grace is a special help which God gives, to attain the end for which He instituted each Sacrament.

147. Q. Do the Sacraments always give grace?

A. The Sacraments always give grace, if we receive them with the right dispositions.

148. Q. Can we receive the Sacraments more than once?

A. We can receive the Sacraments more than once, except Baptism. Confirmation, and Holy Orders.

149. Q. Why can we not receive Baptism, Confirmation, and Holy Orders more than once?

A. We cannot receive Baptism, Confirmation, and Holy Orders more than once, because they imprint a character in the soul.

150. Q. What is the character which these Sacraments imprint in the soul?

A. The character which these Sacraments imprint in the soul is a spiritual mark which remains forever.

151. Q. Does this character remain in the soul even after death?

A. This character remains in the soul even after death: for the honor and glory of those who are saved; for the shame and punishment of those who are lost.

Lesson Fourteenth: On Baptism

152. Q. What is Baptism?

A. Baptism is a Sacrament which cleanses us from original sin, makes us Christians, children of God, and heirs of heaven.

153. Q Are actual sins ever remitted by Baptism?

A. Actual sins and all the punishment due to them are remitted by Baptism, if the person baptized be guilty of any.

154. Q. Is Baptism necessary to salvation?

A. Baptism is necessary to salvation, because without it we cannot enter into the kingdom of heaven.

155. Q. Who can administer Baptism?

A. The priest is the ordinary minister of Baptism; but in case of necessity any one who has the use of reason may baptize.

156. Q. How is Baptism given?

A. Whoever baptizes should pour water on the head of the person to be baptized, and say, while pouring the water: *I baptize thee in the name of the Father, and of the Son, and of the Holy Ghost.*

157. Q. How many kinds of Baptism are there?

A. There are three kinds of Baptism: Baptism of water, of desire, and of blood.

158. Q. What is Baptism of water?

A. Baptism of water is that which is given by pouring water on the head of the person to be baptized, and saying at the same time: *I baptize thee in the name of the Father, and of the Son, and of the Holy Ghost.*

159. Q. What is Baptism of desire?

A. Baptism of desire is an ardent wish to receive Baptism, and to do all that God has ordained for our salvation.

160. Q. What is Baptism of blood?

A. Baptism of blood is the shedding of one's blood for the faith of Christ.

161. Q. Is Baptism of desire or of blood sufficient to produce the effects of Baptism of water?

A. Baptism of desire or of blood is sufficient to produce the effects of the Baptism of water, if it is impossible to receive the Baptism of water.

162. Q. What do we promise in Baptism?

A. In Baptism we promise to renounce the devil with all his works and pomps.

163. Q. Why is the name of a saint given in Baptism?

A. The name of a saint is given in Baptism in order that the person baptized may imitate his virtues and have him for a protector.

164. Q. Why are godfathers and godmothers given in Baptism?

A. Godfathers and godmothers are given in Baptism in order that they may promise, in the name of the child, what the child itself would promise if it had the use of reason.

165. Q. What is the obligation of a godfather and a godmother?

A. The obligation of a godfather and a godmother is to instruct the child in its religious duties, if the parents neglect to do so or die.

Lesson Fifteenth: On Confirmation

166. Q. What is Confirmation?

A. Confirmation is a Sacrament through which we receive the Holy Ghost to make us strong and perfect Christians and soldiers of Jesus Christ.

167. Q. Who administers Confirmation?

A. The bishop is the ordinary minister of Confirmation.

168. Q. How does the bishop give Confirmation?

A. The bishop extends his hands over those who are to be confirmed, prays that they may receive the Holy Ghost, and anoints the forehead of each with holy chrism in the form of a cross.

169. Q. What is holy chrism?

A. Holy chrism is a mixture of olive-oil and balm, consecrated by the bishop.

170. Q. What does the bishop say in anointing the person he confirms?

A. In anointing the person he confirms the bishop says: *I sign thee with the sign of the cross, and I confirm thee with the chrism of salvation, in the name of the Father, and of the Son, and of the Holy Ghost.*

171. Q. What is meant by anointing the forehead with chrism in the form of a cross?

A. By anointing the forehead with chrism in the form of a cross is meant, that the Christian who is confirmed must openly profess and practice his faith, never be ashamed of it, and rather die than deny it.

172. Q. Why does the bishop give the person he confirms a slight blow on the cheek?

A. The bishop gives the person he confirms a slight blow on the cheek, to put him in mind that he must be ready to suffer everything, even death, for the sake of Christ.

173. Q. To receive Confirmation worthily is it necessary to be in the state of grace?

A. To receive Confirmation worthily it is necessary to be in the state of grace.

174. Q. What special preparation should be made to receive Confirmation?

A. Persons of an age to learn should know the chief mysteries of faith and the duties of a Christian, and be instructed in the nature and effects of this Sacrament.

175. Q. Is it a sin to neglect Confirmation?

A. It is a sin to neglect Confirmation, especially in these evil days when faith and morals are exposed to so many and such violent temptations.

Lesson Sixteenth: On the Gifts and Fruits of the Holy Ghost

176. Q. Which are the effects of Confirmation?

A. The effects of Confirmation are an increase of sanctifying grace, the strengthening of our faith, and the gifts of the Holy Ghost.

177. Q. Which are the gifts of the Holy Ghost?

A. The gifts of the Holy Ghost are Wisdom, Understanding, Counsel, Fortitude, Knowledge, Piety and Fear of the Lord.

178. Q. Why do we receive the gift of Fear of the Lord?
A. We receive the gift of Fear of the Lord to fill us with a dread of sin.

179. Q. Why do we receive the gift of Piety?
A. We receive the gift of Piety to make us love God as a Father and obey Him because we love Him.

180. Q. Why do we receive the gift of Knowledge?
A. We receive the gift of Knowledge to enable us to discover the will of God in all things.

181. Q. Why do we receive the gift of Fortitude?
A. We receive the gift of Fortitude to strengthen us to do the will of God in all things.

182. Q Why do we receive the gift of Counsel?
A. We receive the gift of Counsel to warn us of the deceits of the devil, and of the dangers to salvation.

183. Q. Why do we receive the gift of Understanding?
A. We receive the gift of Understanding to enable us to know more clearly the mysteries of faith.

184. Q. Why do we receive the gift of Wisdom?
A. We receive the gift of Wisdom to give us a relish for the things of God, and to direct our whole life and all our actions to His honor and glory.

185. Q. Which are the Beatitudes?
A. The Beatitudes are:
- Blessed are the poor in spirit, for theirs is the kingdom of heaven.
- Blessed are the meek, for they shall possess the land.
- Blessed are they that mourn, for they shall be comforted.
- Blessed are they that hunger and thirst after justice, for they shall be filled.
- Blessed are the merciful, for they shall obtain mercy.
- Blessed are the clean of heart, for they shall see God.
- Blessed are the peacemakers, for they shall be called the children of God.
- Blessed are they that suffer persecution for justice sake, for theirs is the kingdom of heaven.

186. Q. Which are the twelve fruits of the Holy Ghost?
A. The twelve fruits of the Holy Ghost are Charity, Joy, Peace, Patience, Benignity, Goodness, Long-suffering, Mildness, Faith, Modesty, Continency, and Chastity.

Lesson Seventeenth: On the Sacrament of Penance

187. Q. What is the Sacrament of Penance?
A. Penance is a Sacrament in which the sins committed after Baptism are forgiven.

188. Q. How does the Sacrament of Penance remit sin, and restore to the soul the friendship of God?

A. The Sacrament of Penance remits sins and restores the friendship of God to the soul by means of the absolution of the priest.

189. Q. How do you know that the priest has the power of absolving from the sins committed after Baptism?

A. I know that the priest has the power of absolving from the sins committed after Baptism, because Jesus Christ granted that power to the priests of His Church when He said: *"Receive ye the Holy Ghost. Whose sins you shall forgive, they are forgiven them; whose sins you shall retain, they are retained."*

190. Q. How do the priests of the Church exercise the power of forgiving sins?

A. The priests of the Church exercise the power of forgiving sins by hearing the confession of sins, and granting pardon for them as ministers of God and in His name.

191. Q. What must we do to receive the Sacrament of Penance worthily?

A. To receive the Sacrament of Penance worthily we must do five things:

- We must examine our conscience.
- We must have sorrow for our sins.
- We must make a firm resolution never more to offend God.
- We must confess our sins to the priest.
- We must accept the penance which the priest gives us.

192. Q. What is the examination of conscience?

A. The examination of conscience is an earnest effort to recall to mind all the sins we have committed since our last worthy confession.

193. Q. How can we make a good examination of conscience?

A. We can make a good examination of conscience by calling to memory the commandments of God, the precepts of the Church, the seven capital sins, and the particular duties of our state in life, to find out the sins we have committed.

194. Q. What should we do before beginning the examination of conscience?

A. Before beginning the examination of conscience we should pray to God to give us light to know our sins and grace to detest them.

Lesson Eighteenth: On Contrition

195. Q. What is Contrition, or sorrow for sin?

A. Contrition, or sorrow for sin, is a hatred of sin and a true grief of the soul for having offended God, with a firm purpose of sinning no more.

196. Q. What kind of sorrow should we have for our sins?

A. The sorrow we should have for our sins should be interior, supernatural, universal, and sovereign.

197. Q. What do you mean by saying that our sorrow should be interior?

A. When I say that our sorrow should be interior, I mean that it should come from the heart, and not merely from the lips.

198. Q. What do you mean by saying that our sorrow should be supernatural?

A. When I say that our sorrow should be supernatural, I mean that it should be prompted by the grace of God, and excited by motives which spring from faith, and not by merely natural motives.

199. Q. What do you mean by saying that our sorrow should be universal?

A. When I say that our sorrow should be universal, I mean that we should be sorry for all our mortal sins without exception.

200. Q. What do you mean when you say that our sorrow should be sovereign?

A. When I say that our sorrow should be sovereign, I mean that we should grieve more for having offended God than for any other evil that can befall us.

201. Q. Why should we be sorry for our sins?

A. We should be sorry for our sins, because sin is the greatest of evils and an offense against God our Creator, Preserver, and Redeemer, and because it shuts us out of heaven and condemns us to the eternal pains of hell.

202. Q. How many]kinds of contrition are there?

A. There are two kinds of contrition: perfect contrition and imperfect contrition.

203. Q. What is perfect contrition?

A. Perfect contrition is that which fills us with sorrow and hatred for sin, because it offends God, who is infinitely good in Himself and worthy of all love.

204. Q. What is imperfect contrition?

A. Imperfect contrition is that by which we hate what offends God, because by it we lose heaven and deserve hell; or because sin is so hateful in itself.

205. Q. Is imperfect contrition sufficient for a worthy confession?

A. Imperfect contrition is sufficient for a worthy confession, but we should endeavor to have perfect contrition.

206. Q. What do you mean by a firm purpose of sinning no more?

A. By a firm purpose of sinning no more I mean a fixed resolve not only to avoid all mortal sin, but also its near occasions.

207. Q. What do you mean by the near occasions of sin?

A. By the near occasions of sin I mean all the persons, places, and things that may easily lead us into sin.

Lesson Nineteenth: On Confession

208. Q. What is Confession?

A. Confession is the telling of our sins to a duly authorized priest, for the purpose of obtaining forgiveness.

209. Q. What sins are we bound to confess?

A. We are bound to confess all our mortal sins. but it is well also to confess our venial sins.

210. Q. Which are the chief qualities of a good Confession?

A. The chief qualities of a good Confession are three: it must be humble, sincere, and entire.

211. Q. When is our Confession humble?

A. Our Confession is humble, when we accuse our selves of our sins, with a deep sense of shame and sorrow for having offended God.

212. Q. When is our Confession sincere?

A. Our Confession is sincere, when we tell our sins honestly and truthfully, neither exaggerating nor excusing them.

213. Q. When is our Confession entire?

A. Our Confession is entire, when we tell the number and kinds of our sins and the circumstances which change their nature.

214. Q. What should we do if we cannot remember the number of our sins?

A. If we cannot remember the number of our sins, we should tell the number as nearly as possible, and say how often we may have sinned in a day, a week, or a month, and how long the habit or practice has lasted.

215. Q. Is our Confession worthy if, without our fault, we forget to confess a mortal sin?

A. If without our fault we forget to confess a mortal sin, Tour Confession is worthy, and the sin is forgiven; but it must be told in Confession if it again comes to our mind.

216. Q. Is it a grievous offense willfully to conceal a mortal sin in Confession?

A. It is a grievous offense willfully to conceal a mortal sin in Confession, because we thereby tell a lie to the Holy Ghost, and make our Confession worthless.

217. Q. What must he do who has willfully concealed a mortal sin in Confession?

A. He who has willfully concealed a mortal sin in Confession must not only confess it, but must also repeat all the sins he has committed since his last worthy Confession.

218. Q. Why does the priest give us a penance after Confession?

A. The priest gives us a penance after Confession, that we may satisfy God for the temporal punishment due to our sins.

219. Q. Does not the Sacrament of Penance remit all punishment duo to sin?

A. The Sacrament of Penance remits the eternal punishment due to sin, but it does not always remit the temporal punishment which God requires as satisfaction for our sins.

220. Q. Why does God require a temporal punishment as a satisfaction for sin?

A. God requires a temporal punishment as a satisfaction for sin, to teach us the great evil of sin and to prevent us from falling again.

221. Q. Which are the chief means by which we satisfy God for the temporal punishment due to sin?

A. The chief means by which we satisfy God for the temporal punishment due to sin are: Prayer, Fasting, Almsgiving, all spiritual and corporal works of mercy, and the patient suffering of the ills of life.

222. Q. Which are the chief spiritual works of mercy?

A. The chief spiritual works of mercy are seven: To admonish the sinner, to instruct the ignorant, to counsel the doubtful, to comfort the sorrowful, to bear wrongs patiently, to forgive all injuries, and to pray for the living and the dead.

223. Q. Which are the chief corporal works of mercy?

A. The chief corporal works of mercy are seven: To feed the hungry, to give drink to the thirsty, to clothe the naked, to ransom the captive, to harbor the harborless, to visit the sick, and to bury the dead.

Lesson Twentieth: On the Manner of Making A Good Confession

224. Q. What should we do on entering the confessional?

A. On entering the confessional we should kneel, make the sign of the Cross, and say to the priest, Bless me, Father; then add, I confess to Almighty God and to you, Father, that I have sinned.

225. Q. Which are the first things we should tell. the priest in Confession?

A. The first things we should tell the priest in Confession are the time of our last Confession, and whether we said the penance and went to Holy Communion.

226. Q. After telling the time of our last Confession and Communion what should we do?

A. After telling the time of our last Confession and Communion we should confess all the mortal sins we have since committed, and all the venial sins we may wish to mention.

227. Q. What must we do when the confessor asks us questions?

A. When the confessor asks us questions we must answer them truthfully and clearly.

228. Q. What should we do after telling our sins?

A. After telling our sins we should listen with attention to the advice which the confessor may think proper to give.

229. Q. How should we and our Confession?

A. We should end our Confession by saying, *I also accuse myself of all the sins of my past life,* telling, if we choose, one or several of our past sins.

230. Q. What should we do while the priest is giving us absolution?

A. While the priest is giving us absolution we should from our heart renew the Act of Contrition.

Lesson Twenty-First: On Indulgences

231. Q. What is an Indulgence?

A. An Indulgence is the remission in whole or in part of the temporal punishment due to sin.

232. Q. Is an Indulgence a pardon of sin, or a license to commit sin?

A. An Indulgence is not a pardon of sin, nor a license to commit sin, and one who is in a state of mortal sin cannot gain an Indulgence.

233. Q. How many kinds of Indulgences are there?

A. There are two kinds of Indulgences-Plenary and Partial.

234. Q. What is a Plenary Indulgence?

A. A Plenary Indulgence is the full remission of the temporal punishment due to sin.

235. Q. What is a Partial Indulgence?

A. A Partial Indulgence is the remission of a part of the temporal punishment due to sin.

236. Q. How does the Church by means of Indulgences remit the temporal punishment due to sin?

A. The Church by means of Indulgences remits the temporal punishment due to sin by applying to us the merits of Jesus Christ, and the superabundant satisfactions of the Blessed Virgin Mary and of the saints; which merits and satisfactions are its spiritual treasury.

237. Q. What must we do to gain an Indulgence?

A. To gain an Indulgence we must be in the state of grace and perform the works enjoined.

Lesson Twenty-Second: On the Holy Eucharist

238. Q. What is the Holy Eucharist?

A. The Holy Eucharist is the Sacrament which contains the body and blood, soul and divinity, of our Lord Jesus Christ under the appearances of bread and wine.

239. Q. When did Christ institute the Holy Eucharist?

A. Christ instituted the Holy Eucharist at the Last Supper, the night before He died.

240. Q. Who were present when our Lord instituted the Holy Eucharist?

A. When our Lord instituted the Holy Eucharist the twelve Apostles were present.

241. Q. How did our Lord institute the Holy Eucharist?

A. Our Lord instituted the Holy Eucharist by taking bread, blessing, breaking, and giving to His Apostles, saying: *Take ye and eat. This is My body;* and then by taking the cup of wine, blessing and giving it, saying to them: *Drink ye all of this. This is My blood which shall be shed for the remission of Sins. Do this for a commemoration of Me.*

242. Q. What happened when our Lord said, This is My body; this is My blood?

A. When our Lord said, *This is My body,* the substance of the bread was changed into the substance of His body; when He said, *This is My blood,* the substance of the wine was changed into the substance of His blood.

243. Q. Is Jesus Christ whole and entire both under the form of bread and under the form of wine?

A. Jesus Christ is whole and entire both under the form of bread and Under the form of wine.

244. Q. Did anything remain of the bread and wine after their substance had been changed into the substance of the body and blood of our Lord?

A. After the substance of the bread and wine had been changed into the substance of the body and blood of our Lord there remained only the appearances **of** bread and wine.

245. Q. What do you mean by the appearances of bread and wine?

A. By the appearances of bread and wine I mean the figure, the color, the taste, and whatever appears to the senses.

246. Q. What is this change of the bread and wine into the body and blood of our Lord called?

A. This change of the bread and wine into the body and blood of our Lord is called Transubstantiation.

247. Q. How was the substance of the bread and wine changed into the substance of the body and blood of Christ?

A. The substance **of** the bread and wine was changed into the substance of the body and blood of Christ by His almighty power.

248. Q. Does this change of bread and wine into the body and blood of Christ continue to be made in the Church?

A. This change of bread and wine into the body and blood of Christ continues to be made in the Church by Jesus Christ through the ministry of His priests.

249. Q. When did Christ give His priests the power to change bread and wine into His body and blood?

A. Christ gave His priests the power to change bread and wine into His body and blood when He said to the Apostles, *Do this in commemoration of Me.*

250. Q. How do the priests exercise this power of changing broad and wine into the body and blood of Christ?

A. The priests exercise this power of changing bread and wine into the body and blood of Christ through the words of consecration in the Mass, which are the words of Christ: *This is My body; this is My blood.*

Lesson Twenty-Third: On the Ends for Which the Holy Eucharist Was Instituted

251. Q. Why did Christ institute the Holy Eucharist?

A. Christ instituted the Holy Eucharist:

1. To unite us to Himself and to nourish our soul with His divine life.
2. To increase sanctifying grace and all virtues in our soul.
3. To lessen our evil inclinations.
4. To be a pledge of everlasting life.
5. To fit our bodies for a glorious resurrection.
6. To continue the sacrifice of the Cross in His Church.

252. Q. How are we united to Jesus Christ in the Holy Eucharist?

A. We are united to Jesus Christ in the Holy Eucharist by means of Holy Communion.

253. Q. What is Holy Communion?

A. Holy Communion is the receiving of the body and blood of Christ.

254. Q. What is necessary to make a good Communion?

A. To make a good Communion it is necessary to be in the state of sanctifying grace, to have a right intention, and to obey the laws of fasting. (See Q. 257.)

255. Q. Does he who receives Communion in mortal sin receive the body and blood of Christ?

A. He who receives Communion in mortal sin receives the body and blood of Christ, but does not receive His grace, and he commits a great sacrilege.

256. Q. Is it enough to be free from mortal sin to receive Plentifully the graces of Holy Communion?

A. To receive plentifully the graces of Holy Communion it is not enough to be free from mortal sin, but we should be free from all affection to venial sin, and should make acts of faith, hope, and love.

257. Q. What is the fast necessary for Holy Communion?

A. The fast necessary for Holy Communion is to abstain from all food, beverages, and alcoholic drinks for one hour before Holy Communion. Water

33

may be taken at any time. The sick may take food, non-alcoholic drinks, and any medicine up to Communion time.

258. Q. Is any one ever allowed to receive Holy Communion when not fasting?

A. Any one in danger of death is allowed to receive Holy Communion when not fasting or when it is necessary to save the Blessed Sacrament from insult or injury.

259. Q. When are we bound to receive Holy Communion?

A. We are bound to receive Holy Communion, under pain of mortal sin, during the Easter time and when in danger of death.

260. Q. Is it well to receive Holy Communion often?

A. It is well to receive Holy Communion often, as nothing is a greater aid to a holy life than often to receive the Author of all grace and the Source of all good.

261. Q. What should we do after Holy Communion?

A. After Holy Communion we should spend some time in adoring our Lord, in thanking Him for the grace we have received, and in asking Him for the blessings we need.

Lesson Twenty-Fourth: On the Sacrifice of The Mass

262. Q. When and where are the bread and wine changed into the body and blood of Christ?

A. The bread and wine are changed into the body and blood of Christ at the Consecration in the Mass.

263. Q. What is the Mass?

A. The Mass is the unbloody sacrifice of the body and blood of Christ.

264. Q. What is a sacrifice?

A. A sacrifice is the offering of an object by a priest to God alone, and the consuming of it to acknowledge that He is the Creator and Lord of all things.

265. Q. Is the Mass the same sacrifice as that of the Cross?

A. The Mass is the same sacrifice as that of the Cross.

266. Q. How is the Mass the same sacrifice as that of the Cross?

A. The Mass is the same sacrifice as that of the Cross because the offering and the priest are the same-Christ our Blessed Lord; and the ends for which the sacrifice of the Mass is offered are the same as those of the sacrifice of the Cross.

267. Q. What were the ends for which the sacrifice of the Cross was offered?

A. The ends for which the sacrifice of the Cross was offered were:

1. To honor and glorify God;
2. To thank Him for all the graces bestowed on the whole world;
3. To satisfy God's justice for the sins of men;
4. To obtain all graces and blessings.

268. Q. Is there any difference between the sacrifice of the Cross and the sacrifice of the Mass?

A. Yes; the manner in which the sacrifice is offered is different. On the Cross Christ really shed His blood and was really slain; in the Mass there is no real shedding of blood nor real death, because Christ can die no more; but the sacrifice of the Mass, through the separate consecration of the bread and the wine, represents His death on the Cross.

269. Q. How should we assist at Mass?

A. We should assist at Mass with great interior recollection and piety and with every outward mark of respect and devotion.

270. Q. Which is the best manner of hearing Mass?

A. The best manner of hearing Mass is to offer it to God with the priest for the same purpose for which it is said, to meditate on Christ's sufferings and death, and to go to Holy Communion.

Lesson Twenty-Fifth: On Extreme Unction and Holy Orders

271. Q. What is the Sacrament of Extreme Unction?

A. Extreme Unction is the Sacrament which, through the anointing and prayer of the priest, gives health and strength to the soul, and sometimes to the body, when we are in danger of death from sickness.

272. Q. When should we receive Extreme Unction?

A. We should receive Extreme Unction when we are in danger of death from sickness, or from a wound or accident.

273. Q. Should we wait until we are in extreme danger before we receive Extreme Unction?

A. We should not wait until we are in extreme danger before we receive Extreme Unction, but if possible we should receive it whilst we have the use of our senses.

274. Q. Which are the effects of the Sacrament of Extreme Unction?

A. The effects of Extreme Unction are:

1. To comfort us in the pains of sickness and to strengthen us against temptation;

2. To remit venial sins and to cleanse our soul from the remains of sin;

3. To restore us to health, when God sees fit.

275. Q. What do you mean by the remains of sin?

A. By the remains of sin I mean the inclination to evil and the weakness of the will which are the result of our sins, and which remain after our sins have been forgiven.

276. Q. How should we receive the Sacrament of Extreme Unction?

A. We should receive the Sacrament of Extreme Unction in the state of grace, and with lively faith and resignation to the will of God.

277. Q. Who is the minister of the Sacrament of Extreme Unction?
A. The priest is the minister of the Sacrament of Extreme Unction.

278. Q. What is the Sacrament of Holy Orders?
A. Holy Orders is a Sacrament by which bishops, priests, and other ministers of the Church are ordained and receive the power and grace to perform their sacred duties.

279. Q. What is necessary to receive Holy orders worthily?
A. To receive Holy Orders worthily it is necessary to be in the state of grace, to have the necessary knowledge and a divine call to this sacred office.

280. Q. How should Christians look upon the priests of the Church?
A. Christians should look upon the priests of the Church as the messengers of God and the dispensers of His mysteries.

281. Q. Who can confer the Sacrament of Holy Orders?
A. Bishops can confer the Sacrament of Holy Orders.

Lesson Twenty-Sixth: On Matrimony

282. Q. What is the Sacrament of Matrimony?
A. The Sacrament of Matrimony is the Sacrament which unites a Christian man and woman in lawful marriage.

283. Q. Can a Christian man and woman be united in lawful marriage in any other way than by the Sacrament of Matrimony?
A. A Christian man and woman cannot be united in lawful marriage in any other way than by the Sacrament of Matrimony, because Christ raised marriage to the dignity of a Sacrament.

284. Q. Can the bond of Christian marriage be dissolved by any human power?
A. The bond of Christian marriage cannot be dissolved by any human power.

285. Q. Which are the effects of the Sacrament of Matrimony?
A. The effects of the Sacrament of Matrimony are:
1. To sanctify the love of husband and wife;
2. To give them grace to bear with each other's weaknesses;
3. To enable them to bring up their children in the fear and love of God.

286. Q. To receive the Sacrament of matrimony worthily is it necessary to be in the state of grace?
A. To receive the Sacrament of Matrimony worthily it is necessary to be in the state of grace, and it is necessary also to comply with the laws of the Church.

287. Q. Who has the right to make laws concerning the Sacrament of marriage?
A. The Church alone has the right to make laws concerning the Sacrament of marriage, though the state also has the right to make laws concerning the civil effects of the marriage contract.

288. Q. Does the Church forbid the marriage of Catholics with persons who have a different religion or no religion at all?

A. The Church does forbid the marriage of Catholics with persons who have a different religion or no religion at all.

289. Q. Why does the Church forbid the marriage of Catholics with persons who have a different religion or no religion at all?

A. The Church forbids the marriage of Catholics with persons who have a different religion or no religion at all, because such marriages generally lead to indifference, loss of faith, and to the neglect of the religious education of the children.

290. Q. Why do many marriages prove unhappy?

A. Many marriages prove unhappy because they are entered into hastily and without worthy motives.

291. Q. How should Christians prepare for a holy and happy marriage?

A. Christians should prepare for a holy and happy marriage by receiving the Sacraments of Penance and Holy Eucharist; by begging God to grant them a pure intention and to direct their choice; and by seeking the advice of their parents and the blessing of their pastors.

Lesson Twenty-Seventh: On the Sacramentals

292. Q. What is a sacramental?

A. A sacramental is anything set apart or blessed by the Church to excite good thoughts and to increase devotion, and through these movements of the heart to remit venial sin.

293. Q. What is the difference between the Sacraments and the sacramentals?

A. The difference between the Sacraments and the sacramentals is:

1. The Sacraments were instituted by Jesus Christ and the sacramentals were instituted by the Church;

2. The Sacraments give grace of themselves when we place no obstacle in the way; the sacramentals excite in us pious dispositions, by means of which we may obtain grace.

294. Q. Which is the chief sacramental used in the Church?

A. The chief sacramental used in the Church is the sign of the Cross.

295. Q. How do we make the sign of the Cross?

A. We make the sign of the Cross by putting the right hand to the forehead, then on the breast, and then to the left and right shoulders, saying, *In the name of the Father and of the Son, and of the Holy Ghost. Amen.*

296. Q. Why do we make the sign of the Cross?

A. We make the sign of the Cross to show that we are Christians and to profess our belief in the chief mysteries of our religion.

297. Q. How is the sign of the Cross a profession of faith in the chief mysteries of our religion?

A. The sign of the Cross is a profession of faith in the chief mysteries of our religion because it expresses the mysteries of the Unity and Trinity of God and of the Incarnation and death of our Lord.

298. Q. How does the sign of the Cross express the mystery of the Unity and Trinity of God?

A. The words, *In the name*, express the Unity of God; the words that follow, *of the Father, and of the Son*, and *of the Holy Ghost*, express the mystery of the Trinity.

299. Q. How does the sign of the Cross express the mystery of the Incarnation and death of our Lord?

A. The sign of the Cross expresses the mystery of the Incarnation by reminding us that the Son of God, having become man, suffered death on the cross.

300. Q. What other sacramental is in very frequent use?

A. Another sacramental in very frequent use is holy water.

301. Q. What is holy water?

A. Holy water is water blessed by the priest with solemn prayer to beg God's blessing on those who use it, and protection from the powers of darkness.

302. Q. Are there other sacramentals besides the sign of the Cross and holy water?

A. Besides the sign of the Cross and holy water there are many other sacramentals, such as blessed candles, ashes, palms, crucifixes, images of the Blessed Virgin and of the saints, rosaries, and scapulars.

Lesson Twenty-Eighth: On Prayer

303. Q. Is there any other means of obtaining God's grace than the Sacraments?

A. There is another means of obtaining God's grace, and it is prayer.

304. Q. What is prayer?

A. Prayer is the lifting up of our minds and hearts to God to adore Him, to thank Him for His benefits, to ask His forgiveness, and to beg of Him all the graces we need whether for soul or body.

305. Q. Is prayer necessary to salvation?

A. Prayer is necessary to salvation, and without it no one having the use of reason can be saved.

306. Q. At what particular times should we pray?

A. We should pray particularly on Sundays and holydays, every morning and night, in all dangers, temptations, and afflictions.

307. Q. How should we pray?

A. We should pray:

1. With attention;
2. With a sense of our own helplessness and dependence upon God;
3. With a great desire for the graces we beg of God;
4. With trust in God's goodness;
5. With perseverance.

308. Q. Which are the prayers most recommended to Us?

A. The prayers most recommended to us are the Lord's Prayer, the Hail Mary, the Apostles' Creed, the Confiteor, and the Acts of Faith, Hope, Love, and Contrition.

309. Q. Are prayers said with distractions of any avail?

A. Prayers said with willful distractions are of no avail.

Lesson Twenty-Ninth: On the Commandments of God

310. Q. is it enough to belong to God's Church in order to be saved?

A. It is not enough to belong to the Church in order to be saved, but we must also keep the Commandments of God and of the Church.

311. Q. Which are the Commandments that contain the whole law of God?

A. The Commandments which contain the whole law of God are these two:

1. Thou shalt love the Lord thy God with thy whole heart, with thy whole soul, with thy whole strength, and with thy whole mind;
2. Thou shalt love thy neighbor as thyself.

312. Q. Why do these two Commandments of the love of God and of our neighbor contain the whole law of God?

A. These two Commandments of the love of God and of our neighbor contain the whole law of God because all the other Commandments are given either to help us to keep these two, or to direct us how to shun what is opposed to them.

313. Q. Which are the Commandments of God?

A. The Commandments of God are these ten.

1. I am the Lord thy God, who brought thee out of the land of Egypt, out of the house of bondage. Thou shalt not have strange gods before Me. Thou shalt not make to thyself a graven thing, nor the likeness of anything that is in heaven above, or in the earth beneath, nor of those things that are in the waters under the earth. Thou shalt not adore them, nor serve them.
2. Thou shalt not take the name of the Lord thy God in vain.
3. Remember thou keep holy the Sabbath day.
4. Honor thy father and thy mother.
5. Thou shalt not kill.
6. Thou shalt not commit adultery.
7. Thou shalt not steal.

8. Thou shalt not bear false witness against thy neighbor.

9. Thou shalt not covet thy neighbor's wife.

10. Thou shalt not covet thy neighbor's goods.

314. Q. Who gave the Ten Commandments?

A. God Himself gave the Ten Commandments to Moses on Mount Sinai. and Christ our Lord confirmed them.

Lesson Thirtieth: On the First Commandment

315. Q. What is the first Commandment?

A. The first Commandment is: I am the Lord thy God: thou shalt not have strange gods before Me.

316. Q. How does the first Commandment help us to keep the great Commandment of the love of God?

A. The first Commandment helps us to keep the great Commandment of the love of God because it commands us to adore God alone.

317. Q. How do we adore God?

A. We adore God by faith, hope, and charity, by prayer and sacrifice.

318. Q. How may the first Commandment be broken?

A. The first Commandment may be broken by giving to a creature the honor which belongs to God alone; by false worship; and by attributing to a creature a perfection which belongs to God alone.

319. Q. Do those who make use of spells and charms, or who believe in dreams, in mediums, spiritists, fortune-tellers, and the like, sin against the first Commandment?

A. Those who make use of spells and charms, or who believe in dreams, in mediums, spiritists, fortunetellers and the like, sin against the first Commandment, because they attribute to creatures perfections which belong to God alone.

320. Q. Are sins against faith, hope and charity also sins against the first Commandment?

A. Sins against faith, hope, and charity are also sins against the first Commandment.

321. Q. How does a person sin against faith?

A. A person sins against faith:

1. by not trying to know what God has taught;

2. by refusing to believe all that God has taught;

3. by neglecting to profess his belief in what God has taught.

322. Q. How do we fail to try to know what God has taught?

A. We fail to try to know what God has taught by neglecting to learn the Christian doctrine.

323. Q. Who are they who do not believe all that God has taught?

A. They who do not believe all that God has taught are the heretics and infidels.

324. Q. Who are they who neglect to profess their belief in what-God has taught?

A. They who neglect to profess their belief in what God has taught are all those who fail to acknowledge the true Church in which they really believe.

325. Q. Can they who fail to profess their faith in the true Church in which they believe expect to be saved while in that state?

A. They who fail to profess their faith in the true Church in which they believe cannot expect to be saved while in that state, for Christ has said: " Whoever shall deny Me before men, I will also deny him before My Father who is in heaven."

326. Q. Are we obliged to make open profession of our faith?

A. We are obliged to make open profession of our faith as often as God's honor, our neighbor's spiritual good, or our own requires it. "Whosoever," says Christ, "shall confess Me before men, I will also confess him before My Father who is in heaven."

327. Q. Which are the sins against hope?

A. The sins against hope are presumption and despair.

328. Q. What is presumption?

A. Presumption is a rash expectation of salvation without making proper use of the necessary means to obtain it.

329. Q. What is despair?

A. Despair is the loss of hope in God's mercy.

330. Q. How do we sin against the love of God?

A. We sin against the love of God by all sin, but particularly by mortal sin.

Lesson Thirty-First: The First Commandment--On the Honor and Invocation of Saints

331. Q. Does the first Commandment forbid the honoring of the saints?

A. The first Commandment does not forbid the honoring of the saints, but rather approves of it; because by honoring the saints, who are the chosen friends of God, we honor God Himself.

332. Q. Does the first Commandment forbid us to pray to the saints?

A. The first Commandment does not forbid us to pray to the saints.

333. Q. What do we mean by praying to the saints?

A. By praying to the saints we mean the asking of their help and prayers.

334. Q. How do we know that the saints hear us?

A. We know that the saints hear us, because they are with God, who makes our prayers known to them.

335. Q. Why do we believe that the saints will help us?

A. We believe that the saints will help us because both they and we are members of the same Church. and they love us as their brethren.

336. Q. How are the saints and we members of the same Church?

A. The saints and we are members of the same Church, because the Church in heaven and the Church on earth are one and the same Church, and all its members are in communion with one another.

337. Q. What is the communion of the members of the Church called?

A. The communion of the members of the Church is called the communion of saints.

338. Q. What does the communion of saints mean?

A. The communion of saints means the union which **exists** between the members of the Church on earth with one another, and with the blessed in heaven and with the suffering souls in purgatory.

339. Q. What benefits are derived from the communion of saints?

A. The following benefits are derived from the communion of saints:--the faithful on earth assist one another by their prayers and good works, and they are aided by the intercession of the saints in heaven, while both the saints in heaven and the faithful on earth help the souls in purgatory.

340. Q. Does the first Commandment forbid us. to honor relics?

A. The first Commandment does not forbid us to honor relics, because relics are the bodies of the saints, or objects directly connected with them or with our Lord.

341. Q. Does the first Commandment forbid the making of images?

A. The first Commandment does forbid the making of images if they are made to be adored as gods, but it does not forbid the making of them to put us in mind of Jesus Christ, His Blessed Mother, and the saints.

342. Q. Is it right to show respect to the pictures and images of Christ and His saints?

A. It is right to show respect to the pictures and images of Christ and His saints, because they are the representations and memorials of them.

343. Q. Is it allowed to pray to the crucifix or to the images and relics of the saints?

A. It is not allowed to pray to the crucifix or images and relics of the saints, for they have no life, nor power to help us, nor sense to hear us.

344. Q. Why do we pray before the crucifix and the images and relics of the saints?

A. We pray before the crucifix and images and relics of the saints because they enliven our devotion by exciting pious affections and desires, and by reminding us of Christ and of the saints, that we may imitate their virtues.

Lesson Thirty-Second: From the Second to the Fourth Commandment

345. Q. What is the second Commandment?

A. The second Commandment is: Thou shalt not take the name of the Lord thy God in vain.

346. Q. What are we commanded by the second Commandment?

A. We are commanded by the second Commandment to speak with reverence of God and of the saints, and of all holy things, and to keep our lawful oaths and vows.

347. Q. What is an oath?

A. An oath is the calling upon God to witness the truth of what we say.

348. Q. When may we take an oath?

A. We may take an oath when it is ordered by lawful authority or required for God's honor or for our own or our neighbor's good.

349. Q. What is necessary to make an oath lawful?

A. To make an oath lawful it is necessary that what we swear to, be true, and that there be a sufficient cause for taking an oath.

350. Q. What is a vow?

A. A vow is a deliberate promise made to God to do something that is pleasing to Him.

351. Q. Is it a sin not to fulfill our vows?

A. Not to fulfill our vows is a sin, mortal or venial, according to the nature of the vow and the intention we had in making it.

352. Q. What is forbidden by the second Commandment?

A. The second Commandment forbids all false, rash, unjust, and unnecessary oaths, blasphemy, cursing, and profane words.

353. Q. What is the third Commandment?

A. The third Commandment is: Remember thou keep holy the Sabbath day.

354. Q. What are we commanded by the third Commandment?

A. By the third Commandment we are commanded to keep holy the Lord's day and the holydays of obligation, on which we are to give our time to the service and worship of God.

355. Q. How are we to worship God on Sundays and holydays of obligation?

A. We are to worship God on Sundays and holydays of obligation by hearing Mass, by prayer, and by other good works.

356. Q. Are the Sabbath day and the Sunday the same?

A. The Sabbath day and the Sunday are not the same. The Sabbath is the seventh day of the week, and is the day which was kept holy in the Old Law; the Sunday is the first day of the week, and is tile day which is kept holy in the New Law.

357. Q. Why does the Church command us to keep the Sunday holy instead of the Sabbath?

A. The Church commands us to keep the Sunday holy instead of the Sabbath because on Sunday Christ rose from the dead, and on Sunday He sent the Holy Ghost upon the Apostles.

358. Q. What is forbidden by the third Commandment?

A. The third Commandment forbids all unnecessary servile work and whatever else may hinder the due observance of the Lord's day.

359. Q. What are servile works?

A. Servile works are those which require labor rather of body than of mind.

360. Q. Are servile works on Sunday ever lawful?

A. Servile works are lawful on Sunday when the honor of God, the good of our neighbor, or necessity requires them.

Lesson Thirty-Third: From the Fourth to the Seventh Commandment

361. Q. What is the fourth Commandment?

A. The fourth Commandment is: Honor thy father and thy mother.

362. Q. What are we commanded by the fourth Commandment?

A. We are commanded by the fourth Commandment to honor, love, and obey our parents in all that is not sin.

363. Q. Are we bound to honor and obey others than our parents?

A. We are also bound to honor and obey our bishops, pastors, magistrates, teachers, and other lawful superiors.

364. Q. Have parents and superiors any duties towards those who are under their charge?

A. It is the duty of parents and superiors to take good care of all under their charge and give them proper direction and example.

365. Q. What is forbidden by the fourth Commandment?

A. The fourth Commandment forbids all disobedience, contempt, and stubbornness towards our parents or lawful superiors.

366. Q. What is the fifth Commandment?

A. The fifth Commandment is: Thou shalt not kill.

367. Q. What are we commanded by the fifth Commandment?

A. We are commanded by the fifth Commandment to live in peace and union with our neighbor, to respect his rights, to seek his spiritual and bodily welfare, and to take proper care of our own life and health.

368. Q. What is forbidden by the fifth Commandment?

A. The fifth Commandment forbids all willful murder, fighting, anger, hatred, revenge, and bad example.

369. Q. What is the sixth Commandment?

A. The sixth Commandment is: Thou shalt not commit adultery.

370. Q. What are we commanded by the sixth Commandment?

A. We are commanded by the sixth Commandment to be pure in thought and modest in all our looks, words, and actions.

371. Q. What is forbidden by the sixth Commandment?

A. The sixth commandment forbids all unchaste freedom with anothers wife or husband; also all immodesty with ourselves or others in looks, dress, words, or actions.

372. Q. Does the sixth Commandment forbid the reading of bad and immodest books and newspapers?

A. The sixth Commandment does forbid the reading of bad and immodest books and newspapers.

Lesson Thirty-Fourth: From the Seventh to the End of the Tenth Commandment

373. Q. What is the seventh Commandment?
A. The seventh Commandment is: Thou shalt not steal.
374. Q. What are we commanded by the seventh Commandment?
A. By the seventh Commandment we are commanded to give to all men what belongs to them and to respect their property.
375. Q. What is forbidden by the seventh Commandment?
A. The seventh Commandment forbids all unjust taking or keeping what belongs to another.
376. Q. Are we bound to restore ill-gotten goods?
A. We are bound to restore ill-gotten goods, or the value of them, as far as we are able; otherwise we can. not be forgiven.
377. Q. Are we obliged to repair the damage we have unjustly caused?
☐We are bound to repair the damage we have unjustly caused.
378. Q. What is the eighth Commandment?
A. The eighth Commandment is: Thou shalt not bear false witness against thy neighbor.
379. Q. What are we commanded by the eighth Commandment?
A. We are commanded by the eighth Commandment to speak the truth in all things and to be careful of the honor and reputation of every one.
380. Q. What is forbidden by the eighth Commandment?
A. The eighth Commandment forbids all rash judgments, backbiting, slanders, and lies.
381. Q. What must they do who have lied about their neighbor and seriously injured his character?
A. They who have lied about their neighbor and seriously injured his character must repair the injury done as far as they are able, otherwise they will not be forgiven.
382. Q. What is the ninth Commandment?
A. The ninth Commandment is: Thou shalt not covet thy neighbor's wife.
383. Q. What are we commanded by the ninth Commandment?
A. We are commanded by the ninth Commandment to keep ourselves pure in thought and desire.
384. Q. What is forbidden by the ninth Commandment?
A. The ninth Commandment forbids unchaste thoughts, desires of anothers wife or husband, and all other unlawful impure thoughts and desires.
385. Q. Are impure thoughts and desires always sins?

A. Impure thoughts and desires are always sins, unless they displease us and we try to banish them.

386. Q. What is the tenth Commandment?

A. The tenth Commandment is: Thou shalt not covet thy neighbor's goods.

387. Q. What are we commanded by the tenth Commandment?

A. By the tenth Commandment we are commanded to be content with what we have. and to rejoice in our neighbor's welfare.

389. Q. What is forbidden by the tenth Commandment?

A. The tenth Commandment forbids all desires to take or keep wrongfully what belongs to another.

Lesson Thirty-Fifth: On the First and Second Commandments of the Church

389. Q. Which are the chief commandments of the Church?

A. The chief commandments of the Church are six:

1. To hear Mass on Sundays and holydays of obligation.
2. To fast and abstain on the days appointed.
3. To confess at least once a year.
4. To receive the Holy Eucharist during the Easter time.
5. To contribute to the support of our pastors.
6. Not to marry persons who are not Catholics, or who are related to us within the third degree of kindred, nor privately without witnesses, nor to solemnize marriage at forbidden times.

390. Q. Is it a mortal sin not to hear Mass on a Sunday or a holyday of obligation?

A. It is a mortal sin not to hear Mass on a Sunday or a holyday of obligation, unless we are excused for a serious reason. They also commit a mortal sin who, having others under their charge, hinder them from hearing Mass, without a sufficient reason.

391. Q. Why were holydays instituted by the Church?

A. Holydays were instituted by the Church to recall to our minds the great mysteries of religion and the virtues and rewards of the saints.

392. Q. How should we keep the holydays of obligation?

A. We should keep the holydays of obligation as we should keep the Sunday.

393. Q. What do you mean by fast-days?

A. By fast-days I mean days on which we are allowed but one full meal.

394. Q. What do you mean by days of abstinence?

A. By days of abstinence I mean days on which we are forbidden to eat flesh-meat, but are allowed the usual number of meals.

395. Q. Why does the Church command us to fast and abstain?

A. The Church commands us to fast and abstain, in order that we may mortify our passions and satisfy for our sins.

396. Q. Why does the Church command us to abstain from flesh-meat on Fridays?

A. The Church commands us to abstain from flesh-meat on Fridays, in honor of the day on which our Saviour died.

Lesson Thirty-Sixth: On the Third, Fourth, Fifth and Sixth Commandments of the Church

397. Q. What is meant by the command of confessing at least once a year?

A. By the command of confessing at least once a year is meant that we are obliged, under pain of mortal sin, to go to confession within the year.

398. Q. Should we confess only once a year?

A. We should confess frequently, if we wish to lead a good life.

399. Q. Should children go to Confession?

A. Children should go to Confession when they are old enough to commit sin, which is commonly about the age of seven years.

400. Q. What sin does he commit who neglects to receive Communion during the Easter time?

A. He who neglects to receive Communion during the Easter time commits a mortal sin.

401. Q. What is the Easter time?

A. The Easter time is, in this country, the time between the first Sunday of Lent and Trinity Sunday.

402. Q. Are we obliged to contribute to the support of our pastors?

A. We are obliged to contribute to the support of our pastors, and to bear our share in the expenses of the church and school.

403. Q. What is the meaning of the commandment not to marry within the third degree of kindred?

A. The meaning of the commandment not to marry within the third degree of kindred is that no one is allowed to marry another within the third degree of blood relationship.

404. Q. What is the meaning of the command not to marry privately?

A. The command not to marry privately means that none should marry without the blessing of God's priests or without witnesses.

405. Q. What is the meaning of the precept not to solemnize marriage at forbidden times?

A. The meaning of the precept not to solemnize marriage at forbidden times is that during Lent and Advent the marriage ceremony should not be performed with pomp or a nuptial Mass.

406. Q. What is the nuptial Mass?

A. A nuptial Mass is a Mass appointed by the Church to invoke a special blessing upon the married couple.

407. Q. Should Catholics be married at a nuptial Mass?

A. Catholics should be married at a nuptial Mass, because they thereby show greater reverence for the holy Sacrament and bring richer blessings upon their wedded life.

Lesson Thirty-Seventh: On the Last Judgment and the Resurrection, Hell, Purgatory, and Heaven

408. Q. When will Christ judge us?

A. Christ will judge us immediately after our death, and on the last day.

409. Q. What is the judgment called which we have to undergo immediately after death?

A. The judgment we have to undergo immediately after death is called the Particular Judgment.

410. Q. What is the judgment called which all men have to undergo on the last day?

A. The judgment which all men have to undergo on the last day is called the General Judgment.

411. Q. Why does Christ judge men immediately after death?

A. Christ judges men immediately after death to reward or punish them according to their deeds.

412. Q. What are the rewards or punishments appointed for men's souls after the Particular Judgment?

A. The rewards or punishments appointed for men's souls after the Particular Judgment are Heaven, Purgatory, and Hell.

413. Q. What is Hell?

A. Hell is a state to which the wicked are condemned, and in which they are deprived of the sight of God for all eternity, and are in dreadful torments.

414. Q. What is Purgatory?

A. Purgatory is a state in which those suffer for a time who die guilty of venial sins, or without having satisfied for the punishment due to their sins.

415. Q. Can the faithful on earth help the souls in Purgatory?

A. The faithful on earth can help the souls in Purgatory by their prayers, fasts, alms-deeds; by indulgences, and by having Masses said for them.

416. Q. If every one is judged immediately after death, what need is there of a General Judgment?

A. There is need of a General Judgment, though every one is judged immediately after death, that the providence of God, which, on earth, often permits the good to suffer and the wicked to prosper, may in the end appear just before all men.

417. Q. Will our bodies share in the reward or punishment of our souls?

A. Our bodies will share in the reward or punishment of our souls, because through the resurrection they will again be united to them.

418. Q. In what state will the bodies of the just rise?

A. The bodies of the just will rise glorious and immortal.

419. Q. Will the bodies of the damned also rise?

A. The bodies of the damned will also rise, but they will be condemned to eternal punishment.

420. Q. What is Heaven?

A. Heaven is the state of everlasting life in which we see God face to face, are made like unto Him in glory. and enjoy eternal happiness.

421. Q. What words should we bear always in mind?

A. We should bear always in mind these words of our Lord and Saviour Jesus Christ: *"What doth it profit a man if he gain the whole world and suffer the loss of his own soul, or what exchange shall a man give for his soul? For the Son of man shall come in the glory of His Father with His angels; and then will He render to every man according to his works."*

Prayers

The Lord's Prayer

Our Father, who art in heaven, hallowed be Thy name. Thy kingdom come; Thy will be done on earth as it is in heaven. Give us this day our daily bread; and forgive us our trespasses as we forgive those who trespass against us; and lead us not into temptation, but deliver us from evil. Amen.

The Angelical Salutation

Hail Mary, full of grace! the Lord is with thee: blessed art thou amongst women, and blessed is the fruit of thy womb, Jesus. Holy Mary, Mother of God, pray for us sinners, now and at the hour of our death. Amen.

The Apostles' Creed

I believe in God, the Father Almighty, Creator of heaven and earth; and in Jesus Christ, His only Son, our Lord; who was conceived by the Holy Ghost, born of the Virgin Mary, suffered under Pontius Pilate, was crucified; died, and was buried. He descended into hell; the third day He arose again from the dead; He ascended into heaven, sitteth at the right hand of God, the Father Almighty; from thence He shall come to judge the living and the dead. I believe in the Holy Ghost the Holy Catholic Church, the communion of Saints, the forgiveness of sins, the resurrection of the body, and the life everlasting. Amen.

The Confiteor

I confess to Almighty God, to blessed Mary, ever Virgin, to blessed Michael the Archangel, to blessed John the Baptist, to the holy Apostles Peter and Paul, and to all the Saints, that I have sinned exceedingly in thought, word and deed, through, my fault, through my fault, through my most grievous fault. Therefore, I beseech blessed Mary, ever Virgin, blessed Michael the Archangel, blessed John the Baptist, the holy Apostles Peter and Paul, and all the Saints, to pray to the Lord our God for me. May the Almighty God have mercy on me, and forgive me my sins, and bring me to everlasting life. Amen.

May the Almighty and merciful Lord grant me pardon, absolution, and remission of all my sins. Amen.

An Act of Faith

O my God! I firmly believe that Thou art one God in three Divine persons, Father, Son, and Holy Ghost; I believe that Thy Divine Son became man, and died for our sins, and that he will come to, judge the living and the dead. I believe these and all the truths which the Holy Catholic Church teaches, because Thou hast revealed them, who canst neither deceive nor be deceived.

An Act of Hope

O my God! relying on Thy infinite goodness and promises, I hope to obtain pardon of my sins, the help of Thy grace, and life everlasting, through the merits of Jesus Christ, my Lord and Redeemer.

An Act of Love

O my God! I love Thee above all things, with my whole heart and soul, because Thou art all-good and worthy of all love. I love my neighbor as myself for the love of Thee. I forgive all who have injured me, and ask pardon of all whom I have injured.

An Act of Contrition

O my God! I am heartily sorry for having offended Thee, and I detest all my sins, because I dread the loss of heaven and the pains of hell; but most of all because they offend Thee, my God, who art all-good and deserving of all my love. I firmly resolve, with the help of Thy grace, to confess my sins, to do penance, and to amend my life.

The Blessing before Meals

† Bless us, o Lord! and these Thy gifts, which we are about to receive from Thy bounty, through Christ our Lord. Amen.

Grace after Meals

† We give Thee thanks for all Thy benefits, O Almighty God, who livest and reignest for ever; and may the souls of the faithful departed, through the mercy of God, rest in peace.
Amen.
The Manner in which a Lay Person is to Baptize in Case of Necessity:

Pour common water on the head or face of the person to be baptized say while pouring it:

"I baptize thee in the name of the Father, and of the Son, and of the Holy Ghost."

N.B. Any person of either sex who has reached the use of reason can baptize in case of necessity.

The Lessons of the Catechism

Lesson First: On the End of Man

Q. 126. What do we mean by the "end of man"?
A. By the "end of man" we mean the purpose for which he was created: namely, to know, love, and serve God.

Q. 127. How do you know that man was created for God alone?
A. I know that man was created for God alone because everything in the world was created for something more perfect than itself: but there is nothing in the world more perfect than man; therefore, he was created for something outside this world, and since he was not created for the Angels, he must have been created for God.

Q. 128. In what respect are all men equal?
A. All men are equal in whatever is necessary for their nature and end. They are all composed of a body and soul; they are all created to the image and likeness of God; they are all gifted with understanding and free will; and they have all been created for the same end -- God.

Q. 129. Do not men differ in many things?
A. Men differ in many things, such as learning, wealth, power, etc.; but these things belong to the world and not man's nature. He came into this world without them and he will leave it without them. Only the consequences of good or evil done in this world will accompany men to the next.

Q. 130. Who made the world?
A. God made the world.

Q. 131. What does "world" mean in this question?
A. In this question "world" means the universe; that is, the whole creation; all that we now see or may hereafter see.

Q. 132. Who is God?
A. God is the Creator of heaven and earth, and of all things.

Q. 133. What is man?
A. Man is a creature composed of body and soul, and made to the image and likeness of God.

Q. 134. Does "man" in the Catechism mean all human beings?
A. "Man" in the Catechism means all human beings, either men or women, boys, girls, or children.

Q. 135. What is a creature?

A. A creature is anything created, whether it has life or not; body or no body. Every being, person, or thing except God Himself may be called a creature.

Q. 136. Is this likeness in the body or in the soul?

A. This likeness is chiefly in the soul.

Q. 137. How is the soul like to God?

A. The soul is like to God because it is a spirit that will never die, and has understanding and free will.

Q. 138. Is every invisible thing a spirit?

A. Every spirit is invisible -- which means can not be seen; but every invisible thing is not a spirit. The wind is invisible, and it is not a spirit.

Q. 139. Has a spirit any other quality?

A. A spirit is also indivisible; that is, it can not be divided into parts, as we divide material things.

Q. 140. What do the words "will never die" mean?

A. By the words "will never die" we mean that the soul, when once created, will never cease to exist, whatever be its condition in the next world. Hence we say the soul is immortal or gifted with immortality.

Q. 141. Why then do we say a soul is dead while in a state of mortal sin?

A. We say a soul is dead while in a state of mortal sin, because in that state it is as helpless as a dead body, and can merit nothing for itself.

Q. 142. What does our "understanding" mean?

A. Our "understanding" means the "gift of reason," by which man is distinguished from all other animals, and by which he is enabled to think and thus acquire knowledge and regulate his actions.

Q. 143. Can we learn all truths by our reason alone?

A. We can not learn all truths by our reason alone, for some truths are beyond the power of our reason and must be taught to us by God.

Q. 144. What do we call the truths God teaches us?

A. Taken together, we call the truths God teaches us revelation, and we call the manner by which He teaches them also revelation.

Q. 145. What is "Free Will"?

A. "Free Will" is that gift of God by which we are enabled to choose between one thing and another; and to do good or evil in spite of reward or punishment.

Q. 146. Have brute animals "understanding" and "free will"?

A. Brute animals have not "understanding" and "free will." They have not "understanding" because they never change their habits or better their condition. They have not "free will" because they never show it in their actions.

Q. 147. What gift in animals supplies the place of reason?

A. In animals the gift of "instinct" supplies the place of reason in guiding their actions.

Q. 148. What is instinct?

A. "Instinct" is a gift by which all animals are impelled to follow the laws and habits that God has given to their nature.

Q. 149. Have men as well as brutes "instinct"?

A. Men have "instinct," and they show it when placed in sudden danger, when they have not time to use their reason. A falling man instantly grasps for something to support him.

Q. 150. Why did God make you?

A. God made me to know Him, to love Him, and to serve Him in this world, and to be

happy with Him forever in the next.

Q. 151. Why is it necessary to know God?

A. It is necessary to know God because without knowing Him we cannot love Him; and without loving Him we cannot be saved. We should know Him because He is infinitely true; love Him because He is infinitely beautiful; and serve Him because He is infinitely good.

Q. 152. Of which must we take more care, our soul or our body?

A. We must take more care of our soul than of our body.

Q. 153. Why must we take more care of our soul than of our body?

A. We must take more care of our soul than of our body, because in losing our soul we lose God and everlasting happiness.

Q. 154. What must we do to save our souls?

A. To save our souls, we must worship God by faith, hope, and charity; that is, we must believe in Him, hope in Him, and love Him with all our heart.

Q. 155. What does "worship" mean?

A. "Worship" means to give divine honor by acts such as the offering of prayer or sacrifice.

Q. 156. How shall we know the things which we are to believe?

A. We shall know the things which we are to believe from the Catholic Church, through which God speaks to us.

Q. 157. What do we mean by the "Church, through which God speaks to us"?

A. By the "Church, through which God speaks to us," we mean the "teaching Church"; that is, the Pope, Bishops, and priests, whose duty it is to instruct us in the truths and practices of our religion.

Q. 158. Where shall we find the chief truths which the Church teaches?

A. We shall find the chief truths which the Church teaches in the Apostles' Creed.

Q. 159. If we shall find only the "chief truths" in the Apostles' Creed, where shall we find the remaining truths?

A. We shall find the remaining truths of our Faith in the religious writings and preachings

that have been sanctioned by the authority of the Church.

Q. 160. Name some sacred truths not mentioned in the Apostles' Creed.

mention of the Real Presence of Our
nfallibility of the Pope, nor of the Im-
in Mary, nor of some other truths

reator of heaven and earth; and
was conceived by the Holy Ghost,
us Pilate, was crucified; died,
ird day He arose again from
he right hand of God, the Fa-
judge the living and the dead. I
ic Church, the communion of Saints,
on of the body, and the life everlasting.

son Second: On God and His Perfections

Q. 162. What is a perfection?
A. A perfection is any good quality a thing should have. A thing is perfect when it has all the good qualities it should have.

Q. 163. What is God?
A. God is a spirit infinitely perfect.

Q. 164. What do we mean when we say God is "infinitely perfect"?
A. When we say God is "infinitely perfect" we mean there is no limit or bounds to His perfection; for He possesses all good qualities in the highest possible degree and He alone is "infinitely perfect."

Q. 165. Had God a beginning?
A. God had no beginning; He always was and He always will be.

Q. 166. Where is God?
A. God is everywhere.

Q. 167. How is God everywhere?
A. God is everywhere whole and entire as He is in any one place. This is true and we must believe it, though we cannot understand it.

Q. 168. If God is everywhere, why do we not see Him?
A. We do not see God, because He is a pure spirit and cannot be seen with bodily eyes.

Q. 169. Why do we call God a "pure spirit'?
A. We call God a pure spirit because He has no body. Our soul is a spirit, but not a "pure" spirit, because it was created for union with our body.

Q. 170. Why can we not see God with the eyes of our body?
A. We cannot see God with the eyes of our body because they are created to see only material things, and God is not material but spiritual.

Q 171. Does God see us?
A. God sees us and watches over us.

Q. 172. Is it necessary for God to watch over u

A. It is necessary for God to watch over us, for with

we could not exist.

Q. 173. Does God know all things?

A. God knows all things, even our most secret thoughts,

Q. 174. Can God do all things?

A. God can do all things, and nothing is hard or impossible t

Q. 175. When is a thing said to be "impossible"?

A. A thing is said to be "impossible" when it cannot be done. Ma

that are impossible for creatures are possible for God.

Q. 176. Is God just, holy, and merciful?

A. God is all just, all holy, all merciful, as He is infinitely perfect.

Q. 177. Why must God be "just" as well as "merciful"?

A. God must be just as well as merciful because He must fulfill His promis

to punish those who merit punishment, and because He cannot be infinite in

one perfection without being infinite in all.

Q. 178. Into what sins will the forgetfulness of God's justice lead us?

A. The forgetfulness of God's justice will lead us into sins of presumption.

Q 179. Into what sins will the forgetfulness of God's mercy lead us?

A. The forgetfulness of God's mercy will lead us into sins of despair.

Lesson Third: On the Unity and Trinity of God

Q. 180. What does "unity," and what does "trinity" mean?

A. "Unity" means being one, and "trinity" means three-fold or three in one.

Q. 181. Can we find an example to fully illustrate the mystery of the Blessed Trinity?

A. We cannot find an example to fully illustrate the mystery of the Blessed Trinity, because the mysteries of our

holy religion are beyond comparison.

Q. 182. Is there but one God?

A. Yes; there is but one God.

Q. 183. Why can there be but one God?

A. There can be but one God because God, being supreme and infinite, cannot have an equal.

Q. 184. What does "supreme" mean?

A. "Supreme" means the highest in authority; also the most excellent or greatest possible in anything. Thus in all things God is supreme, and in the Church the Pope is supreme.

Q. 185. When are two persons said to be equal?

A. Two persons are said to be equal when one is in no way greater than or inferior to the other.

Q. 186. How many persons are there in God?

A. In God there are three Divine persons, really distinct, and equal in all things --the Father, the Son, and the Holy Ghost.

Q. 187. What do "divine" and "distinct" mean?

A. "Divine" means pertaining to God, and "distinct" means separate; that is, not confounded or mixed with any other thing.

Q. 188. Is the Father God?

A. The Father is God and the first Person of the Blessed Trinity.

Q. 189. Is the Son God?

A. The Son is God and the second Person of the Blessed Trinity.

Q. 190. Is the Holy Ghost God?

A. The Holy Ghost is God and the third Person of the Blessed Trinity.

Q. 191. Do "first," "second," and "third" with regard to the persons of the Blessed Trinity mean that one

person existed before the other or that one is greater than the other?

A. "First," "second," and "third" with regard to the persons of the Blessed Trinity do not mean that one person was before the other or that one is greater than the other; for all the persons of the Trinity are eternal and equal in every respect. These numbers are used to mark the distinction between the persons, and they show the order in which the one proceeded from the other.

Q. 192. What do you mean by the Blessed Trinity?

A. By the Blessed Trinity I mean one God in three Divine Persons.

Q. 193. Are the three Divine Persons equal in all things?

A. The three Divine Persons are equal in all things.

Q. 194. Are the three Divine Persons one and the same God?

A. The three Divine Persons are one and the same God, having one and the same Divine nature and substance.

Q. 195. What do we mean by the "nature" and "substance" of a thing?

A. By the "nature" of a thing we mean the combination of all the qualities that make the thing what it is. By the "substance" of a thing we mean the part that never changes, and which cannot be changed without destroying the nature of the thing.

Q. 196. Can we fully understand how the three Divine Persons are one and the same God?

A. We cannot fully understand how the three Divine Persons are one and the same God, because this is a mystery.

Q. 197. What is a mystery?

A. A mystery is a truth which we cannot fully understand.

Q. 198. Is every truth which we cannot understand a mystery?

A. Every truth which we cannot understand is not a mystery; but every revealed truth which no one can understand is a mystery.

Q. 199. Should we believe truths which we cannot understand?

A. We should and often do believe truths which we cannot understand when we have proof of their existence.

Q. 200. Give an example of truths which all believe, though many do not understand them.

A. All believe that the earth is round and moving, though many do not understand it. All believe that a seed planted in the ground will produce a flower or tree often with more than a thousand other seeds equal to itself, though many cannot understand how this is done.

Q. 201. Why must a divine religion have mysteries?

A. A divine religion must have mysteries because it must have supernatural truths and God Himself must teach them. A religion that has only natural truths, such as man can know by reason alone, fully understand and teach, is only a human religion.

Q. 202. Why does God require us to believe mysteries?

A. God requires us to believe mysteries that we may submit our understanding to Him.

Q. 203. By what form of prayer do we praise the Holy Trinity?

A. We praise the Holy Trinity by a form of prayer called the Doxology, which has come down to us almost from the time of the Apostles.

Q. 204. Say the Doxology.

A. The Doxology is: "Glory be to the Father, and to the Son, and to the Holy Ghost. As it was in the beginning, is now, and ever shall be, world without end. Amen."

Q. 205. Is there any other form of the Doxology?

A. There is another form of the Doxology, which is said in the celebration of the Mass. It is called the "Gloria in excelsis" or "Glory be to God on high," etc., the words sung by the Angels at the birth of Our Lord.

Lesson Fourth: On Creation

Q. 206. What is the difference between making and creating?

A. "Making" means bringing forth or forming out of some material already existing, as workmen do. "Creating" means bringing forth out of nothing, as God alone can do.

Q. 207. Has everything that exists been created?

A. Everything that exists except God Himself has been created.

Q. 208. Who created heaven and earth, and all things?

A. God created heaven and earth, and all things.

Q. 209. From what do we learn that God created heaven and earth and all things?

A. We learn that God created heaven and earth and all things from the Bible or Holy Scripture, in which the account of the Creation is given.

Q. 210. Why did God create all things?

A. God created all things for His own glory and for their or our good.

Q. 211. Did God leave all things to themselves after He had created them?

A. God did not leave all things to themselves after He had created them; He continues to preserve and govern them.

Q. 212. What do we call the care by which God preserves and governs the world and all it contains?

A. We call the care by which God preserves and governs the world and all it contains His providence.

Q. 213. How did God create heaven and earth?

A. God created heaven and earth from nothing by His word only; that is, by a single act of His all-powerful will.

Q. 214. Which are the chief creatures of God?

A. The chief creatures of God are angels and men.

Q. 215. How may God's creatures on earth be divided?

A. God's creatures on earth may be divided into four classes:

1.(1) Things that exist, as air;

2.(2) Things that exist, grow and live, as plants and trees;

3.(3) Things that exist, grow, live and feel, as animals;

4.(4) Things that exist, grow, live, feel and understand, as man.

Q. 216. What are angels?

A. Angels are pure spirits without a body, created to adore and enjoy God in heaven.

Q. 217. If Angels have no bodies, how could they appear?

A. Angels could appear by taking bodies to render themselves visible for a time; just as the Holy Ghost took the form of a dove and the devil took the form of a serpent.

Q. 218. Name some persons to whom Angels appeared.

A. Angels appeared to the Blessed Virgin and St. Joseph; also to Abraham, Lot, Jacob, Tobias and others.

Q. 219. Were the angels created for any other purpose?

A. The angels were also created to assist before the throne of God and to minister unto Him; they have often been sent as messengers from God to man; and are also appointed our guardians.

Q. 220. Are all the Angels equal in dignity?

A. All the Angels are not equal in dignity. There are nine choirs or classes mentioned in the Holy Scripture. The highest are called Seraphim and the lowest simply Angels. The Archangels are one class higher than ordinary Angels.

Q. 221. Mention some Archangels and tell what they did.

A. The Archangel Michael drove Satan out of heaven; the Archangel Gabriel announced to the Blessed Virgin that she was to become the Mother of God. The Archangel Raphael guided and protected Tobias.

Q. 222. Were Angels ever sent to punish men?

A. Angels were sometimes sent to punish men. An Angel killed 185,000 men in the army of a wicked king who had blasphemed God; an Angel also slew the first-born in the families of the Egyptians who had persecuted God's people.

Q. 223. What do our guardian Angels do for us?

A. Our guardian Angels pray for us, protect and guide us, and offer our prayers, good works and desires to God.

Q. 224. How do we know that Angels offer our prayers and good works to God?

A. We know that Angels offer our prayers and good works to God because it is so stated in Holy Scripture, and Holy Scripture is the Word of God.

Q. 225. Why did God appoint guardian Angels if He watches over us Himself?

A. God appointed guardian Angels to secure for us their help and prayers, and also to show His great love for us in giving us these special servants and faithful friends.

Q. 226. Were the angels, as God created them, good and happy?

A. The angels, as God created them, were good and happy.

Q. 227. Did all the angels remain good and happy?

A. All the angels did not remain good and happy; many of them sinned and were cast into hell, and these are called devils or bad angels.

Q. 228. Do we know the number of good and bad Angels?

A. We do not know the number of the good or bad Angels, but we know it is very great.

Q. 229. What was the devil's name before he fell, and why was he cast out of heaven?

A. Before he fell, Satan, or the devil, was called Lucifer, or light-bearer, a name which indicates great beauty. He was cast out of heaven because through pride he rebelled against God.

Q. 230. How do the bad Angels act toward us?

A. The bad Angels try by every means to lead us into sin. The efforts they make are called temptations of the devil.

Q. 231. Why does the devil tempt us?

A. The devil tempts us because he hates goodness, and does not wish us to enjoy the happiness which he himself has lost.

Q. 232. Can we by our own power overcome the temptations of the devil?

A. We cannot by our own power overcome the temptations of the devil, because the devil is wiser than we are;

for, being an Angel, he is more intelligent, and he did not lose his intelligence by falling into sin any more than we do now. Therefore, to overcome his temptations we need the help of God.

Lesson Fifth: On our First Parents and the Fall

Q. 233. Who were the first man and woman?

A. The first man and woman were Adam and Eve.

Q. 234. Are there any persons in the world who are not the descendants of Adam and Eve?

A. There are no persons in the world now, and there never have been any, who are not the descendants of Adam and Eve, because the whole human race had but one origin.

Q. 235. Do not the differences in color, figure, etc., which we find in distinct races indicate a difference in first parents?

A. The differences in color, figure, etc., which we find in distinct races do not indicate a difference in first parents, for these differences have been brought about in the lapse of time by other causes, such as climate, habits, etc.

Q. 236. Were Adam and Eve innocent and holy when they came from the hand of God?

A. Adam and Eve were innocent and holy when they came from the hand of God.

Q. 237. What do we mean by saying Adam and Eve "were innocent" when they came from the hand of
God?

A. When we say Adam and Eve "were innocent" when they came from the hand of God we mean they were in the state of original justice; that is, they were gifted with every virtue and free from every sin.

Q. 238. How was Adam's body formed?

A. God formed Adam's body out of the clay of the earth and then breathed into it a living soul.

Q. 239. How was Eve's body formed?

A. Eve's body was formed from a rib taken from Adam's side during a deep sleep which God caused to come upon him.

Q. 240. Why did God make Eve from one of Adam's ribs?

A. God made Eve from one of Adam's ribs to show the close relationship existing between husband and wife in their marriage union which God then instituted.

Q. 241. Could man's body be developed from the body of an inferior animal?

A. Man's body could be developed from the body of an inferior animal if God so willed; but science does not prove that man's body was thus formed, while revelation teaches that it was formed directly by God from the clay of the earth.

Q. 242. Could man's soul and intelligence be formed by the development of animal life and instinct?

A. Man's soul could not be formed by the development of animal instinct; for, being entirely spiritual, it must be created by God, and it is united to the body as soon as the body is prepared to receive it.

Q. 243. Did God give any command to Adam and Eve?

A. To try their obedience, God commanded Adam and Eve not to eat of a certain fruit which grew in the garden of Paradise.

Q. 244. What was the Garden of Paradise?

A. The Garden of Paradise was a large and beautiful place prepared for man's habitation upon earth. It was supplied with every species of plant and animal and with everything that could contribute to man's happiness.

Q. 245. Where was the Garden of Paradise situated?

A. The exact place in which the Garden of Paradise -- called also the Garden of Eden -- was situated is not known, for the deluge may have so changed the surface of the earth that old landmarks were wiped out. It was

probably some place in Asia, not far from the river Euphrates.

Q. 246. What was the tree bearing the forbidden fruit called?

A. The tree bearing the forbidden fruit was called "the tree of knowledge of good and evil."

Q. 247. Do we know the name of any other tree in the garden?

A. We know the name of another tree in the Garden called the "tree of life." Its fruit kept the bodies of our first parents in a state of perfect health.

Q. 248. Which were the chief blessings intended for Adam and Eve had they remained faithful to God?

A. The chief blessings intended for Adam and Eve, had they remained faithful to God, were a constant state of happiness in this life and everlasting glory in the next.

Q. 249. Did Adam and Eve remain faithful to God?

A. Adam and Eve did not remain faithful to God, but broke His command by eating the forbidden fruit.

Q. 250. Who was the first to disobey God?

A. Eve was the first to disobey God, and she induced Adam to do likewise.

Q. 251. How was Eve tempted to sin?

A. Eve was tempted to sin by the devil, who came in the form of a serpent and persuaded her to break God's command.

Q. 252. Which were the chief causes that led Eve into sin?

A. The chief causes that led Eve into sin were:

1.(1) She went into the danger of sinning by admiring what was forbidden, instead of avoiding it.

2.(2) She did not fly from the temptation at once, but debated about yielding to it.

Similar conduct on our part will lead us also into sin.

Q. 253. What befell Adam and Eve on account of their sin?

A. Adam and Eve, on account of their sin, lost innocence and holiness, and were doomed to sickness and death.

Q. 254. What other evils befell Adam and Eve on account of their sin?

A. Many other evils befell Adam and Eve on account of their sin. They were driven out of Paradise and condemned to toil. God also ordained that henceforth the earth should yield no crops without cultivation, and that

the beasts, man's former friends, should become his savage enemies.

Q. 255. Were we to remain in the Garden of Paradise forever if Adam had not sinned?

A. We were not to remain in the Garden of Paradise forever even if Adam had not sinned, but after passing through the years of our probation or trial upon earth we were to be taken, body and soul, into heaven without suffering death.

Q. 256. What evil befell us on account of the disobedience of our first parents?

A. On account of the disobedience of our first parents, we all share in their sin and punishment, as we should have shared in their happiness if they had remained faithful.

Q. 257. Is it not unjust to punish us for the sin of our first parents?

A. It is not unjust to punish us for the sin of our first parents, because their punishment consisted in being deprived of a free gift of God; that is, of the gift of original justice to which they had no strict right and which they willfully forfeited by their act of disobedience.

Q. 258. But how did the loss of the gift of original justice leave our first parents and us in mortal sin?

A. The loss of the gift of original justice left our first parents and us in mortal sin because it deprived them of the Grace of God, and to be without this gift of Grace which they should have had was to be in mortal sin. As all their children are deprived of the same gift, they, too, come into the world in a state of mortal sin.

Q. 259. What other effects followed from the sin of our first parents?

A. Our nature was corrupted by the sin of our first parents, which darkened our understanding, weakened our will, and left in us a strong inclination to evil.

Q. 260. What do we mean by "our nature was corrupted"?

A. When we say "our nature was corrupted" we mean that our whole being, body and soul, was injured in all its parts and powers.

Q. 261. Why do we say our understanding was darkened?

A. We say our understanding was darkened because even with much learning we have not the clear knowledge, quick perception and retentive memory that Adam had before his fall from grace.

Q. 262. Why do we say our will was weakened?

A. We say our will was weakened to show that our free will was not entirely taken away by Adam's sin, and that we have it still in our power to use our free will in doing good or evil.

Q. 263. In what does the strong inclination to evil that is left in us consist?

A. This strong inclination to evil that is left in us consists in the continual efforts our senses and appetites make to lead our souls into sin. The body is inclined to rebel against the soul, and the soul itself to rebel against God.

Q. 264. What is this strong inclination to evil called, and why did God permit it to remain in us?

A. This strong inclination to evil is called concupiscence, and God permits it to remain in us that by His grace we may resist it and thus increase our merits.

Q. 265. What is the sin called which we inherit from our first parents?

A. The sin which we inherit from our first parents is called original sin.

Q. 266. Why is this sin called original?

A. This sin is called original because it comes down to us from our first parents, and we are brought into the world with its guilt on our soul.

Q. 267. Does this corruption of our nature remain in us after original sin is forgiven?

A. This corruption of our nature and other punishments remain in us after original sin is forgiven.

Q. 268. Was any one ever preserved from original sin?

A. The Blessed Virgin Mary, through the merits of her Divine Son, was preserved free from the guilt of original sin, and this privilege is called her Immaculate Conception.

Q. 269. Why was the Blessed Virgin preserved from original sin?

A. The Blessed Virgin was preserved from original sin because it would not be consistent with the dignity of the Son of God to have His Mother, even for an instant, in the power of the devil and an enemy of God.

Q. 270. How could the Blessed Virgin be preserved from sin by her Divine Son, before her Son was born?

A. The Blessed Virgin could be preserved from sin by her Divine Son before He was born as man, for He always existed as God and foresaw His own future merits and the dignity of His Mother. He therefore by His future merits provided for her privilege of exemption from original sin.

Q. 271. What does the "Immaculate Conception" mean?

A. The Immaculate Conception means the Blessed Virgin's own exclusive privilege of coming into existence, through the merits of Jesus Christ, without the stain of original sin. It does not mean, therefore, her sinless life, perpetual virginity or the miraculous conception of Our Divine Lord by the power of the Holy Ghost.

Q. 272. What has always been the belief of the Church concerning this truth?

A. The Church has always believed in the Immaculate Conception of the Blessed Virgin and to place this truth beyond doubt has declared it an Article of Faith.

Q. 273. To what should the thoughts of the Immaculate Conception lead us?

A. The thoughts of the Immaculate Conception should lead us to a great love of purity and to a desire of imitating the Blessed Virgin in the practice of that holy virtue.

Lesson Sixth: On Sin and Its Kinds

Q. 274. How is sin divided?

A.

1.(1) Sin is divided into the sin we inherit called original sin, and the sin we commit ourselves, called actual sin.

2.(2) Actual sin is sub-divided into greater sins, called mortal, and lesser sins, called venial.

Q. 275. In how many ways may actual sin be committed?

A. Actual sin may be committed in two ways: namely, by willfully doing things forbidden, or by willfully neglecting things commanded.

Q. 276. What is our sin called when we neglect things commanded?

A. When we neglect things commanded our sin is called a sin of omission. Such sins as willfully neglecting to hear Mass on Sundays, or neglecting to go to Confession at least once a year, are sins of omission.

Q. 277. Is original sin the only kind of sin?

A. Original sin is not the only kind of sin; there is another kind of sin, which we commit ourselves, called actual sin.

Q. 278. What is actual sin?

A. Actual sin is any willful thought, word, deed, or omission contrary to the law of God.

Q. 279. How many kinds of actual sin are there?

A. There are two kinds of actual sin -- mortal and venial.

Q. 280. What is mortal sin?

A. Mortal sin is a grievous offense against the law of God.

Q. 281. Why is this sin called mortal?

A. This sin is called mortal because it deprives us of spiritual life, which is sanctifying grace, and brings everlasting death and damnation on the soul.

Q. 282. How many things are necessary to make a sin mortal?

A. To make a sin mortal, three things are necessary:

1.a grievous matter, sufficient reflection, and full consent of the will.

Q. 283. What do we mean by "grievous matter" with regard to sin?

A. By "grievous matter" with regard to sin we mean that the thought, word or deed by which mortal sin is committed must be either very bad in itself or severely prohibited, and therefore sufficient to make a mortal sin if we deliberately yield to it.

Q. 284. What does "sufficient reflection and full consent of the will" mean?

A. "Sufficient reflection" means that we must know the thought, word or deed to be sinful at the time we are guilty of it; and "full consent of the will" means that we must fully and willfully yield to it.

Q. 285. What are sins committed without reflection or consent called?

A. Sins committed without reflection or consent are called material sins; that is, they would be formal or real sins if we knew their sinfulness at the time we committed them. Thus to eat flesh meat on a day of abstinence without knowing it to be a day of abstinence or without thinking of the prohibition, would be a material sin.

Q. 286. Do past material sins become real sins as soon as we discover their sinfulness?

A. Past material sins do not become real sins as soon as we discover their sinfulness, unless we again repeat them with full knowledge and consent.

Q. 287. How can we know what sins are considered mortal?

A. We can know what sins are considered mortal from Holy Scripture; from the teaching of the Church, and from the writings of the Fathers and Doctors of the Church.

Q. 288. Why is it wrong to judge others guilty of sin?

A. It is wrong to judge others guilty of sin because we cannot know for certain that their sinful act was committed with sufficient reflection and full consent of the will.

Q. 289. What sin does he commit who without sufficient reason believes another guilty of sin?

A. He who without sufficient reason believes another guilty of sin commits a sin of rash judgment.

Q. 290. What is venial sin?

A. Venial sin is a slight offense against the law of God in matters of less importance, or in matters of great importance it is an offense committed without sufficient reflection or full consent of the will.

Q. 291. Can we always distinguish venial from mortal sin?

A. We cannot always distinguish venial from mortal sin, and in such cases we must leave the decision to our confessor.

Q. 292. Can slight offenses ever become mortal sins?

A. Slight offenses can become mortal sins if we commit them through defiant contempt for God or His law; and also when they are followed by very evil consequences, which we foresee in committing them.

Q. 293. Which are the effects of venial sin?

A. The effects of venial sin are the lessening of the love of God in our heart, the making us less worthy of His help, and the weakening of the power to resist mortal sin.

Q. 294. How can we know a thought, word or deed to be sinful?

A. We can know a thought, word or deed to be sinful if it, or the neglect of it, is forbidden by any law of God or of His Church, or if it is opposed to any supernatural virtue.

Q. 295. Which are the chief sources of sin?

A. The chief sources of sin are seven:

1.Pride, Covetousness, Lust, Anger, Gluttony, Envy, and Sloth, and they are commonly called capital sins.

Q. 296. What is pride?

A. Pride is an excessive love of our own ability; so that we would rather sinfully disobey than humble ourselves.

Q. 297. What effect has pride on our souls?

A. Pride begets in our souls sinful ambition, vainglory, presumption and hypocrisy.

Q. 298. What is covetousness?

A. Covetousness is an excessive desire for worldly things.

Q. 299. What effect has covetousness on our souls?

A. Covetousness begets in our souls unkindness, dishonesty, deceit and want of charity.

Q. 300. What is lust?

A. Lust is an excessive desire for the sinful pleasures forbidden by the Sixth Commandment.

Q. 301. What effect has lust on our souls?

A. Lust begets in our souls a distaste for holy things, a perverted conscience, a hatred for God, and it very frequently leads to a complete loss of faith.

Q. 302. What is anger?

A. Anger is an excessive emotion of the mind excited against any person or thing, or it is an excessive desire for revenge.

Q. 303. What effect has anger on our soul?

A. Anger begets in our souls impatience, hatred, irreverence, and too often the habit of cursing.

Q. 304. What is gluttony?

A. Gluttony is an excessive desire for food or drink.

Q. 305. What kind of a sin is drunkenness?

A. Drunkenness is a sin of gluttony by which a person deprives himself of the use of his reason by the excessive taking of intoxicating drink.

Q. 306. Is drunkenness always a mortal sin?

A. Deliberate drunkenness is always a mortal sin if the person be completely deprived of the use of reason by it, but drunkenness that is not intended or desired may be excused from mortal sin.

Q. 307. What are the chief effects of habitual drunkenness?

A. Habitual drunkenness injures the body, weakens the mind, leads its victim into many vices and exposes him to
the danger of dying in a state of mortal sin.

Q. 308. What three sins seem to cause most evil in the world?

A. Drunkenness, dishonesty and impurity seem to cause most evil in the world, and they are therefore to be carefully avoided at all times.

Q. 309. What is envy?

A. Envy is a feeling of sorrow at another's good fortune and joy at the evil which befalls him; as if we ourselves were injured by the good and benefited by the evil that comes to him.

Q. 310. What effect has envy on the soul?

A. Envy begets in the soul a want of charity for our neighbor and produces a spirit of detraction, back-biting and slander.

Q. 311. What is sloth?

A. Sloth is a laziness of the mind and body, through which we neglect our duties on account of the labor they require.

Q. 312. What effect has sloth upon the soul?

A. Sloth begets in the soul a spirit of indifference in our spiritual duties and a disgust for prayer.

Q. 313. Why are the seven sources of sin called capital sins?

A. The seven sources of sin are called capital sins because they rule over our other sins and are the causes of them.

Q. 314. What do we mean by our predominant sin or ruling passion?

A. By our predominant sin, or ruling passion, we mean the sin into which we fall most frequently and which we find it hardest to resist.

Q. 315. How can we best overcome our sins?

A. We can best overcome our sins by guarding against our predominant or ruling sin.

Q. 316. Should we give up trying to be good when we seem not to succeed in overcoming our faults?

A. We should not give up trying to be good when we seem not to succeed in overcoming our faults, because our efforts to be good will keep us from becoming worse than we are.

Q. 317. What virtues are opposed to the seven capital sins?

A. Humility is opposed to pride; generosity to covetousness; chastity to lust; meekness to anger; temperance to gluttony; brotherly love to envy, and diligence to sloth.

Lesson Seventh: On the Incarnation and Redemption

Q. 318. What does "incarnation" mean, and what does "redemption" mean?

A. "Incarnation" means the act of clothing with flesh. Thus Our Lord clothed His divinity with a human body. "Redemption" means to buy back again.

Q. 319. Did God abandon man after he fell into sin?

A. God did not abandon man after he fell into sin, but promised him a Redeemer, who was to satisfy for man's sin and reopen to him the gates of heaven.

Q. 320. What do we mean by the "gates of heaven"?

A. By the "gates of heaven" we mean the divine power by which God keeps us out of heaven or admits us into it, at His pleasure.

Q. 321. Who is the Redeemer?

A. Our Blessed Lord and Saviour Jesus Christ is the Redeemer of mankind.

Q. 322. What does the name "Jesus" signify and how was this name given to Our Lord?

A. The name "Jesus" signifies Saviour or Redeemer, and this name was given to Our Lord by an Angel who appeared to Joseph and said: "Mary shall bring forth a Son; and thou shalt call His name Jesus."

Q. 323. What does the name "Christ" signify?

A. The name "Christ" means the same as Messias, and signifies Anointed; because, as in the Old Law, Prophets, High Priests and Kings were anointed with oil; so Jesus, the Great Prophet, High Priest and King of the New Law, was anointed as man with the fullness of divine power.

Q. 324. How did Christ show and prove His divine power?

A. Christ showed and proved His divine power chiefly by His miracles, which are extraordinary works that can be performed only by power received from God, and which have, therefore, His sanction and authority.

Q. 325. What, then, did the miracles of Jesus Christ prove?

A. The miracles of Jesus Christ proved that whatever He said was true, and that when He declared Himself to be the Son of God He really was what He claimed to be.

Q. 326. Could not men have been deceived in the miracles of Christ?

A. Men could not have been deceived in the miracles of Christ because they were performed in the most open manner and usually in the presence of great multitudes of people, among whom were many of Christ's enemies, ever ready to expose any deceit. And if Christ performed no real miracles, how, then, could He have converted the world and have persuaded sinful men to give up what they loved and do the difficult things that the Christian religion imposes?

Q. 327. Could not false accounts of these miracles have been written after the death of Our Lord?

A. False accounts of these miracles could not have been written after the death of Our Lord; for then neither His friends nor His enemies would have believed them without proof. Moreover, the enemies of Christ did not deny the miracles, but tried to explain them by attributing them to the power of the devil or other causes. Again, the Apostles and the Evangelists who wrote the accounts suffered death to testify their belief in the words and works of Our Lord.

Q. 328. Did Jesus Christ die to redeem all men of every age and race without exception?

A. Jesus Christ died to redeem all men of every age and race without exception; and every person born into the world should share in His merits, without which no one can be saved.

Q. 329. How are the merits of Jesus Christ applied to our souls?

A. The merits of Jesus Christ are applied to our souls through the Sacraments, and especially through Baptism and Penance, which restore us to the friendship of God.

Q. 330. What do you believe of Jesus Christ?

A. I believe that Jesus Christ is the Son of God, the second Person of the Blessed Trinity, true God and true man.

Q. 331. Cannot we also be called the Children of God, and therefore His sons and daughters?

A. We can be called the Children of God because He has adopted us by His grace or because He is the Father who has created us; but we are not, therefore, His real Children; whereas, Jesus Christ, His only real and true Son, was neither adopted nor created, but was begotten of His Father from all eternity.

Q. 332. Why is Jesus Christ true God?

A. Jesus Christ is true God because He is the true and only Son of God the Father.

Q. 333. Why is Jesus Christ true man?

A. Jesus Christ is true man because He is the Son of the Blessed Virgin Mary and has a body and soul like ours.

Q. 334. Who was the foster father or guardian of Our Lord while on earth?

A. St. Joseph, the husband of the Blessed Virgin, was the foster-father or guardian of Our Lord while on earth.

Q. 335. Is Jesus Christ in heaven as God or as man?

A. Since His Ascension Jesus Christ is in heaven both as God and as man.

Q. 336. How many natures are there in Jesus Christ?

A. In Jesus Christ there are two natures, the nature of God and the nature of man.

Q. 337. Is Jesus Christ more than one person?

A. No. Jesus Christ is but one Divine Person.

Q. 338. From what do we learn that Jesus Christ is but one person?

A. We learn that Jesus Christ is but one person from Holy Scripture and from the constant teaching of the Church, which has condemned all those who teach the contrary.

Q. 339. Was Jesus Christ always God?

A. Jesus Christ was always God, as He is the second person of the Blessed Trinity, equal to His Father from all eternity.

Q. 340. Was Jesus Christ always man?

A. Jesus Christ was not always man, but became man at the time of His Incarnation.

Q. 341. What do you mean by the Incarnation?

A. By the Incarnation I mean that the Son of God was made man.

Q. 342. How was the Son of God made man?

A. The Son of God was conceived and made man by the power of the Holy Ghost, in the womb of the Blessed Virgin Mary.

Q. 343. Is the Blessed Virgin Mary truly the Mother of God?

A. The Blessed Virgin Mary is truly the Mother of God, because the same Divine Person who is the Son of God is also the Son of the Blessed Virgin Mary.

Q. 344. Did the Son of God become man immediately after the sin of our first parents?

A. The Son of God did not become man immediately after the sin of our first parents, but was promised to them as a Redeemer.

Q. 345. How many years passed from the time Adam sinned till the time the Redeemer came?

A. About 4,000 years passed from the time Adam sinned till the time the Redeemer came.

Q. 346. What was the moral condition of the world just before the coming of Our Lord?

A. Just before the coming of Our Lord the moral condition of the world was very bad. Idolatry, injustice, cruelty, immorality and horrid vices were common almost everywhere.

Q. 347. Why was the coming of the Redeemer so long delayed?

A. The coming of the Redeemer was so long delayed that the world -- suffering from every misery -- might learn the great evil of sin and know that God alone could help fallen man.

Q. 348. When was the Redeemer promised to mankind?

A. The Redeemer was first promised to mankind in the Garden of Paradise, and often afterward through Abraham and his descendants, the patriarchs, and through numerous prophets.

Q. 349. Who were the prophets?

A. The prophets were inspired men to whom God revealed the future, that they might with absolute certainty make it known to the people.

Q. 350. What did the prophets foretell concerning the Redeemer?

A. The prophets, taken together, foretold so accurately all the circumstances of the birth, life, death, resurrection and glory of the Redeemer that no one who carefully studied their writings could fail to recognize Him when He came.

Q. 351. Have all these prophecies concerning the Redeemer been fulfilled?

A. All the prophecies concerning the Redeemer have been fulfilled in every point by the circumstances of Christ's birth, life, death, resurrection and glory; and He is, therefore, the Redeemer promised to mankind from the time of Adam.

Q. 352. Where shall we find these prophecies concerning the Redeemer?

A. We shall find these prophecies concerning the Redeemer in the prophetic books of the Bible or Holy Scripture.

Q. 353. If the Redeemer's coming was so clearly foretold, why did not all recognize Him when He came?

A. All did not recognize the Redeemer when He came, because many knew only part of the prophecies; and taking those concerning His glory and omitting those concerning His suffering, they could not understand His life.

Q. 354. How could they be saved who lived before the Son of God became man?

A. They who lived before the Son of God became man could be saved by believing in a Redeemer to come, and
    by keeping the Commandments.

Q. 355. On what day was the Son of God conceived and made man?

A. The Son of God was conceived and made man on Annunciation Day -- the day on which the Angel Gabriel announced to the Blessed Virgin Mary that she was to be the Mother of God.

Q. 356. On what day was Christ born?

A. Christ was born on Christmas Day, in a stable at Bethlehem, over nineteen hundred years ago.

Q. 357. Why did the Blessed Virgin and St. Joseph go to Bethlehem just before the birth of Our Lord?

A. The Blessed Virgin and St. Joseph went to Bethlehem in obedience to the Roman Emperor, who ordered all his subjects to register their names in the towns or cities of their ancestors. Bethlehem was the City of David, the royal ancestor of Mary and Joseph, hence they had to register there. All this was done by the Will of God, that the prophecies concerning the birth of His Divine Son might be fulfilled.

Q. 358. Why was Christ born in a stable?

A. Christ was born in a stable because Joseph and Mary were poor and strangers in Bethlehem, and without money they could find no other shelter. This was permitted by Our Lord that we might learn a lesson from His great humility.

Q. 359. In giving the ancestors or forefathers of Our Lord, why do the Gospels give the ancestors of

Joseph, who was only Christ's foster-father, and not the ancestors of Mary, who was Christ's real parent?

A. In giving the ancestors of Our Lord, the Gospels give the ancestors of Joseph:

1.(1) Because the ancestors of women were not usually recorded by the Jews; and

2.(2) Because Mary and Joseph were members of the same tribe, and had, therefore, the same ancestors; so that, in giving the ancestors of Joseph, the Gospels give also those of Mary; and this was understood by those for whom the Gospels were intended.

Q. 360. Had Our Lord any brothers or sisters ?

A. Our Lord had no brothers or sisters. When the Gospels speak of His brethren they mean only His near relations. His Blessed Mother Mary was always a Virgin as well before and at His birth as after it.

Q. 361. Who were among the first to adore the Infant Jesus?

A. The shepherds of Bethlehem, to whom His birth was announced by Angels; and the Magi or three wise men, who were guided to His crib by a miraculous star, were among the first to adore the Infant Jesus. We recall the adoration of the Magi on the feast of the Epiphany, which means appearance or manifestation, namely, of Our Saviour.

Q. 362. Who sought to kill the Infant Jesus?

A. Herod sought to kill the Infant Jesus because he thought the influence of Christ -- the new-born King – would deprive him of his throne.

Q. 363. How was the Holy Infant rescued from the power of Herod?

A. The Holy Infant was rescued from the power of Herod by the flight into Egypt, when St. Joseph -- warned by an Angel -- fled hastily into that country with Jesus and Mary.

Q. 364. How did Herod hope to accomplish his wicked designs?

A. Herod hoped to accomplish his wicked designs by murdering all the infants in and near Bethlehem. The day on which we commemorate the death of these first little martyrs, who shed their blood for Christ's sake, is called the feast of Holy Innocents.

Q. 365. How may the years of Christ's life be divided?

A. The years of Christ's life may be divided into three parts:

1.(1) His childhood, extending from His birth to His twelfth year, when He went with his parents to worship in the Temple of Jerusalem.

2.(2) His hidden life, which extends from His twelfth to His thirtieth year, during which time He dwelt with His parents at Nazareth.

3.(3) His public life, extending from His thirtieth year -- or from His baptism by St. John the Baptist to His death; during which time He taught His doctrines and established His Church.

Q. 366. Why is Christ's life thus divided?

A. Christ's life is thus divided to show that all classes find in Him their model. In childhood He gave an example to the young; in His hidden life an example to those who consecrate themselves to the service of God in a religious state; and in His public life an example to all Christians without exception.

Q. 367. How long did Christ live on earth?

A. Christ lived on earth about thirty-three years, and led a most holy life in poverty and suffering.

Q. 368. Why did Christ live so long on earth?

A. Christ lived so long on earth to show us the way to heaven by His teachings and example.

Lesson Eighth: On Our Lord's Passion, Death, Resurrection, and Ascension

Q. 369. What do we mean by Our Lord's Passion?

A. By Our Lord's Passion we mean His dreadful sufferings from His agony in the garden till the moment of His death.

Q. 370. What did Jesus Christ suffer?

A. Jesus Christ suffered a bloody sweat, a cruel scourging, was crowned with thorns, and was crucified.

Q. 371. When did Our Lord suffer the "bloody sweat"?

A. Our Lord suffered the "bloody sweat" while drops of blood came forth from every pore of His body, during His agony in the Garden of Olives, near Jerusalem, where He went to pray on the night His Passion began.

Q. 372. Who accompanied Our Lord to the Garden of Olives on the night of His Agony?

A. The Apostles Peter, James and John, the same who had witnessed His transfiguration on the mount, accompanied Our Lord to the Garden of Olives, to watch and pray with Him on the night of His agony.

Q. 373. What do we mean by the transfiguration of Our Lord?

A. By the transfiguration of Our Lord we mean the supernatural change in His appearance when He showed Himself to His Apostles in great glory and brilliancy in which "His face did shine as the sun and His garments became white as snow."

Q. 374. Who were present at the transfiguration?

A. There were present at the transfiguration -- besides the Apostles Peter, James and John, who witnessed it -- the two great and holy men of the Old Law, Moses and Elias, talking with Our Lord.

Q. 375. What caused Our Lord's agony in the garden?

A It is believed Our Lord's agony in the garden was caused:

1.(1) By his clear knowledge of all He was soon to endure;

2.(2) By the sight of the many offenses committed against His Father by the sins of the whole world;

3.(3) By His knowledge of men's ingratitude for the blessings of redemption.

Q. 376. Why was Christ cruelly scourged?

A. Christ was cruelly scourged by Pilate's orders, that the sight of His bleeding body might move His enemies to spare His life.

Q. 377. Why was Christ crowned with thorns?

A. Christ was crowned with thorns in mockery because He had said He was a King.

Q. 378. Could Christ, if He pleased, have escaped the tortures of His Passion?

A. Christ could, if He pleased, have escaped the tortures of His Passion, because He foresaw them and had it in His power to overcome His enemies.

Q. 379. Was it necessary for Christ to suffer so much in order to redeem us?

A. It was not necessary for Christ to suffer so much in order to redeem us, for the least of His sufferings was more than sufficient to atone for all the sins of mankind. By suffering so much He showed His great love for us.

Q. 380. Who betrayed Our Lord?

A. Judas, one of His Apostles, betrayed Our Lord, and from His sin we may learn that even the good may become very wicked by the abuse of their free will.

Q. 381. How was Christ condemned to death?

A. Through the influence of those who hated Him, Christ was condemned to death, after an unjust trial, at which false witnesses were induced to testify against Him.

Q. 382. On what day did Christ die?

A. Christ died on Good Friday.

Q. 383. Why do you call that day "good" on which Christ died so sorrowful a death?

A. We call that day good on which Christ died because by His death He showed His great love for man, and purchased for him every blessing.

Q. 384. How long was Our Lord hanging on the cross before He died?

A. Our Lord was hanging on the Cross about three hours before He died. While thus suffering, His enemies stood around blaspheming and mocking Him. By His death He proved Himself a real mortal man, for He could not die in His divine nature.

Q. 385. What do we call the words Christ spoke while hanging on the Cross?

A. We call the words Christ spoke while hanging on the Cross "the seven last words of Jesus on the Cross." They teach us the dispositions we should have at the hour of death.

Q. 386. Repeat the seven last words or sayings of Jesus on the Cross.

A. The seven last words or sayings of Jesus on the Cross are:

1.(1) "Father, forgive them, for they know not what they do," in which He forgives and prays for His enemies.

2.(2) "Amen, I say to thee, this day thou shalt be with Me in Paradise," in which He pardons the penitent sinner.

3.(3) "Woman, behold thy Son" -- "Behold thy Mother," in which He gave up what was dearest to Him on earth, and gave us Mary for our Mother.

4.(4) "My God, my God, why hast Thou forsaken Me?" from which we learn the suffering of His mind.

5.(5) "I thirst," from which we learn the suffering of His body.

6.(6) "All is consummated," by which He showed the fulfillment of all the prophecies concerning Him and the completion of the work of our redemption.

7.(7) "Father, into Thy hands I commend my spirit," by which He showed His perfect resignation to the Will of His Eternal Father.

Q. 387. What happened at the death of Our Lord?

A. At the death of Our Lord there were darkness and earthquake; many holy dead came forth from their graves, and the veil concealing the Holy of Holies, in the Temple of Jerusalem, was torn asunder.

Q. 388. What was the Holy of Holies in the temple?

A. The Holy of Holies was the sacred part of the Temple, in which the Ark of the Covenant was kept, and where the high priest consulted the Will of God.

Q. 389. What was the "Ark of the Covenant"?

A. The Ark of the Covenant was a precious box in which were kept the tablets of stone bearing the written Commandments of God, the rod which Aaron changed into a serpent before King Pharao, and a portion of the manna with which the Israelites were miraculously fed in the desert. The Ark of the Covenant was a figure of the Tabernacle in which we keep the Holy Eucharist.

Q. 390. Why was the veil of the Temple torn asunder at the death of Christ?

A. The veil of the Temple was torn asunder at the death of Christ because at His death the Jewish religion ceased to be the true religion, and God no longer manifested His presence in the Temple.

Q. 391. Why did the Jewish religion, which up to the death of Christ had been the true religion, cease at that time to be the true religion?

A. The Jewish religion, which, up to the death of Christ, had been the true religion, ceased at that time to be the true religion, because it was only a promise of the redemption and figure of the Christian religion, and when the redemption was accomplished and the Christian religion established by the death of Christ, the promise and the figure were no longer necessary.

Q. 392. Were all the laws of the Jewish religion abolished by the establishment of Christianity?

A. The moral laws of the Jewish religion were not abolished by the establishment of Christianity, for Christ came not to destroy these laws, but to make them more perfect. Its ceremonial laws were abolished when the Temple of Jerusalem ceased to be the House of God.

Q. 393. What do we mean by moral and ceremonial laws?

A. By "moral" laws we mean laws regarding good and evil. By "ceremonial" laws we mean laws regulating the manner of worshipping God in Temple or Church.

Q. 394. Where did Christ die?

A. Christ died on Mount Calvary.

Q. 395. Where was Mount Calvary, and what does the name signify?

A. Mount Calvary was the place of execution, not far from Jerusalem; and the name signifies the "place of skulls."

Q. 396. How did Christ die?

A. Christ was nailed to the Cross, and died on it between two thieves.

Q. 397. Why was Our Lord crucified between thieves?

A. Our Lord was crucified between thieves that His enemies might thus add to His disgrace by making Him equal to the worst criminals.

Q. 398. Why did Christ suffer and die?

A. Christ suffered and died for our sins.

Q. 399. How was Our Lord's body buried?

A. Our Lord's body was wrapped in a clean linen cloth and laid in a new sepulchre or tomb cut in a rock, by Joseph of Arimathea and other pious persons who believed in Our Divine Lord.

Q. 400. What lessons do we learn from the sufferings and death of Christ?

A. From the sufferings and death of Christ we learn the great evil of sin, the hatred God bears to it, and the necessity of satisfying for it.

Q. 401. Whither did Christ's soul go after His death?

A. After Christ's death His soul descended into hell.

Q. 402. Did Christ's soul descend into the hell of the damned?

A. The hell into which Christ's soul descended was not the hell of the dammed, but a place or state of rest called Limbo, where the souls of the just were waiting for Him.

Q. 403. Why did Christ descend into Limbo?

A. Christ descended into Limbo to preach to the souls who were in prison -- that is, to announce to them the joyful tidings of their redemption.

Q. 404. Where was Christ's body while His soul was in Limbo?

A. While Christ's soul was in Limbo His body was in the holy sepulchre.

Q. 405. On what day did Christ rise from the dead?

A. Christ rose from the dead, glorious and immortal, on Easter Sunday, the third day after His death.

Q. 406. Why is the Resurrection the greatest of Christ's miracles?

A. The Resurrection is the greatest of Christ's miracles because all He taught and did is confirmed by it and depends upon it. He promised to rise from the dead and without the fulfillment of that promise we could not believe in Him.

Q. 407. Has any one ever tried to disprove the miracle of the resurrection?

A. Unbelievers in Christ have tried to disprove the miracle of the resurrection as they have tried to disprove all His other miracles; but the explanations they give to prove Christ's miracles false are far more unlikely and harder to believe than the miracles themselves.

Q. 408. What do we mean when we say Christ rose "glorious" from the dead?

A. When we say Christ rose "glorious" from the dead we mean that His body was in a glorified state; that is, gifted with the qualities of a glorified body.

Q. 409. What are the qualities of a glorified body?

A. The qualities of a glorified body are:

1.(1) Brilliancy, by which it gives forth light;
2.(2) Agility, by which it moves from place to place as rapidly as an angel;
3.(3) Subtility, by which material things cannot shut it out;
4.(4) Impassibility, by which it is made incapable of suffering.

Q. 410. Was Christ three full days in the tomb?

A. Christ was not three full days, but only parts of three days in the tomb.

Q. 411. How long did Christ stay on earth after His resurrection?

A. Christ stayed on earth forty days after His resurrection, to show that He was truly risen from the dead, and to instruct His apostles.

Q. 412. Was Christ visible to all and at all times during the forty days He remained on earth after His resurrection?

A. Christ was not visible to all nor at all times during the forty days He remained on earth after His resurrection. We know that He appeared to His apostles and others at least nine times, though He may have appeared oftener.

Q. 413. How did Christ show that He was truly risen from the dead?

A. Christ showed that He was truly risen from the dead by eating and conversing with His Apostles and others to whom He appeared. He showed the wounds in His hands, feet and side, and it was after His resurrection that He gave to His Apostles the power to forgive sins.

Q. 414. After Christ had remained forty days on earth, whither did He go?

A. After forty days Christ ascended into heaven, and the day on which be ascended into heaven is called Ascension Day.

Q. 415. Where did the ascension of Our Lord take place?

A. Christ ascended into heaven from Mount Olivet, the place made sacred by His agony on the night before His death.

Q. 416. Who were present at the ascension and who ascended with Christ?

A. From various parts of Scripture we may conclude there were about 125 persons -- though traditions tell us there was a greater number -- present at the Ascension. They were the Apostles, the Disciples, the pious women and others who had followed Our Blessed Lord. The souls of the just who were waiting in Limbo for the redemption ascended with Christ.

Q. 417. Why is the paschal candle which is lighted on Easter morning extinguished at the Mass on Ascension Day?

A. The paschal candle which is lighted on Easter morning signifies Christ's visible presence on earth, and it is extinguished on Ascension Day to show that He, having fulfilled all the prophecies concerning Himself and having accomplished the work of redemption, has transferred the visible care of His Church to His Apostles and returned in His body to heaven.

Q. 418. Where is Christ in heaven?

A. In heaven Christ sits at the right hand of God the Father Almighty.

Q. 419. What do you mean by saying that Christ sits at the right hand of God?

A. When I say that Christ sits at the right hand of God I mean that Christ as God is equal to His Father in all things, and that as man He is in the highest place in heaven next to God.

Lesson Ninth: On the Holy Ghost and His Descent upon the Apostles

Q. 420. Who is the Holy Ghost?

A. The Holy Ghost is the third Person of the Blessed Trinity.

Q. 421. Did the Holy Ghost ever appear?

A. The Holy Ghost appeared at times under the form of a dove, and again under the form of tongues of fire; for, being a pure spirit without a body, He can take any form.

Q. 422. Is the Holy Ghost called by other names?

A. The Holy Ghost is called also the Holy Spirit, the Paraclete, the Spirit of Truth and other names given in Holy Scripture.

Q. 423. From whom does the Holy Ghost proceed?

A. The Holy Ghost proceeds from the Father and the Son.

Q. 424. Is the Holy Ghost equal to the Father and the Son?

A. The Holy Ghost is equal to the Father and the Son, being the same Lord and God as they are.

Q. 425. On what day did the Holy Ghost come down upon the Apostles?

A. The Holy Ghost came down upon the Apostles ten days after the Ascension of our Lord; and the day on which He came down upon the Apostles is called Whitsunday, or Pentecost.

Q. 426. Why is the day on which the Holy Ghost came down upon the Apostles called Whitsunday?

A. The day on which the Holy Ghost came down upon the Apostles is called Whitsunday or White Sunday, probably because the Christians who were baptized on the eve of Pentecost wore white garments for some time afterward, as a mark of the purity bestowed upon their souls by the Sacrament of Baptism.

Q. 427. Why is this feast called also Pentecost?

A. This feast is called also Pentecost because Pentecost means the fiftieth; and the Holy Ghost came down upon the Apostles fifty days after the resurrection of Our Lord.

Q. 428. How did the Holy Ghost come down upon the Apostles?

A. The Holy Ghost came down upon the Apostles in the form of tongues of fire.

Q. 429. What did the form of tongues of fire denote?

A. The form of tongues of fire denoted the sacred character and divine authority of the preaching and teaching of the Apostles, by whose words and fervor all men were to be converted to the love of God.

Q. 430. Who sent the Holy Ghost upon the Apostles?

A. Our Lord Jesus Christ sent the Holy Ghost upon the Apostles.

Q. 431. Did the Apostles know that the Holy Ghost would come down upon them?

A. The Apostles knew that the Holy Ghost would come down upon them; for Christ promised His Apostles that after His Ascension He would send the Holy Ghost, the Spirit of Truth, to teach them all truths and to abide with them forever.

Q. 432. Has any one ever denied the existence of the Holy Ghost?

A. Some persons have denied the existence of the Holy Ghost; others have denied that He is a real person equal to the Father and the Son; but all these assertions are shown to be false by the words of Holy Scripture and the infallible teaching of the Church.

Q. 433. What are the sins against the Holy Ghost which Our Lord said will not be forgiven either in this world or in the next?

A. The sins against the Holy Ghost which Our Lord said will not be forgiven either in this world or in the next, are sins committed out of pure malice, and greatly opposed to the mercy of God, and are, therefore, seldom forgiven.

Q. 434. Why did Christ send the Holy Ghost?

A. Christ sent the Holy Ghost to sanctify His Church, to enlighten and strengthen the Apostles, and to enable them to preach the Gospel.

Q. 435. How was the Church sanctified through the coming of the Holy Ghost?

A. The Church was sanctified through the coming of the Holy Ghost by receiving those graces which Christ had merited for His ministers, the bishops and priests, and for the souls of all those committed to their care.

Q. 436. How were the Apostles enlightened through the coming of the Holy Ghost?

A. The Apostles were enlightened through the coming of the Holy Ghost by receiving the grace to remember and understand in its true meaning all that Christ had said and done in their presence.

Q. 437. How were the Apostles strengthened through the coming of the Holy Ghost?

A. The Apostles were strengthened through the coming of the Holy Ghost by receiving the grace to brave every danger, even death itself, in the performance of their sacred duties.

Q. 438. What does "Apostle," and what does "Gospel" mean?

A. "Apostle" means a person sent, and "Gospel" means good tidings or news. Hence the name "Gospel" is given to the inspired history of Our Lord's life and works upon earth.

Q. 439. Name the Apostles.

A. The Apostles were: Peter, Andrew, James, John, Philip, Bartholomew, Thomas, Matthew, James, Thaddeus, Simon, and Judas Iscariot, in whose place Mathias was chosen.

Q. 440. Was St. Paul an Apostle?

A. St. Paul was an Apostle, but as he was not called till after the Ascension of Our Lord he is not numbered among the twelve. He is called the Apostle of the Gentiles; that is, of all those who were not of the Jewish religion or members of the Church of the Old Law.

Q. 441. How did St. Paul become an Apostle?

A. While on his way to persecute the Christians St. Paul was miraculously converted and called to be an Apostle by Our Lord Himself, who spoke to him. St. Paul was called Saul before his conversion.

Q. 442. Who were the Evangelists?

A. St. Matthew, St. Mark, St. Luke and St. John are called Evangelists, because they wrote the four Gospels bearing their names, and Evangelia is the Latin name for Gospels. St. Mark and St. Luke were not Apostles, but St. Matthew and St. John were both Apostles and Evangelists.

Q. 443. Why did not the Apostles fully understand when Christ Himself taught them?

A. The Apostles did not fully understand when Christ Himself taught them because during His stay with them on earth they were only preparing to become Apostles; and their minds were yet filled with many worldly thoughts and desires that were to be removed at the coming of the Holy Ghost.

Q. 444. Will the Holy Ghost abide with the Church forever?

A. The Holy Ghost will abide with the Church forever, and guide it in the way of holiness and truth.

Q. 445. What benefit do we derive from the knowledge that the Holy Ghost will abide with the Church forever?

A. From the knowledge that the Holy Ghost will abide with the Church forever we are made certain that the Church can never teach us falsehood, and can never be destroyed by the enemies of Our Faith.

Q. 446. What visible power was given to the Apostles through the coming of the Holy Ghost?

A. Through the coming of the Holy Ghost the Apostles received the "gift of tongues," by which they could be understood in every language, though they preached in only one.

Q. 447. Why did such wonderful gifts accompany confirmation, or the coming of the Holy Ghost, in the first ages of the Church?

A. Such wonderful gifts accompanied Confirmation in the first ages of the Church to prove the power, truth and divine character of Christianity to those who otherwise might not believe, and to draw the attention of all to the establishment of the Christian Church.

Q. 448. Why are these signs not continued everywhere at the present time?

A. These signs are not continued everywhere at the present time, because now that the Church is fully established and its divine character and power proved in other ways, such signs are no longer necessary.

Q. 449. Were such powers as the "gift of tongues" a part of the Sacrament of Confirmation?

A. Such powers as the "gift of tongues" were not a part of the Sacrament of Confirmation, but they were added to it by the Holy Ghost when necessary for the good of the Church.

Lesson Tenth: On the Effects of the Redemption

Q. 450. What is an effect?

A. An effect is that which is caused by something else, as smoke, for example, is an effect of fire.

Q. 451. What does redemption mean?

A. Redemption means the buying back of a thing that was given away or sold.

Q. 452. What did Adam give away by his sin, and what did Our Lord buy back for him and us?

A. By his sin Adam gave away all right to God's promised gifts of grace in this world and of glory in the next, and Our Lord bought back the right that Adam threw away.

Q. 453. Which are the chief effects of the Redemption?

A. The chief effects of the Redemption are two: The satisfaction of God's justice by Christ's sufferings and death, and the gaining of grace for men.

Q. 454. Why do we say "chief effects"?

A. We say "chief effects" to show that these are the most important but not the only effects of the Redemption -- for all the benefits of our holy religion and of its influence upon the world are the effects of the redemption.

Q. 455. Why did God's justice require satisfaction?

A. God's justice required satisfaction because it is infinite and demands reparation for every fault. Man in his state of sin could not make the necessary reparation, so Christ became man and made it for him.

Q. 456. What do you mean by grace?

A. By grace I mean a supernatural gift of God bestowed on us, through the merits of Jesus Christ, for our salvation.

Q. 457. What does "supernatural" mean?

A. Supernatural means above or greater than nature. All gifts such as health, learning or the comforts of life, that affect our happiness chiefly in this world, are called natural gifts, and all gifts such as blessings that affect our happiness chiefly in the next world are called supernatural or spiritual gifts.

Q. 458. What do you mean by "merit"?

A. Merit means the quality of deserving well or ill for our actions. In the question above it means a right to reward for good deeds done.

Q. 459. How many kinds of grace are there?

A. There are two kinds of grace, sanctifying grace and actual grace.

Q. 460. What is the difference between sanctifying grace and actual grace?

A. Sanctifying grace remains with us as long as we are not guilty of mortal sin; and hence, it is often called habitual grace; but actual grace comes to us only when we need its help in doing or avoiding an action, and it remains with us only while we are doing or avoiding the action.

Q. 461. What is sanctifying grace?

A. Sanctifying grace is that grace which makes the soul holy and pleasing to God.

Q. 462. What do you call those graces or gifts of God by which we believe in Him, hope in Him, and love Him?

A. Those graces or gifts of God by which we believe in Him, and hope in Him, and love Him, are called the Divine virtues of Faith, Hope, and Charity.

Q. 463. What do you mean by virtue and vice?

A. Virtue is the habit of doing good, and vice is the habit of doing evil. An act, good or bad, does not form a habit; and hence, a virtue or a vice is the result of repeated acts of the same kind.

Q. 464. Does habit excuse us from the sins committed through it?

A. Habit does not excuse us from the sins committed through it, but rather makes us more guilty by showing how often we must have committed the sin to acquire the habit. If, however, we are seriously trying to overcome a bad habit, and through forgetfulness yield to it, the habit may sometimes excuse us from the sin.

Q. 465. What is Faith?

A. Faith is a Divine virtue by which we firmly believe the truths which God has revealed.

Q. 466. What is Hope?

A. Hope is a Divine virtue by which we firmly trust that God will give us eternal life and the means to obtain it.

Q. 467. What is Charity?

A. Charity is a Divine virtue by which we love God above all things for His own sake, and our neighbor as ourselves for the love of God.

Q. 468. Why are Faith, Hope and Charity called virtues?

A. Faith, Hope and Charity are called virtues because they are not mere acts, but habits by which we always and in all things believe God, hope in Him, and love Him.

Q. 469. What kind of virtues are Faith, Hope and Charity?

A. Faith, Hope and Charity are called infused theological virtues to distinguish them from the four moral virtues -- Prudence, Justice, Fortitude and Temperance.

Q. 470. Why do we say the three theological virtues are infused and the four moral virtues acquired?

A. We say the three theological virtues are infused; that is, poured into our souls, because they are strictly gifts of God and do not depend upon our efforts to obtain them, while the four moral virtues -- Prudence, Justice, Fortitude and Temperance -- though also gifts of God, may, as natural virtues, be acquired by our own efforts.

Q. 471. Why do we believe God, hope in Him, and love Him?

A. We believe God and hope in Him because He is infinitely true and cannot deceive us. We love Him because He is infinitely good and beautiful and worthy of all love.

Q. 472. What mortal sins are opposed to Faith?

A. Atheism, which is a denial of all revealed truths, and heresy, which is a denial of some revealed truths, and superstition, which is a misuse of religion, are opposed to Faith.

Q. 473. Who is our neighbor?

A. Every human being capable of salvation of every age, country, race or condition, especially if he needs our help, is our neighbor in the sense of the Catechism.

Q. 474. Why should we love our neighbor?

A. We should love our neighbor because he is a child of God, redeemed by Jesus Christ, and because he is our brother created to dwell in heaven with us.

Q. 475. What is actual grace?

A. Actual grace is that help of God which enlightens our mind and moves our will to shun evil and do good.

Q. 476. Is grace necessary to salvation?

A. Grace is necessary to salvation, because without grace we can do nothing to merit heaven.

Q. 477. Can we resist the grace of God?

A. We can, and unfortunately often do, resist the grace of God.

Q. 478. Is it a sin knowingly to resist the grace of God?

A. It is a sin, knowingly, to resist the grace of God, because we thereby insult Him and reject His gifts without which we cannot be saved.

Q. 479. Does God give His grace to every one?

A. God gives to everyone He creates sufficient grace to save his soul; and if persons do not save their souls, it is because they have not used the grace given.

Q. 480. What is the grace of perseverance?

A. The grace of perseverance is a particular gift of God which enables us to continue in the state of grace till death.

Q. 481. Can we merit the grace of final perseverance or know when we possess it?

A. We cannot merit the grace of final perseverance, or know when we possess it, because it depends entirely upon God's mercy and not upon our actions. To imagine we possess it would lead us into the sin of presumption.

Q. 482. Can a person merit any supernatural reward for good deeds performed while he is in mortal sin?

A. A person cannot merit any supernatural reward for good deeds performed while he is in mortal sin; nevertheless, God rewards such good deeds by giving the grace of repentance; and, therefore, all persons, even those in mortal sin, should ever strive to do good.

Q. 483. Does God reward anything but our good works?

A. God rewards our good intention and desire to serve Him, even when our works are not successful. We should make this good intention often during the day, and especially in the morning.

Lesson Eleventh: On the Church

Q. 484. How was the true religion preserved from Adam till the coming of Christ?

A. The true religion was preserved from Adam till the coming of Christ by the patriarchs, prophets and other holy men whom God appointed and inspired to teach His Will and Revelations to the people, and to remind them of the promised Redeemer.

Q. 485. Who were the prophets, and what was their chief duty?

A. The prophets were men to whom God gave a knowledge of future events connected with religion, that they might foretell them to His people and thus give proof that the message came from God. Their chief duty was to foretell the time, place and circumstances of Our Saviour's coming into the world, that men might know when and where to look for Him, and might recognize Him when He came.

Q. 486. How could they be saved who lived before Christ became man?

A. They who lived before Christ became man could be saved by belief in the Redeemer to come and by keeping the Commandments of God.

Q. 487. Was the true religion universal before the coming of Christ?

A. The true religion was not universal before the coming of Christ. It was confined to one people – the descendants of Abraham. All other nations worshipped false gods.

Q. 488. Which are the means instituted by Our Lord to enable men at all times to share in the fruits of the Redemption?

A. The means instituted by Our Lord to enable men at all times to share in the fruits of His Redemption are the Church and the Sacraments.

Q. 489. What is the Church?

A. The Church is the congregation of all those who profess the faith of Christ, partake of the same Sacraments, and are governed by their lawful pastors under one visible Head.

Q. 490. How may the members of the Church on earth be divided?

A. The members of the Church on earth may be divided into those who teach and those who are taught. Those who teach, namely, the Pope, bishops and priests, are called the Teaching Church, or simply the Church. Those who are taught are called the Believing Church, or simply the faithful.

Q. 491. What is the duty of the Teaching Church?

A. The duty of the Teaching Church is to continue the work Our Lord began upon earth, namely, to teach revealed truth, to administer the Sacraments and to labor for the salvation of souls.

Q. 492. What is the duty of the faithful?

A. The duty of the faithful is to learn the revealed truths taught; to receive the Sacraments, and to aid in saving souls by their prayers, good works and alms.

Q. 493. What do you mean by "profess the faith of Christ"?

A. By "profess the faith of Christ" we mean, believe all the truths and practice the religion He has taught.

Q. 494. What do we mean by "lawful pastors"?

A. By "lawful pastors" we mean those in the Church who have been appointed by lawful authority and who have, therefore, a right to rule us. The lawful pastors in the Church are: Every priest in his own parish; every bishop in his own diocese, and the Pope in the whole Church.

Q. 495. Who is the invisible Head of the Church?

A. Jesus Christ is the invisible Head of the Church.

Q. 496. Who is the visible Head of the Church?

A. Our Holy Father the Pope, the Bishop of Rome, is the Vicar of Christ on earth and the visible Head of the Church.

Q. 497. What does "vicar" mean?

A. Vicar is a name used in the Church to designate a person who acts in the name and authority of another. Thus a Vicar Apostolic is one who acts in the name of the Pope, and a Vicar General is one who acts in the name of the bishop.

Q. 498. Could any one be Pope without being Bishop of Rome?

A. One could not be Pope without being Bishop of Rome, and whoever is elected Pope must give up his title to any other diocese and take the title of Bishop of Rome.

Q. 499. Why is the Pope, the Bishop of Rome, the visible Head of the Church?

A. The Pope, the Bishop of Rome, is the visible Head of the Church because he is the successor of St. Peter, whom Christ made the chief of the Apostles and the visible Head of the Church.

Q. 500. Why are Catholics called "Roman"?

A. Catholics are called Roman to show that they are in union with the true Church founded by Christ and governed by the Apostles under the direction of St. Peter, by divine appointment the Chief of the Apostles, who founded the Church of Rome and was its first bishop.

Q. 501. By what name is a bishop's diocese sometimes called?

A. A bishop's diocese is sometimes called his see. The diocese of Rome, on account of its authority and dignity, is called the Holy See, and its bishop is called the Holy Father or Pope. Pope means father.

Q. 502. What do we call the right by which St. Peter or his successor has always been the head of the Church and of all its bishops?

A. We call the right by which St. Peter or his successor has always been the head of the Church, and of all its bishops, the Primacy of St. Peter or of the Pope. Primacy means holding first place.

Q. 503. How is it shown that St. Peter or his successor has always been the head of the Church?

A. It is shown that St. Peter or his successor has always been the head of the Church:

1.(1) From the words of Holy Scripture, which tell how Christ appointed Peter Chief of the Apostles and head of the Church.

2.(2) From the history of the Church, which shows that Peter and his successors have always acted and have always been recognized as the head of the Church.

Q. 504. How do we know that the rights and privileges bestowed on St. Peter were given also to his successors -- the Popes?

A. We know that the rights and privileges bestowed on St. Peter were given also to his successors, the Popes, because the promises made to St. Peter by Our Lord were to be fulfilled in the Church till the end of time, and as Peter was not to live till the end of time, they are fulfilled in his successors.

Q. 505. Did St. Peter establish any Church before he came to Rome?

A. Before he came to Rome, St. Peter established a Church at Antioch and ruled over it for several years.

Q. 506. Who are the successors of the other Apostles?

A. The successors of the other Apostles are the Bishops of the Holy Catholic Church.

Q. 507. How do we know that the bishops of the Church are the successors of the Apostles?

A. We know that the bishops of the Church are the successors of the Apostles because they continue the work of the Apostles and give proof of the same authority. They have always exercised the rights and powers that belonged to the Apostles in making laws for the Church, in consecrating bishops and ordaining priests.

Q. 508. Why did Christ found the Church?

A. Christ founded the Church to teach, govern, sanctify, and save all men.

Q. 509. Are all bound to belong to the Church?

A. All are bound to belong to the Church, and he who knows the Church to be the true Church and remains out of it cannot be saved.

Q. 510. Is it ever possible for one to be saved who does not know the Catholic Church to be the true Church?

A. It is possible for one to be saved who does not know the Catholic Church to be the true Church, provided that person:

1.(1) Has been validly baptized;

2.(2) Firmly believes the religion he professes and practices to be the true religion, and

3.(3) Dies without the guilt of mortal sin on his soul.

Q. 511. Why do we say it is only possible for a person to be saved who does not know the Catholic Church to be the true Church?

A. We say it is only possible for a person to be saved who does not know the Catholic Church to be the true Church, because the necessary conditions are not often found, especially that of dying in a state of grace without making use of the Sacrament of Penance.

Q. 512. How are such persons said to belong to the Church?

A. Such persons are said to belong to the "soul of the church"; that is, they are really members of the Church without knowing it. Those who share in its Sacraments and worship are said to belong to the body or visible part of the Church.

Q. 513. Why must the true Church be visible?

A. The true Church must be visible because its founder, Jesus Christ, commanded us under pain of condemnation to hear the Church; and He could not in justice command us to hear a Church that could not be seen and known.

Q. 514. What excuses do some give for not becoming members of the true Church?

A. The excuses some give for not becoming members of the true church are:

1.(1) They do not wish to leave the religion in which they were born.

2.(2) There are too many poor and ignorant people in the Catholic Church.

3.(3) One religion is as good as another if we try to serve God in it, and be upright and honest in our lives.

Q. 515. How do you answer such excuses?

A.

1.(1) To say that we should remain in a false religion because we were born in it is as untrue as to say we

should not heal our bodily diseases because we were born with them.

2.(2) To say there are too many poor and ignorant in the Catholic Church is to declare that it is Christ's

Church; for He always taught the poor and ignorant and instructed His Church to continue the work.

3.(3) To say that one religion is as good as another is to assert that Christ labored uselessly and taught falsely; for He came to abolish the old religion and found the new in which alone we can be saved as He Himself declared.

Q. 516. Why can there be only one true religion?

A. There can be only one true religion, because a thing cannot be false and true at the same time, and, therefore, all religions that contradict the teaching of the true Church must teach falsehood. If all religions in which men seek to serve God are equally good and true, why did Christ disturb the Jewish religion and the Apostles condemn heretics?

Lesson Twelfth: On the Attributes and Marks of the Church

Q. 517. What is an attribute?

A. An attribute is any characteristic or quality that a person or thing may be said to have. All perfections or imperfections are attributes.

Q. 518. What is a mark?

A. A mark is a given and known sign by which a thing can be distinguished from all others of its kind. Thus a trademark is used to distinguish the article bearing it from all imitations of the same article.

Q. 519. How do we know that the Church must have the four marks and three attributes usually ascribed or given to it?

A. We know that the Church must have the four marks and three attributes usually ascribed or given to it from the words of Christ given in the Holy Scripture and in the teaching of the Church from its beginning.

Q. 520. Can the Church have the four marks without the three attributes?

A. The Church cannot have the four marks without the three attributes, because the three attributes necessarily

come with the marks and without them the marks could not exist.

Q. 521. Why are both marks and attributes necessary in the Church?

A. Both marks and attributes are necessary in the Church, for the marks teach us its external or visible qualities, while the attributes teach us its internal or invisible qualities. It is easier to discover the marks than the attributes; for it is easier to see that the Church is one than that it is infallible.

Q. 522. Which are the attributes of the Church?

A. The attributes of the Church are three:

1.authority, infallibility, and indefectibility.

Q. 523. What is authority?

A. Authority is the power which one person has over another so as to be able to justly exact obedience. Rulers have authority over their subjects, parents over their children, and teachers over their scholars.

Q. 524. From whom must all persons derive whatever lawful authority they possess?

A. All persons must derive whatever lawful authority they possess from God Himself, from whom they receive it directly or indirectly. Therefore, to disobey our lawful superiors is to disobey God Himself, and hence such disobedience is always sinful.

Q. 525. What do you mean by the authority of the Church?

A. By the authority of the Church I mean the right and power which the Pope and the Bishops, as the successors of the Apostles, have to teach and to govern the faithful.

Q. 526. What do you mean by the infallibility of the Church?

A. By the infallibility of the Church I mean that the Church can not err when it teaches a doctrine of faith or morals.

Q. 527. What do we mean by a "doctrine of faith or morals"?

A. By a doctrine of faith or morals we mean the revealed teaching that refers to whatever we must believe and do in order to be saved.

Q. 528. How do you know that the Church can not err?

A. I know that the Church can not err because Christ promised that the Holy Ghost would remain with it forever and save it from error. If, therefore, the Church has erred, the Holy Ghost must have abandoned it and Christ has failed to keep His promise, which is a thing impossible.

Q. 529. Since the Church can not err, could it ever be reformed in its teaching of faith or morals?

A. Since the Church can not err, it could never be reformed in its teaching of faith or morals. Those who say the Church needed reformation in faith or morals accuse Our Lord of falsehood and deception.

Q. 530. When does the Church teach infallibly?

A. The Church teaches infallibly when it speaks through the Pope and Bishops united in general council, or through the Pope alone when he proclaims to all the faithful a doctrine of faith or morals.

Q. 531. What is necessary that the Pope may speak infallibly or ex-cathedra?

A. That the Pope may speak infallibly, or ex-cathedra:

1.(1) He must speak on a subject of faith or morals;

2.(2) He must speak as the Vicar of Christ and to the whole Church;

3.(3) He must indicate by certain words, such as, we define, we proclaim, etc., that he intends to speak infallibly.

Q. 532. Is the Pope infallible in everything he says and does?

A. The Pope is not infallible in everything he says and does, because the Holy Ghost was not promised to make him infallible in everything, but only in matters of faith and morals for the whole Church. Nevertheless, the Pope's opinion on any subject deserves our greatest respect on account of his learning, experience and dignity.

Q. 533. Can the Pope commit sin?

A. The Pope can commit sin and he must seek forgiveness in the Sacrament of Penance as others do. Infallibility does not prevent him from sinning, but from teaching falsehood when he speaks ex-cathedra.

Q. 534. What does ex-cathedra mean?

A. "Cathedra" means a seat, and "ex" means out of. Therefore, ex-cathedra means speaking from the seat or official place held by St. Peter and his successors as the head of the whole Church.

Q. 535. Why is the chief Church in a diocese called a Cathedral?

A. The chief Church in a diocese is called a Cathedral because the bishop's cathedra, that is, his seat or throne, is erected in it, and because he celebrates all important feasts and performs all his special duties in it.

Q. 536. How many Popes have governed the Church from St. Peter to Pius XI.?

A. From St. Peter to Pius XI., 261 Popes have governed the Church; and many of them have been remarkable for their zeal, prudence, learning and sanctity.

Q. 537. What does anti-pope mean, and who were the anti-popes?

A. Anti-pope means a pretended pope. The anti-popes were men who by the aid of faithless Christians or others unlawfully seized and claimed the papal power while the lawful pope was in prison or exile.

Q. 538. Why must the Pope sometimes warn us on political and other matters?

A. The Pope must sometimes warn us on political and other matters, because whatever nations or men do is either good or bad, just or unjust, and wherever the Pope discovers falsehood, wickedness or injustice he must speak against it and defend the truths of faith and morals. He must protect also the temporal rights and property of the Church committed to his care.

Q. 539. What do we mean by the "temporal power" of the Pope?

A. By the temporal power of the Pope we mean the right which the Pope has as a temporal or ordinary ruler to govern the states and manage the properties that have rightfully come into the possession of the Church.

Q. 540. How did the Pope acquire and how was he deprived of the temporal power?

A. The Pope acquired the temporal power in a just manner by the consent of those who had a right to bestow it.

He was deprived of it in an unjust manner by political changes.

Q. 541. How was the temporal power useful to the Church?

A. The temporal power was useful to the Church:

1.(1) Because it gave the Pope the complete independence necessary for the government of the Church and for the defense of truth and virtue.

2.(2) It enabled him to do much for the spread of the true religion by giving alms for the establishment and support of Churches and schools in poor or pagan countries.

Q. 542. What name do we give to the offerings made yearly by the faithful for the support of the Pope and the government of the Church?

A. We call the offerings made yearly by the faithful for the support of the Pope and government of the Church "Peter's pence." It derives its name from the early custom of sending yearly a penny from every house to the successor of St. Peter, as a mark of respect or as an alms for some charity.

Q. 543. What do you mean by the indefectibility of the Church?

A. By the indefectibility of the Church I mean that the Church, as Christ founded it, will last till the end of time.

Q. 544. What is the difference between the infallibility and indefectibility of the Church?

A. When we say the Church is infallible we mean that it can never teach error while it lasts; but when we say the Church is indefectible, we mean that it will last forever and be infallible forever; that it will always remain as Our Lord founded it and never change the doctrines He taught.

Q. 545. Did Our Lord Himself make all the laws of the Church?

A. Our Lord Himself did not make all the laws of the Church. He gave the Church also power to make laws to suit the needs of the times, places or persons as it judged necessary.

Q. 546. Can the Church change its laws?

A. The Church can, when necessary, change the laws it has itself made, but it cannot change the laws that Christ has made. Neither can the Church change any doctrine of faith or morals.

Q. 547. In whom are these attributes found in their fullness?

A. These attributes are found in their fullness in the Pope, the visible Head of the Church, whose infallible authority to teach bishops, priests, and people in matters of faith or morals will last to the end of the world.

Q. 548. Has the Church any marks by which it may be known?

A. The Church has four marks by which it may be known: it is One; it is Holy; it is Catholic; it is Apostolic.

Q. 549. How is the Church One?

A. The Church is One because all its members agree in one faith, are all in one communion, and are all under one head.

Q. 550. How is it evident that the Church is one in government?

A. It is evident that the Church is one in government, for the faithful in a parish are subject to their pastors, the pastors are subject to the bishops of their dioceses, and the bishops of the world are subject to the Pope.

Q. 551. What is meant by the Hierarchy of the Church?

A. By the Hierarchy of the Church is meant the sacred body of clerical rules who govern the Church.

Q. 552. How is it evident that the Church is one in worship?

A. It is evident that the Church is one in worship because all its members make use of the same sacrifice and receive the same Sacraments.

Q. 553. How is it evident that the Church is one in faith?

A. It is evident the Church is one in faith because all Catholics throughout the world believe each and every article of faith proposed by the Church.

Q. 554. Could a person who denies only one article of our faith be a Catholic?

A. A person who denies even one article of our faith could not be a Catholic; for truth is one and we must accept it whole and entire or not at all.

Q. 555. Are there any pious beliefs and practices in the Church that are not articles of faith?

A. There are many pious beliefs and practices in the Church that are not articles of faith; that is, we are not bound under pain of sin to believe in them; yet we will often find them useful aids to holiness, and hence they are recommended by our pastors.

Q. 556. Of what sin are persons guilty who put firm belief in religious or other practices that are either
forbidden or useless?

A. Persons who put a firm belief in religious or other practices that are forbidden or useless are guilty of the sin of superstition.

Q. 557. Where does the Church find the revealed truths it is bound to teach?

A. The Church finds the revealed truths it is bound to teach in the Holy Scripture and revealed traditions.

Q. 558. What is the Holy Scripture or Bible?

A. The Holy Scripture or Bible is the collection of sacred, inspired writings through which God has made known to us many revealed truths. Some call them letters from Heaven to earth, that is, from God to man.

Q. 559. What is meant by the Canon of the Sacred Scriptures?

A. The Canon of Sacred Scriptures means the list the Church has prepared to teach us what sacred writings are Holy Scripture and contain the inspired word of God.

Q. 560. Where does the Church find the revealed traditions?

A. The Church finds the revealed traditions in the decrees of its councils; in its books of worship; in its paintings and inscriptions on tombs and monuments; in the lives of its Saints; the writings of its Fathers, and in its own history.

Q. 561. Must we ourselves seek in the Scriptures and traditions for what we are to believe?

A. We ourselves need not seek in the Scriptures and traditions for what we are to believe. God has appointed the Church to be our guide to salvation and we must accept its teaching us our infallible rule of faith.

Q. 562. How do we show that the Holy Scriptures alone could not be our guide to salvation and infallible rule of faith?

A. We show that the Holy Scripture alone could not be our guide to salvation and infallible rule of faith:

1.(1) Because all men cannot examine or understand the Holy Scripture; but all can listen to the teaching of the Church;

2.(2) Because the New Testament or Christian part of the Scripture was not written at the beginning of the Church's existence, and, therefore, could not have been used as the rule of faith by the first Christians;

3.(3) Because there are many things in the Holy Scripture that cannot be understood without the explanation given by tradition, and hence those who take the Scripture alone for their rule of faith are constantly disputing about its meaning and what they are to believe.

Q. 563. How is the Church Holy?

A. The Church is Holy because its founder, Jesus Christ, is holy; because it teaches a holy doctrine; invites all to a holy life; and because of the eminent holiness of so many thousands of its children.

Q. 564. How is the Church Catholic or universal?

A. The Church is Catholic or universal because it subsists in all ages, teaches all nations, and maintains all truth.

Q. 565. How do you show that the Catholic Church is universal in time, in place, and in doctrine?

A. 1.(1) The Catholic Church is universal in time, for from the time of the Apostles to the present it has existed, taught and labored in every age;

2.(2) It is universal in place, for it has taught throughout the whole world;

3.(3) It is universal in doctrine, for it teaches the same everywhere, and its doctrines are suited to all classes of persons. It has converted all the pagan nations that have ever been converted.

Q. 566. Why does the Church use the Latin language instead of the national language of its children?

A. The Church uses the Latin language instead of the national language of its children:

1.(1) To avoid the danger of changing any part of its teaching in using different languages;

2.(2) That all its rulers may be perfectly united and understood in their communications;

3.(3) To show that the Church is not an institute of any particular nation, but the guide of all nations.

Q. 567. How is the Church Apostolic?

A. The Church is Apostolic because it was founded by Christ on His Apostles, and is governed by their lawful successors, and because it has never ceased, and never will cease, to teach their doctrine.

Q. 568. Does the Church, by defining certain truths, thereby make new doctrines?

A. The Church, by defining, that is, by proclaiming certain truths, articles of faith, does not make new doctrines, but simply teaches more clearly and with greater effort truths that have always been believed and held by the Church.

Q. 569. What, then, is the use of defining or declaring a truth an article of faith if it has always been believed?

A. The use of defining or declaring a truth an article of faith, even when it has always been believed, is:

1.(1) To clearly contradict those who deny it and show their teaching false;

2.(2) To remove all doubt about the exact teaching of the Church, and to put an end to all discussion about the truth defined.

Q. 570. In which Church are these attributes and marks found?

A. These attributes and marks are found in the Holy Roman Catholic Church alone.

Q. 571. How do you show that Protestant Churches have not the marks of the true Church?

A. Protestant Churches have not the marks of the true Church, because:

1.(1) They are not one either in government or faith; for they have no chief head, and they profess different

beliefs;

2.(2) They are not holy, because their doctrines are founded on error and lead to evil consequences;

3.(3) They are not catholic or universal in time, place or doctrine. They have not existed in all ages nor in all places, and their doctrines do not suit all classes;

4.(4) They are not apostolic, for they were not established for hundreds of years after the Apostles, and they do not teach the doctrines of the Apostles.

Q. 572. From whom does the Church derive its undying life and infallible authority?

A. The Church derives its undying life and infallible authority from the Holy Ghost, the spirit of truth, who abides with it forever.

Q. 573. By whom is the Church made and kept One, Holy, and Catholic?

A. The Church is made and kept One, Holy, and Catholic by the Holy Ghost, the spirit of love and holiness, who unites and sanctifies its members throughout the world.

Lesson Thirteenth: On the Sacraments in General

Q. 574. What is a Sacrament?

A. A Sacrament is an outward sign instituted by Christ to give grace.

Q. 575. Are these three things, namely: An outward or visible sign, the institution of that sign by Christ, and the giving of grace through the use of that sign, always necessary for the existence of a Sacrament?

A. These three things, namely:

1.An outward or visible sign, the institution of that sign by Christ, and the giving of grace through the use of that sign, are always necessary for the existence of a Sacrament, and if any of the three be wanting there can be no Sacrament.

Q. 576. Why does the Church use numerous ceremonies or actions in applying the outward signs of the Sacraments?

A. The Church uses numerous ceremonies or actions in applying the outward signs of the Sacraments to increase our reverence and devotion for the Sacraments, and to explain their meaning and effects.

Q. 577. How many Sacraments are there?

A. There are seven Sacraments:

1.Baptism, Confirmation, Holy Eucharist, Penance, Extreme Unction, Holy Orders, and Matrimony.

Q. 578. Were all the Sacraments instituted by Our Lord?

A. All the Sacraments were instituted by Our Lord, for God alone has power to attach the gift of grace to the use of an outward or visible sign. The Church, however, can institute the ceremonies to be used in administering or giving the Sacraments.

Q. 579. How do we know there are seven Sacraments and no more or less?

A. We know there are seven Sacraments and no more or less because the Church always taught that truth. The number of the Sacraments is a matter of faith, and the Church cannot be mistaken in matters of faith.

Q. 580. Why have the Sacraments been instituted?

A. The Sacraments have been instituted as a special means through which we are to receive the grace merited for us by Christ. As Christ is the giver of the grace, He has the right to determine the manner in which it shall be given, and one who refuses to make use of the Sacraments will not receive God's grace.

Q. 581. Do the Sacraments recall in any way the means by which Our Lord merited the graces we receive through them?

A. The Sacraments recall in many ways the means by which Our Lord merited the graces we receive through them. Baptism recalls His profound humility; Confirmation His ceaseless prayer; Holy Eucharist His care of the needy; Penance His mortified life; Extreme Unction His model death; Holy Orders His establishment of the priesthood, and Matrimony His close union with the Church.

Q. 582. Give, for example, the outward sign in Baptism and Confirmation.

A. The outward sign in Baptism is the pouring of the water and the saying of the words of Baptism. The outward sign in Confirmation is the anointing with oil, the saying of the words of Confirmation and the placing of the bishop's hands over the person he confirms.

Q. 583. What is the use of the outward signs in the Sacraments?

A. Without the outward signs in the Sacraments we could not know when or with what effect the grace of the Sacraments enters into our souls.

Q. 584. Does the outward sign merely indicate that grace has been given, or does the use of the outward sign with the proper intention also give the grace of the Sacrament?

A. The outward sign is not used merely to indicate that grace has been given, for the use of the outward sign with the proper intention also gives the grace of the Sacrament. Hence the right application of the outward sign is always followed by the gift of internal grace if the Sacrament be administered with the right intention and received with the right dispositions.

Q. 585. What do we mean by the "right intention" for the administration of the Sacraments?

A. By the right intention for the administration of the Sacraments we mean that whoever administers a Sacrament must have the intention of doing what Christ intended when He instituted the Sacrament and what the Church intends when it administers the Sacrament.

Q. 586. Is there any likeness between the thing used in the outward sign and the grace given in each Sacrament?

A. There is a great likeness between the thing used in the outward sign and the grace given in each Sacrament; thus water is used for cleansing; Baptism cleanses the soul; Oil gives strength and light; Confirmation strengthens and enlightens the soul; Bread and wine nourish; the Holy Eucharist nourishes the soul.

Q. 587. What do we mean by the "matter and form" of the Sacraments?

A. By the "matter" of the Sacraments we mean the visible things, such as water, oil, bread, wine, etc., used for the Sacraments. By the "form" we mean the words, such as "I baptize thee," "I confirm thee," etc., used in giving or administering the Sacraments.

Q. 588. Do the needs of the soul resemble the needs of the body?

A. The needs of the soul do resemble the needs of the body; for the body must be born, strengthened, nourished, healed in affliction, helped at the hour of death, guided by authority, and given a place in which to dwell. The soul is brought into spiritual life by Baptism; it is strengthened by Confirmation; nourished by the Holy Eucharist; healed by Penance; helped at the hour of our death by Extreme Unction; guided by God's ministers through the Sacrament of Holy Orders, and it is given a body in which to dwell by the Sacrament of Matrimony.

Q. 589. Whence have the Sacraments the power of giving grace?

A. The Sacraments have the power of giving grace from the merits of Jesus Christ.

Q. 590. Does the effect of the Sacraments depend on the worthiness or unworthiness of the one who administers them?

A. The effect of the Sacraments does not depend on the worthiness or unworthiness of the one who administers them, but on the merits of Jesus Christ, who instituted them, and on the worthy dispositions of those who receive them.

Q. 591. What grace do the Sacraments give?

A. Some of the Sacraments give sanctifying grace, and others increase it in our souls.

Q. 592. When is a Sacrament said to give, and when is it said to increase, grace in our souls?

A. A Sacrament is said to give grace when there is no grace whatever in the soul, or in other words, when the soul is in mortal sin. A Sacrament is said to increase grace when there is already grace in the soul, to which more is added by the Sacrament received.

Q. 593. Which are the Sacraments that give sanctifying grace?

A. The Sacraments that give sanctifying grace are Baptism and Penance; and they are called Sacraments of the dead.

Q. 594. Why are Baptism and Penance called Sacraments of the dead?

A. Baptism and Penance are called Sacraments of the dead because they take away sin, which is the death of the soul, and give grace, which is its life.

Q. 595. May not the Sacrament of Penance be received by one who is in a state of grace?

A. The Sacrament of Penance may be and very often is received by one who is in a state of grace, and when thus received it increases -- as the Sacraments of the living do -- the grace already in the soul.

Q. 596. Which are the Sacraments that increase sanctifying grace in our soul?

A. The Sacraments that increase sanctifying grace in our souls are:
1.Confirmation, Holy Eucharist, Extreme Unction, Holy Orders, and Matrimony; and they are called Sacraments of the living.

Q. 597. What do we mean by Sacraments of the dead and Sacraments of the living?

A. By the Sacraments of the dead we mean those Sacraments that may be lawfully received while the soul is in a state of mortal sin. By the Sacraments of the living we mean those Sacraments that can be lawfully received only while the soul is in a state of grace -- i.e., free from mortal sin. Living and dead do not refer here to the persons, but to the condition of the souls; for none of the Sacraments can be given to a dead person.

Q. 598. Why are Confirmation, Holy Eucharist, Extreme Unction, Holy Orders, and Matrimony called Sacraments of the living?

A. Confirmation, Holy Eucharist, Extreme Unction, Holy Orders, and Matrimony are called Sacraments of the living because those who receive them worthily are already living the life of grace.

Q. 599. What sin does he commit who receives the Sacraments of the living in mortal sin?

A. He who receives the Sacraments of the living in mortal sin commits a sacrilege, which is a great sin, because it is an abuse of a sacred thing.

Q. 600. In what other ways besides the unworthy reception of the Sacraments may persons commit sacrilege?

A. Besides the unworthy reception of the Sacraments, persons may commit sacrilege by the abuse of a sacred person, place or thing; for example, by willfully wounding a person consecrated to God; by robbing or destroying a Church; by using the sacred vessels of the Altar for unlawful purposes, etc.

Q. 601. Besides sanctifying grace do the Sacraments give any other grace?

A. Besides sanctifying grace the Sacraments give another grace, called sacramental grace.

Q. 602. What is sacramental grace?

A. Sacramental grace is a special help which God gives, to attain the end for which He instituted each Sacrament.

Q. 603. Is the Sacramental grace independent of the sanctifying grace given in the Sacraments?

A. The Sacramental grace is not independent of the sanctifying grace given in the Sacraments; for it is the sanctifying grace that gives us a certain right to special helps -- called Sacramental grace -- in each Sacrament, as often as we have to fulfill the end of the Sacrament or are tempted against it.

Q. 604. Give an example of how the Sacramental grace aids us, for instance, in Confirmation and Penance.

A. The end of Confirmation is to strengthen us in our faith. When we are tempted to deny our religion by word or deed, the Sacramental Grace of Confirmation is given to us and helps us to cling to our faith and firmly profess it.

The end of Penance is to destroy actual sin. When we are tempted to sin, the Sacramental Grace of Penance is given to us and helps us to overcome the temptation and persevere in a state of grace. The sacramental grace in each of the other Sacraments is given in the same manner, and aids us in attaining the end for which each Sacrament was instituted and for which we receive it.

Q. 605. Do the Sacraments always give grace?

A. The Sacraments always give grace, if we receive them with the right dispositions.

Q. 606. What do we mean by the "right dispositions" for the reception of the Sacraments?

A. By the right dispositions for the reception of the Sacraments we mean the proper motives and the fulfillment of all the conditions required by God and the Church for the worthy reception of the Sacraments.

Q. 607. Give an example of the "right dispositions" for Penance and for the Holy Eucharist.

A. The right dispositions for Penance are:

1.(1) To confess all our mortal sins as we know them;
2.(2) To be sorry for them, and
3.(3) To have the determination never to commit them or others again.

The right dispositions for the Holy Eucharist are:

1.(1) To know what the Holy Eucharist is;
2.(2) To be in a state of grace, and
3.(3) -- except in special cases of sickness -- to be fasting from midnight.

Q. 608. Can we receive the Sacraments more than once?

A. We can receive the Sacraments more than once, except Baptism, Confirmation, and Holy Orders.

Q. 609. Why can we not receive Baptism, Confirmation, and Holy Orders more than once?

A. We cannot receive Baptism, Confirmation, and Holy Orders more than once, because they imprint a character in the soul.

Q. 610. What is the character which these Sacraments imprint in the soul?

A. The character which these Sacraments imprint in the soul is a spiritual mark which remains forever.

Q. 611. Does this character remain in the soul even after death?

A. This character remains in the soul even after death; for the honor and glory of those who are saved; for the shame and punishment of those who are lost.

Q. 612. Can the Sacraments be given conditionally?

A. The Sacraments can be given conditionally as often as we doubt whether they were properly given before, or whether they can be validly given now.

Q. 613. What do we mean by giving a Sacrament conditionally?

A. By giving a Sacrament conditionally we mean that the person administering the Sacrament intends to give it only in case it has not been given already or in case the person has the right dispositions for receiving it, though the dispositions cannot be discovered.

Q. 614. Give an example of how a Sacrament is given conditionally.

A. In giving Baptism, for instance, conditionally -- or what we call conditional Baptism -- the priest, instead of saying absolutely, as he does in ordinary Baptism: "I baptize thee," etc., says: "If you are not already baptized, or if you are capable of being baptized, I baptize thee," etc., thus stating the sole condition on which he intends to administer the Sacrament.

Q. 615. Which of the Sacraments are most frequently given conditionally?

A. The Sacraments most frequently given conditionally are Baptism, Penance and Extreme Unction; because in some cases it is difficult to ascertain whether these Sacraments have been given before or whether they have been validly given, or whether the person about to receive them has the right dispositions for them.

Q. 616. Name some of the more common circumstances in which a priest is obliged to administer the Sacraments conditionally.

A. Some of the more common circumstances in which a priest is obliged to administer the Sacraments conditionally are:

1.(1) When he receives converts into the Church and is not certain of their previous baptism, he must baptize them conditionally.

2.(2) When he is called -- as in cases of accident or sudden illness -- and doubts whether the person be alive or dead, or whether he should be given the Sacraments, he must give absolution and administer Extreme Unction conditionally.

Q. 617. What is the use and effect of giving the Sacraments conditionally?

A. The use of giving the Sacraments conditionally is that there may be no irreverence to the Sacraments in giving them to persons incapable or unworthy of receiving them; and yet that no one who is capable or worthy may be deprived of them. The effect is to supply the Sacrament where it is needed or can be given, and to withhold it where it is not needed or cannot be given.

Q. 618. What is the difference between the powers of a bishop and of a priest with regard to the administration of the Sacraments?

A. The difference between the powers of a bishop and of a priest with regard to the administration of the Sacraments is that a bishop can give all the Sacraments, while a priest cannot give Confirmation or Holy Orders.

Q. 619. Can a person receive all the Sacraments?

A. A person cannot, as a rule, receive all the Sacraments; for a woman cannot receive Holy Orders, and a man who receives priesthood is forbidden to receive the Sacrament of Matrimony.

Lesson Fourteenth: On Baptism

Q. 620. When was baptism instituted?

A. Baptism was instituted, very probably, about the time Our Lord was baptized by St. John, and its reception was commanded when after His resurrection Our Lord said to His Apostles: "All power is given to Me in heaven and in earth. Going, therefore, teach all nations, baptizing them in the name of the Father, and of the Son, and of the Holy Ghost."

Q. 621. What is Baptism?

A. Baptism is a Sacrament which cleanses us from original sin, makes us Christians, children of God, and heirs of heaven.

Q. 622. What were persons called in the first ages of the Church who were being instructed and prepared for baptism?

A. Persons who were being instructed and prepared for baptism, in the first ages of the Church, were called catechumens, and they are frequently mentioned in Church history.

Q. 623. What persons are called heirs?

A. All persons who inherit or come lawfully into the possession of property or goods at the death of another, are called heirs.

Q. 624. Why, then, are we the heirs of Christ?

A. We are the heirs of Christ because at His death we came into the possession of God's friendship, of grace, and of the right to enter heaven, provided we comply with the conditions Our Lord has laid down for the gaining of this inheritance.

Q. 625. What conditions has Our Lord laid down for the gaining of this inheritance?

A. The conditions Our Lord has laid down for the gaining of this inheritance are:

1.(1) That we receive, when possible, the Sacraments He has instituted; and

2.(2) That we believe and practice all He has taught.

Q. 626. Did not St. John the Baptist institute the Sacrament of Baptism?

A. St. John the Baptist did not institute the Sacrament of Baptism, for Christ alone could institute a Sacrament. The baptism given by St. John had the effect of a Sacramental; that is, it did not of itself give grace, but prepared the way for it.

Q. 627. Are actual sins ever remitted by Baptism?

A. Actual sins and all the punishment due to them are remitted by Baptism, if the person baptized be guilty of any.

Q. 628. That actual sins may be remitted by baptism, is it necessary to be sorry for them?

A. That actual sins may be remitted by baptism it is necessary to be sorry for them, just as we must be when they are remitted by the Sacrament of Penance.

Q. 629. What punishments are due to actual sins?

A. Two punishments are due to actual sins: one, called the eternal, is inflicted in hell; and the other, called the temporal, is inflicted in this world or in purgatory. The Sacrament of Penance remits or frees us from the eternal punishment and generally only from part of the temporal. Prayer, good works and indulgences in this world and the sufferings of purgatory in the next remit the remainder of the temporal punishment.

Q. 630. Why is there a double punishment attached to actual sins?

1.There is a double punishment attached to actual sins, because in their commission there is a double guilt:

2.(1) Of insulting God and of turning away from Him;

3.(2) Of depriving Him of the honor we owe Him, and of turning to His enemies.

Q. 631. Is Baptism necessary to salvation?

A. Baptism is necessary to salvation, because without it we cannot enter into the kingdom of heaven.

Q. 632. Where will persons go who -- such as infants -- have not committed actual sin and who, through no fault of theirs, die without baptism?

A. Persons, such as infants, who have not committed actual sin and who, through no fault of theirs, die without baptism, cannot enter heaven; but it is the common belief they will go to some place similar to Limbo, where they will be free from suffering, though deprived of the happiness of heaven.

Q. 633. Who can administer Baptism?

A. A priest is the ordinary minister of baptism; but in case of necessity anyone who has the use of reason may baptize.

Q. 634. What do we mean by the "ordinary minister" of a Sacrament?

A. By the "ordinary minister" of a Sacrament we mean the one who usually does administer the Sacrament, and who has always the right to do so.

Q. 635. Can a person who has not himself been baptized, and who does not even believe in the Sacrament of baptism, give it validly to another in case of necessity?

A. A person who has not himself been baptized, and who does not even believe in the Sacrament of baptism, can give it validly to another in case of necessity, provided:

1.(1) He has the use of reason;

2.(2) Knows how to give baptism, and

3.(3) Intends to do what the Church intends in the giving of the Sacrament. Baptism is so necessary that God affords every opportunity for its reception.

Q. 636. Why do the consequences of original sin, such as suffering, temptation, sickness, and death, remain after the sin has been forgiven in baptism?

A. The consequences of original sin, such as suffering, temptation, sickness and death, remain after the sin has been forgiven in baptism:

1.(1) To remind us of the misery that always follows sin; and

2.(2) To afford us an opportunity of increasing our merit by bearing these hardships patiently.

Q. 637. Can a person ever receive any of the other Sacraments without first receiving baptism?

A. A person can never receive any of the other Sacraments without first receiving baptism, because baptism makes us members of Christ's Church, and unless we are members of His Church we cannot receive His Sacraments.

Q. 638. How is Baptism given?

A. Whoever baptizes should pour water on the head of the person to be baptized, and say, while pouring the water: "I baptize thee in the name of the Father, and of the Son, and of the Holy Ghost."

Q. 639. If water cannot be had, in case of necessity, may any other liquid be used for baptism?

A. If water cannot be had, in case of necessity or in any case, no other liquid can be used, and the baptism cannot be given.

Q. 640. If it is impossible, in case of necessity, to reach the head, may the water be poured on any other part of the body?

A. If it is impossible, in case of necessity, to reach the head, the water should be poured on whatever part of the body can be reached; but then the baptism must be given conditionally; that is, before pronouncing the words of baptism, you must say: "If I can baptize thee in this way, I baptize thee in the name of the Father," etc. If the head can afterward be reached, the water must be poured on the head and the baptism repeated conditionally by saying: "If you are not already baptized, I baptize thee in the name," etc.

Q. 641. Is the baptism valid if we say: "I baptize thee in the name of the Holy Trinity," without naming the Persons of the Trinity?

A. The baptism is not valid if we say: "I baptize thee in the name of the Holy Trinity," without naming the Persons of the Trinity; for we must use the exact words instituted by Christ.

Q. 642. Is it wrong to defer the baptism of an infant?

A. It is wrong to defer the baptism of an infant, because we thereby expose the child to the danger of dying without the Sacrament.

Q. 643. Can we baptize a child against the wishes of its parents?

A. We cannot baptize a child against the wishes of its parents; and if the parents are not Catholics, they must not only consent to the baptism, but also agree to bring the child up in the Catholic religion. But if a child is surely dying, we may baptize it without either the consent or permission of its parents.

Q. 644. How many kinds of Baptism are there?

A. There are three kinds of Baptism:

1.Baptism of water, of desire, and of blood.

Q. 645. What is Baptism of water?

A. Baptism of water is that which is given by pouring water on the head of the person to be baptized, and saying at the same time, "I baptize thee in the name of the Father, and of the Son, and of the Holy Ghost."

Q. 646. In how many ways was the baptism of water given in the first ages of the Church?

A. In the first ages of the Church, baptism of water was given in three ways, namely, by immersion or dipping, by aspersion or sprinkling, and by infusion or pouring. Although any of these methods would be valid, only the method of infusion or pouring is now allowed in the Church.

Q. 647. What are the chief ceremonies used in solemn baptism, and what do they signify?

A. The chief ceremonies used in solemn baptism are:

1.(1) A profession of faith and renouncement of the devil to signify our worthiness;

2.(2) The placing of salt in the mouth to signify the wisdom imparted by faith;

3.(3) The holding of the priest's stole to signify our reception into the Church;

4.(4) The anointing to signify the strength given by the Sacrament;

5.(5) The giving of the white garment or cloth to signify our sinless state after baptism; and

6.(6) The giving of the lighted candle to signify the light of faith and fire of love that should dwell in our souls.

Q. 648. Should one who, in case of necessity, has been baptized with private baptism, be afterwards brought to the Church to have the ceremonies of solemn baptism completed?

A. One who, in case of necessity, has been baptized with private baptism should afterwards be brought to the Church to have the ceremonies of solemn baptism completed, because these ceremonies are commanded by the Church and bring down blessings upon us.

Q. 649. Is solemn baptism given with any special kind of water?

A. Solemn baptism is given with consecrated water; that is, water mixed with holy oil and blessed for baptism on Holy Saturday and on the Saturday before Pentecost. It is always kept in the baptismal font in the baptistry – a place near the door of the Church set apart for baptism.

Q. 650. What is Baptism of desire?

A. Baptism of desire is an ardent wish to receive Baptism, and to do all that God has ordained for our salvation.

Q. 651. What is Baptism of blood?

A. Baptism of blood is the shedding of one's blood for the faith of Christ.

Q. 652. What is the baptism of blood most commonly called?

A. The baptism of blood is most commonly called martyrdom, and those who receive it are called martyrs. It is the death one patiently suffers from the enemies of our religion, rather than give up Catholic faith or virtue. We must not seek martyrdom, though we must endure it when it comes.

Q. 653. Is Baptism of desire or of blood sufficient to produce the effects of Baptism of water?

A. Baptism of desire or of blood is sufficient to produce the effects of the Baptism of water, if it is impossible to receive the Baptism of water.

Q. 654. How do we know that the baptism of desire or of blood will save us when it is impossible to receive the baptism of water?

A. We know that baptism of desire or of blood will save us when it is impossible to receive the baptism of water, from Holy Scripture, which teaches that love of God and perfect contrition can secure the remission of sins ; and also that Our Lord promises salvation to those who lay down their life for His sake or for His teaching.

Q. 655. What do we promise in Baptism?

A. In Baptism we promise to renounce the devil, with all his works and pomps.

Q. 656. What do we mean by the "pomps" of the devil?

A. By the pomps of the devil we mean all worldly pride, vanities and vain shows by which people are enticed into sin, and all foolish or sinful display of ourselves or of what we possess.

Q. 657. Why is the name of a saint given in Baptism?

A. The name of a saint is given in Baptism in order that the person baptized may imitate his virtues and have him for a protector.

Q. 658. What is the Saint whose name we bear called?

A. The saint whose name we bear is called our patron saint -- to whom we should have great devotion.

Q. 659. What names should never be given in baptism?

A. These and similar names should never be given in baptism:

1.(1) The names of noted unbelievers, heretics or enemies of religion and virtue;

2.(2) The names of heathen gods, and

3.(3) Nick-names.

Q. 660. Why are godfathers and godmothers given in Baptism?

A. Godfathers and godmothers are given in Baptism in order that they may promise, in the name of the child, what the child itself would promise if it had the use of reason.

Q. 661. By what other name are godfathers and godmothers called?

A. Godfathers and godmothers are usually called sponsors. Sponsors are not necessary at private baptism.

Q. 662. Can a person ever be sponsor when absent from the baptism?

A. A person can be sponsor even when absent from the baptism, provided he has been asked and has consented to be sponsor, and provided also some one answers the questions and touches the person to be baptized in his name. The absent godfather or godmother is then said to be sponsor by proxy and becomes the real godparent of the one baptized.

Q. 663. With whom do godparents, as well as the one baptizing, contract a relationship?

A. Godparents, as well as the one baptizing, contract a spiritual relationship with the person baptized (not with his parents), and this relationship is an impediment to marriage that must be made known to the priest in case of their future marriage with one another. The godfather and godmother contract no relationship with each other.

Q. 664. What questions should persons who bring a child for baptism be able to answer?

A. Persons who bring a child for baptism should be able to tell:

1.(1) The exact place where the child lives;
2.(2) The full name of its parents, and, in particular, the maiden name, or name before her marriage, of its mother;
3.(3) The exact day of the month on which it was born;
4.(4) Whether or not it has received private baptism, and
5.(5) Whether its parents be Catholics.

Sponsors must know also the chief truths of our religion.

Q. 665. What is the obligation of a godfather and a godmother?

A. The obligation of a godfather and a godmother is to instruct the child in its religious duties, if the parents neglect to do so or die.

Q. 666. Can persons who are not Catholics be sponsors for Catholic children?

A. Persons who are not Catholics cannot be sponsors for Catholic children, because they cannot perform the duties of sponsors; for if they do not know and profess the Catholic religion themselves, how can they teach it to their godchildren? Moreover, they must answer the questions asked at baptism and declare that they believe in the Holy Catholic Church and in all it teaches; which would be a falsehood on their part.

Q. 667. What should parents chiefly consider in the selection of sponsors for their children?

A. In the selection of sponsors for their children parents should chiefly consider the good character and virtue of the sponsors, selecting model

Catholics to whom they would be willing at the hour of death to entrust the care and training of their children.

Q. 668. What dispositions must adults or grown persons, have that they may worthily receive baptism?

A. That adults may worthily receive baptism:

1.(1) They must be willing to receive it;
2.(2) They must have faith in Christ;
3.(3) They must have true sorrow for their sins, and
4.(4) They must solemnly renounce the devil and all his works; that is, all sin.

Q. 669. What is the ceremony of churching?

A. The ceremony of churching is a particular blessing which a mother receives at the Altar, as soon as she is able to present herself in the Church after the birth of her child. In this ceremony the priest invokes God's blessing on the mother and child, while she on her part returns thanks to God.

Lesson Fifteenth: On Confirmation

Q. 670. What is Confirmation?

A. Confirmation is a Sacrament through which we receive the Holy Ghost to make us strong and perfect Christians and soldiers of Jesus Christ.

Q. 671. When was Confirmation instituted?

A. The exact time at which Confirmation was instituted is not known. But as this Sacrament was administered by the Apostles and numbered with the other Sacraments instituted by Our Lord, it is certain that He instituted this Sacrament also and instructed His Apostles in its use, at some time before His ascension into heaven.

Q. 672. Why is Confirmation so called?

A. Confirmation is so called from its chief effect, which is to strengthen or render us more firm in whatever belongs to our faith and religious duties.

Q. 673. Why are we called soldiers of Jesus Christ?

A. We are called soldiers of Jesus Christ to indicate how we must resist the attacks of our spiritual enemies and secure our victory over them by following and obeying Our Lord.

Q. 674. May one add a new name to his own at Confirmation?

A. One may and should add a new name to his own at Confirmation, especially when the name of a saint has not been given in Baptism.

Q. 675. Who administers Confirmation?

A. The bishop is the ordinary minister of Confirmation.

Q. 676. Why do we say the bishop is the "ordinary minister" of Confirmation?

A. We say the bishop is the ordinary minister of Confirmation because in some foreign missions, where bishops have not yet been appointed, the Holy Father permits one of the priests to administer Confirmation with the Holy

Oil blessed by the bishop.

Q. 677. How does the bishop give Confirmation?

A. The bishop extends his hands over those who are to be confirmed, prays that they may receive the Holy Ghost, and anoints the forehead of each with holy chrism in the form of a cross.

Q. 678. In Confirmation, what does the extending of the bishop's hands over us signify?

A. In Confirmation, the extending of the bishop's hands over us signifies the descent of the Holy Ghost upon us and the special protection of God through the grace of Confirmation.

Q. 679. What is holy chrism?

A. Holy chrism is a mixture of olive-oil and balm, consecrated by the bishop.

Q. 680. What do the oil and balm in Holy Chrism signify?

A. In Holy Chrism, the oil signifies strength, and the balm signifies the freedom from corruption and the sweetness which virtue must give to our lives.

Q. 681. How many holy oils are used in the Church?

A. Three holy oils are used in the Church, namely, the oil of the sick, the oil of catechumens, and holy chrism.

Q. 682. What constitutes the difference between these oils?

A. The form of prayer or blessing alone constitutes the difference between these oils; for they are all olive oil, but in the Holy Chrism, balm is mixed with the oil.

Q. 683. When and by whom are the holy oils blessed?

A. The holy oils are blessed at the Mass on Holy Thursday by the bishop, who alone has the right to bless them.

After the blessing they are distributed to the priests of the diocese, who must then burn what remains of the old oils and use the newly blessed oils for the coming year.

Q. 684. For what are the holy oils used?

A. The holy oils are used as follows: The oil of the sick is used for Extreme Unction and for some blessings; the oil of catechumens is used for Baptism and Holy Orders. Holy Chrism is used at Baptism and for the blessing of some sacred things, such as altars, chalices, church-bells, etc., which are usually blessed by a bishop.

Q. 685. What does the bishop say in anointing the person he confirms?

A. In anointing the person he confirms the bishop says: "I sign thee with the sign of the cross, and I confirm thee with the chrism of salvation, in the name of the Father, and of the Son, and of the Holy Ghost."

Q. 686. What is meant by anointing the forehead with chrism in the form of a cross?

A. By anointing the forehead with chrism in the form of a cross is meant that the Christian who is confirmed must openly profess and practice his faith, never be ashamed of it; and rather die than deny it.

Q. 687. When must we openly profess and practice our religion?

A. We must openly profess and practice our religion as often as we cannot do otherwise without violating some law of God or of His Church.

Q. 688. Why have we good reason never to be ashamed of the Catholic faith?

A. We have good reason never to be ashamed of the Catholic Faith because it is the Old Faith established by Christ and taught by His Apostles; it is the Faith for which countless Holy Martyrs suffered and died; it is the Faith that has brought true civilization, with all its benefits, into the world, and it is the only Faith that can truly reform and preserve public and private morals.

Q. 689. Why does the bishop give the person he confirms a slight blow on the cheek?

A. The bishop gives the person he confirms a slight blow on the cheek, to put him in mind that he must be ready to suffer everything, even death, for the sake of Christ.

Q. 690. Is it right to test ourselves through our imagination of what we would be willing to suffer for the sake of Christ?

A. It is not right to test ourselves through our imagination of what we would be willing to suffer for the sake of Christ, for such tests may lead us into sin. When a real test comes we are assured God will give to us, as He did to the Holy Martyrs, sufficient grace to endure it.

Q. 691. To receive Confirmation worthily is it necessary to be in the state of grace?

A. To receive Confirmation worthily it is necessary to be in the state of grace.

Q. 692. What special preparation should be made to receive Confirmation?

A. Persons of an age to learn should know the chief mysteries of faith and the duties of a Christian, and be instructed in the nature and effects of this Sacrament.

Q. 693. Why should we know the chief mysteries of faith and the duties of a Christian before receiving Confirmation?

A. We should know the Chief Mysteries of Faith and the duties of a Christian before receiving Confirmation because as one cannot be a good soldier without knowing the rules of the army to which he belongs and understanding the commands of his leader, so one cannot be a good Christian without knowing the laws of the Church and understanding the commands of Christ.

Q. 694. Is it a sin to neglect Confirmation?

A. It is a sin to neglect Confirmation, especially in these evil days when faith and morals are exposed to so many and such violent temptations.

Q. 695. What do we mean by "these evil days"?

A. By "these evil days" we mean the present age or century in which we are living, surrounded on all sides by unbelief, false doctrines, bad books, bad example and temptation in every form.

Q. 696. Is Confirmation necessary for salvation?

A. Confirmation is not so necessary for salvation that we could not be saved without it, for it is not given to infants even in danger of death; nevertheless, there is a divine command obliging all to receive it, if possible. Persons who have not been confirmed in youth should make every effort to be confirmed later in life.

Q. 697. Are sponsors necessary in Confirmation?

A. Sponsors are necessary in Confirmation, and they must be of the same good character as those required at Baptism, for they take upon themselves the same duties and responsibilities. They also contract a spiritual relationship, which, however, unlike that in Baptism, is not an impediment to marriage.

Q. 698. Which are the effects of Confirmation?

A. The effects of Confirmation are an increase of sanctifying grace, the strengthening of our faith, and the gifts of the Holy Ghost.

Q. 699. Which are the gifts of the Holy Ghost?

A. The gifts of the Holy Ghost are Wisdom, Understanding, Counsel, Fortitude, Knowledge, Piety, and Fear of the Lord.

Q. 700. Why do we receive the gift of Fear of the Lord?

A. We receive the gift of Fear of the Lord to fill us with a dread of sin.

Q. 701. Why do we receive the gift of Piety?

A. We receive the gift of Piety to make us love God as a Father, and obey Him because we love Him.

Q. 702. Why do we receive the gift of Knowledge?

A. We receive the gift of Knowledge to enable us to discover the will of God in all things.

Q. 703. Why do we receive the gift of Fortitude?

A. We receive the gift of Fortitude to strengthen us to do the will of God in all things.

Q. 704. Why do we receive the gift of Counsel?

A. We receive the gift of Counsel to warn us of the deceits of the devil, and of the dangers to salvation.

Q. 705. How is it clear that the devil could easily deceive us if the Holy Ghost did not aid us?

A. It is clear that the devil could easily deceive us if the Holy Ghost did not aid us, for just as our sins do not deprive us of our knowledge, so the devil's sin did not deprive him of the great intelligence and power which he possessed as an angel. Moreover, his experience in the world extends over all ages and places, while ours is confined to a few years and to a limited number of places.

Q. 706. Why do we receive the gift of Understanding?

A. We receive the gift of Understanding to enable us to know more clearly the mysteries of faith.

Q. 707. Why do we receive the gift of Wisdom?

A. We receive the gift of Wisdom to give us a relish for the things of God, and to direct our whole life and all our actions to His honor and glory.

Q. 708. Which are the Beatitudes?

A. The Beatitudes are:

1.1. Blessed are the poor in spirit, for theirs is the kingdom of heaven.

2.2. Blessed are the meek, for they shall possess the land.

3.3. Blessed are they that mourn, for they shall be comforted.

4.4. Blessed are they that hunger and thirst after justice, for they shall be filled.

5.5. Blessed are the merciful, for they shall obtain mercy.

6.6. Blessed are the clean of heart, for they shall see God.

7.7. Blessed are the peacemakers, for they shall be called the children of God.

8.8. Blessed are they that suffer persecution for justice' sake, for theirs is the kingdom of heaven.

Q. 709. What are the Beatitudes and why are they so called?

A. The Beatitudes are a portion of Our Lord's Sermon on the Mount, and they are so called because each of them holds out a promised reward to those who practice the virtues they recommend.

Q. 710. Where did Our Lord usually preach?

A. Our Lord usually preached wherever an opportunity of doing good by His Words presented itself. He preached at times in the synagogues or meeting-houses but more frequently in the open air -- by the seashore or on the mountain, and often by the wayside.

Q. 711. What is the meaning and use of the Beatitudes in general?

A.

1.(1) In general the Beatitudes embrace whatever pertains to the perfection of Christian life, and they invite us to the practice of the highest Christian virtues.

2.(2) In different forms they all promise the same reward, namely, sanctifying grace in this life and eternal glory in the next.

3.(3) They offer us encouragement and consolation for every trial and affliction.

Q. 712. What does the first Beatitude mean by the "poor in spirit"?

A. The first Beatitude means by the "poor in spirit" all persons, rich or poor, who would not offend God to possess or retain anything that this world can give; and who, when necessity or charity requires it, give willingly for the glory of God. It includes also those who humbly submit to their condition in life when it cannot be improved by lawful means.

Q. 713. Who are the mourners who deserve the consolation promised in the third Beatitude?

A. The mourners who deserve the consolation promised in the third Beatitude are they who, out of love for God, bewail their own sins and those of the world; and they who patiently endure all trials that come from God or for His sake.

Q. 714. What lessons do the other Beatitudes convey?

110

A. The other Beatitudes convey these lessons: The meek suppress all feelings of anger and humbly submit to whatever befalls them by the Will of God; and they never desire to do evil for evil. The justice after which we should seek is every Christian virtue included under that name, and we are told that if we earnestly desire and seek it we shall obtain it. The persecuted for justice' sake are they who will not abandon their faith or virtue for any cause.

Q. 715. Who may be rightly called merciful?

A. The merciful are they who practice the corporal and spiritual works of mercy, and who aid by word or deed those who need their help for soul or body.

Q. 716. Why are the clean of heart promised so great a reward?

A. The clean of heart, that is, the truly virtuous, whose thoughts, desires, words and works are pure and modest, are promised so great a reward because the chaste and sinless have always been the most intimate friends of God.

Q. 717. What is the duty of a peacemaker?

A. It is the duty of a peacemaker to avoid and prevent quarrels, reconcile enemies, and to put an end to all evil reports of others or evil speaking against them. As peacemakers are called the children of God, disturbers of peace should be called the children of the devil.

Q. 718. Why does Our Lord speak in particular of poverty, meekness, sorrow, desire for virtue, mercy, purity, peace and suffering?

A. Our Lord speaks in particular of poverty, meekness, sorrow, desire for virtue, mercy, purity, peace and suffering because these are the chief features in His own earthly life; poverty in His birth, life and death; meekness in His teaching; sorrow at all times. He eagerly sought to do good, showed mercy to all, recommended chastity, brought peace, and patiently endured suffering.

Q. 719. Which are the twelve fruits of the Holy Ghost?

A. The twelve fruits of the Holy Ghost are Charity, Joy, Peace, Patience, Benignity, Goodness, Long-suffering, Mildness, Faith, Modesty, Continency, and Chastity.

Q. 720. Why are charity, joy, peace, etc., called fruits of the Holy Ghost?

A. Charity, joy, peace, etc., are called fruits of the Holy Ghost because they grow in our souls out of the seven gifts of the Holy Ghost.

Lesson Seventeenth: On the Sacrament of Penance

Q. 721. What is the Sacrament of Penance?

A. Penance is a Sacrament in which the sins committed after Baptism are forgiven.

Q 722. Has the word Penance any other meaning?

A. The word Penance has other meanings. It means also those punishments we inflict upon ourselves as a means of atoning for our past sins; it means likewise that disposition of the heart in which we detest and bewail our sins because they were offensive to God.

Q. 723. How does the institution of the Sacrament of Penance show the goodness of Our Lord?

A. The institution of the Sacrament of Penance shows the goodness of Our Lord, because having once saved us through Baptism, He might have left us to perish if we again committed sin.

Q. 724. What are the natural benefits of the Sacrament of Penance?

A. The natural benefits of the Sacrament of Penance are: It gives us in our confessor a true friend, to whom we can go in all our trials and to whom we can confide our secrets with the hope of obtaining advice and relief.

Q. 725. How does the Sacrament of Penance remit sin, and restore to the soul the friendship of God?

A. The Sacrament of Penance remits sin and restores the friendship of God to the soul by means of the absolution of the priest.

Q. 726. What is Absolution?

A. Absolution is the form of prayer or words the priest pronounces over us with uplifted hand when he forgives the sins we have confessed. It is given while we are saying the Act of Contrition after receiving our Penance.

Q. 727. Does the priest ever refuse absolution to a penitent?

A. The priest must and does refuse absolution to a penitent when he thinks the penitent is not rightly disposed for the Sacrament. He sometimes postpones the absolution till the next confession, either for the good of the penitent or for the sake of better preparation -- especially when the person has been a long time from confession.

Q. 728. What should a person do when the priest has refused or postponed absolution?

A. When the priest has refused or postponed absolution, the penitent should humbly submit to his decision, follow his instructions, and endeavor to remove whatever prevented the giving of the absolution and return to the same confessor with the necessary dispositions and resolution of amendment.

Q. 729. Can the priest forgive all sins in the Sacrament of Penance?

A. The priest has the power to forgive all sins in the Sacrament of Penance, but he may not have the authority to forgive all. To forgive sins validly in the Sacrament of Penance, two things are required:

1.(1) The power to forgive sins which every priest receives at his ordination, and

2.(2) The right to use that power which must be given by the bishop, who authorizes the priest to hear confessions and pass judgment on the sins.

Q. 730. What are the sins called which the priest has no authority to absolve?

A. The sins which the priest has no authority to absolve are called reserved sins. Absolution from these sins can be obtained only from the bishop, and sometimes only from the Pope, or by his special permission. Persons having a reserved sin to confess cannot be absolved from any of their sins till the priest receives faculties or authority to absolve the reserved sin also.

Q. 731. Why is the absolution from some sins reserved to the Pope or bishop?

A. The absolution from some sins is reserved to the Pope or bishop to deter or prevent, by this special restriction, persons from committing them, either on account of the greatness of the sin itself or on account of its evil consequences.

Q. 732. Can any priest absolve a person in danger of death from reserved sins without the permission of the bishop?

A. Any priest can absolve a person in danger of death from reserved sins without the permission of the bishop, because at the hour of death the Church removes these restrictions in order to save, if possible, the soul of the dying.

Q. 733. How do you know that the priest has the power of absolving from the sins committed after Baptism?

A. I know that the priest has the power of absolving from the sins committed after Baptism, because Jesus Christ granted that power to the priests of His Church when He said: "Receive ye the Holy Ghost. Whose sins you shall forgive, they are forgiven them; whose sins you shall retain, they are retained."

Q. 734. How do we know that Our Lord, while on earth, had the power to forgive sins?

A. We know that Our Lord, while on earth, had the power to forgive sins:

1.(1) Because He was always God, and;
2.(2) Because He frequently did forgive sins and proved their forgiveness by miracles.

Since He had the power Himself, He could give it to His Apostles.

Q. 735. Was the power to forgive sins given to the apostles alone?

A. The power to forgive sins was not given to the apostles alone, because it was not given for the benefit merely of those who lived at the time of the apostles, but for all who, having grievously sinned, after Baptism, should need forgiveness. Since, therefore, Baptism will be given till the end of time, and since the danger of sinning after it always remains the power to absolve from such sins must also remain in the Church till the end of time.

Q. 736. When was the Sacrament of Penance instituted?

A. The Sacrament of Penance was instituted after the resurrection of Our Lord, when He gave to His apostles the power to forgive sins, which He had promised to them before His death.

Q. 737. Are the enemies of our religion right when they say man cannot forgive sins?

A. The enemies of our religion are right when they say man cannot forgive sins if they mean that he cannot forgive them by his own power, but they are certainly wrong if they mean that he cannot forgive them even by the power of God, for man can do anything if God gives him the power. The priest does not forgive sins by his own power as man, but by the authority he receives as the minister of God.

Q. 738. How do the priests of the Church exercise the power of forgiving sins?

A. The priests of the Church exercise the power of forgiving sins by hearing the confession of sins, and granting pardon for them as ministers of God and in His name.

Q. 739. How does the power to forgive sins imply the obligation of going to confession?

A. The power to forgive sins implies the obligation of going to confession because as sins are usually committed secretly, the priest could never know what sins to forgive and what not to forgive, unless the sins committed were made known to him by the persons guilty of them.

Q. 740. Could God not forgive our sins if we confessed them to Himself in secret?

A. Certainly, God could forgive our sins if we confessed them to Himself in secret, but He has not promised to do so; whereas He has promised to pardon them if we confess them to His priests. Since He is free to pardon or not to pardon, He has the right to establish a Sacrament through which alone He will pardon.

Q. 741. What must we do to receive the Sacrament of Penance worthily?

A. To receive the Sacrament of Penance worthily we must do five things:

1.1. We must examine our conscience.

2.2. We must have sorrow for our sins.

3.3. We must make a firm resolution never more to offend God.

4.4. We must confess our sins to the priest.

5.5. We must accept the penance which the priest gives us.

Q. 742. What should we pray for in preparing for confession?

A. In preparing for confession we should pray to the Holy Ghost to give us light to know our sins and to understand their guilt; for grace to detest them; for courage to confess them and for strength to keep our resolutions.

Q. 743. What faults do many commit in preparing for confession?

A. In preparing for confession many commit the faults:

1.(1) Of giving too much time to the examination of conscience and little or none in exciting themselves to true sorrow for the sins discovered;

2.(2) Of trying to recall every trifling circumstance, instead of thinking of the means by which they will avoid their sins for the future.

Q. 744. What, then, is the most important part of the preparation for confession?

A. The most important part of the preparation for confession is sincere sorrow for the sins committed and the firm determination to avoid them for the future.

Q. 745. What is the chief reason that our confessions do not always amend our way of living?

A. The chief reason that our confessions do not always amend our way of living is our want of real earnest preparation for them and the fact that we have not truly convinced ourselves of the need of amendment. We often confess our sins more from habit, necessity or fear than from a real desire of receiving grace and of being restored to the friendship of God.

Q. 746. What faults are to be avoided in making our confession?

A. In making our confession we are to avoid:

1.(1) Telling useless details, the sins of others, or the name of any person;

2.(2) Confessing sins we are not sure of having committed; exaggerating our sins or their number; multiplying the number of times a day by the number of days to get the exact number of habitual sins;

3.(3) Giving a vague answer, such as "sometimes," when asked how often; waiting after each sin to be asked for the next;

4.(4) Hesitating over sins through pretended modesty and thus delaying the priests and others; telling the exact words in each when we have committed several sins of the same kind, cursing, for example; and, lastly, leaving the confessional before the priest gives us a sign to go.

Q. 747. Is it wrong to go to confession out of your turn against the will of others waiting with you?

A. It is wrong to go to confession out of our turn against the will of others waiting with us, because:

1.(1) It causes disorder, quarreling and scandalous conduct in the Church;

2.(2) It is unjust, makes others angry and lessens their good dispositions for confession;

3.(3) It annoys and distracts the priest by the confusion and disorder it creates. It is better to wait than go to confession in an excited and disorderly manner.

Q. 748. What should a penitent do who knows he cannot perform the penance given?

A. A penitent who knows he cannot perform the penance given should ask the priest for one that he can perform. When we forget the penance given we must ask for it again, for we cannot fulfill our duty by giving ourselves a penance. The penance must be performed at the time and in the manner the confessor directs.

Q. 749. What is the examination of conscience?

A. The examination of conscience is an earnest effort to recall to mind all the sins we have committed since our last worthy confession.

Q. 750. When is our confession worthy?

A. Our confession is worthy when we have done all that is required for a good confession, and when, through the absolution, our sins are really forgiven.

Q. 751. How can we make a good examination of conscience?

A. We can make a good examination of conscience by calling to memory the commandments of God, the precepts of the Church, the seven capital sins, and the particular duties of our state in life, to find out the sins we have committed.

Q. 752. What should we do before beginning the examination of conscience?

A. Before beginning the examination of conscience we should pray to God to give us light to know our sins and grace to detest them.

Lesson Eighteenth: On Contrition

Q. 753. What is contrition, or sorrow for sin?

A. Contrition, or sorrow for sin, is a hatred of sin and a true grief of the soul for having offended God, with a firm purpose of sinning no more.

Q. 754. Give an example of how we should hate and avoid sin.

A. We should hate and avoid sin as one hates and avoids a poison that almost caused his death. We may not grieve over the death of our soul as we do over the death of a friend, and yet our sorrow may be true; because the sorrow for sin comes more from our reason than from our feelings.

Q. 755. What kind of sorrow should we have for our sins?

A. The sorrow we should have for our sins should be interior, supernatural, universal, and sovereign.

Q. 756. What do you mean by saying that our sorrow should be interior?

A. When I say that our sorrow should be interior, I mean that it should come from the heart, and not merely from the lips.

Q. 757. What do you mean by saying that our sorrow should be supernatural?

A. When I say that our sorrow should be supernatural, I mean that it should be prompted by the grace of God, and excited by motives which spring from faith, and not by merely natural motives.

Q. 758. What do we mean by "motives that spring from faith" and by "merely natural motives" with regard to sorrow for sin?

A. By sorrow for sin from "motives that spring from faith," we mean sorrow for reasons that God has made known to us, such as the loss of heaven, the fear of hell or purgatory, or the dread of afflictions that come from God in punishment for sin. By "merely natural motives" we mean sorrow for reasons made known to us by our own experience or by the experience of others, such as loss of character, goods or health. A motive is whatever moves our will to do or avoid anything.

Q. 759. What do you mean by saying that our sorrow should be universal?

A. When I say that our sorrow should be universal, I mean that we should be sorry for all our mortal sins without exception.

Q. 760. Why cannot some of our mortal sins be forgiven while the rest remain on our souls?

A. It is impossible for any of our mortal sins to be forgiven unless they are all forgiven, because as light and darkness cannot be together in the same place, so sanctifying grace and mortal sin cannot dwell together. If there be grace in the soul, there can be no mortal sin, and if there be mortal sin, there can be no grace, for one mortal sin expels all grace.

Q. 761. What do you mean when you say that our sorrow should be sovereign?

A. When I say that our sorrow should be sovereign, I mean that we should grieve more for having offended God than for any other evil that can befall us.

Q. 762. Why should we be sorry for our sins?

A. We should be sorry for our sins because sin is the greatest of evils and an offense against God our Creator, Preserver, and Redeemer, and because it shuts us out of heaven and condemns us to the eternal pains of hell.

Q. 763. How do we show that sin is the greatest of all evils?

A. We show that sin is the greatest of evils because its effects last the longest and have the most terrible consequences. All the misfortunes of this world can last only for a time, and we escape them at death, whereas the evils caused by sin keep with us for all eternity and are only increased at death.

Q. 764. How many kinds of contrition are there?

A. There are two kinds of contrition; perfect contrition and imperfect contrition.

Q. 765. What is perfect contrition?

A. Perfect contrition is that which fills us with sorrow and hatred for sin, because it offends God, who is infinitely good in Himself and worthy of all love.

Q. 766. When will perfect contrition obtain pardon for mortal sin without the Sacrament of Penance?

A. Perfect contrition will obtain pardon for mortal sin without the Sacrament of Penance when we cannot go to confession, but with the perfect contrition we must have the intention of going to confession as soon as possible, if we again have the opportunity.

Q. 767. What is imperfect contrition?

A. Imperfect contrition is that by which we hate what offends God because by it we lose heaven and deserve hell; or because sin is so hateful in itself.

Q. 768. What other name is given to imperfect contrition and why is it called imperfect?

A. Imperfect contrition is called attrition. It is called imperfect only because it is less perfect than the highest grade of contrition by which we are sorry for sin out of pure love of God's own goodness and without any consideration of what befalls ourselves.

Q. 769. Is imperfect contrition sufficient for a worthy confession?

A. Imperfect contrition is sufficient for a worthy confession, but we should endeavor to have perfect contrition.

Q. 770. What do you mean by a firm purpose of sinning no more?

A. By a firm purpose of sinning no more I mean a fixed resolve not only to avoid all mortal sin, but also its near occasions.

Q. 771. What do you mean by the near occasions of sin?

A. By the near occasions of sin I mean all the persons, places and things that may easily lead us into sin.

Q. 772. Why are we bound to avoid occasions of sin?

A. We are bound to avoid occasions of sin because Our Lord has said: "He who loves the danger will perish in it"; and as we are bound to avoid the loss of our souls, so we are bound to avoid the danger of their loss. The occasion is the cause of sin, and you cannot take away the evil without removing its cause.

Q. 773. Is a person who is determined to avoid the sin, but who is unwilling to give up its near occasion

when it is possible to do so, rightly disposed for confession?

A. A person who is determined to avoid the sin, but who is unwilling to give up its near occasion when it is possible to do so, is not rightly disposed for confession, and he will not be absolved if he makes known to the priest the true state of his conscience.

Q. 774. How many kinds of occasions of sin are there?

A. There are four kinds of occasions of sin:

1.(1) Near occasions, through which we always fall;

2.(2) Remote occasions, through which we sometimes fall;

3.(3) Voluntary occasions or those we can avoid; and

4.(4) Involuntary occasions or those we cannot avoid.

A person who lives in a near and voluntary occasion of sin need not expect forgiveness while he continues in that state.

Q. 775. What persons, places and things are usually occasions of sin?

A.

1.(1) The persons who are occasions of sin are all those in whose company we sin, whether they be bad of themselves or bad only while in our company, in which case we also become occasions of sin for them;

2.(2) The places are usually liquor saloons, low theaters, indecent dances, entertainments, amusements, exhibitions, and all immoral resorts of any kind, whether we sin in them or not;

3.(3) The things are all bad books, indecent pictures, songs, jokes and the like, even when they are tolerated by public opinion and found in public places.

Lesson Nineteenth: On Confession

Q. 776. What is Confession?

A. Confession is the telling of our sins to a duly authorized priest, for the purpose of obtaining forgiveness.

Q. 777. Who is a duly authorized priest?

A. A duly authorized priest is one sent to hear confessions by the lawful bishop of the diocese in which we are at the time of our confession.

Q. 778. Is it ever allowed to write our sins and read them to the priest in the confessional or give them to him to read?

A. It is allowed, when necessary, to write our sins and read them to the priest, as persons do who have almost entirely lost their memory. It is also allowed to give the paper to the priest, as persons do who have lost the use of their speech. In such cases the paper must, after the confession, be carefully destroyed either by the priest or the penitent.

Q. 779. What is to be done when persons must make their confession and cannot find a priest who understands their language?

A. Persons who must make their confession and who cannot find a priest who understands their language, must confess as best they can by some signs, showing what sins they wish to confess and how they are sorry for them.

Q. 780. What sins are we bound to confess?

A. We are bound to confess all our mortal sins, but it is well also to confess our venial sins.

Q. 781. Why is it well to confess also the venial sins we remember?

A. It is well to confess also the venial sins we remember:

1.(1) Because it shows our hatred of all sin, and

2.(2) Because it is sometimes difficult to determine just when a sin is venial and when mortal.

Q. 782. What should one do who has only venial sins to confess?

A. One who has only venial sins to confess should tell also some sin already confessed in his past life for which he knows he is truly sorry; because it is not easy to be truly sorry for slight sins and imperfections, and yet we must be sorry for the sins confessed that our confession may be valid -- hence we add some past sin for which we are truly sorry to those for which we may not be sufficiently sorry.

Q. 783. Should a person stay from confession because he thinks he has no sin to confess?

A. A person should not stay from confession because he thinks he has no sin to confess, for the Sacrament of Penance, besides forgiving sin, gives an increase of sanctifying grace, and of this we have always need, especially to resist temptation. The Saints, who were almost without imperfection, went to confession frequently.

Q. 784. Should a person go to Communion after confession even when the confessor does not bid him go?

A. A person should go to Communion after confession even when the confessor does not bid him go, because the confessor so intends unless he positively forbids his penitent to receive Communion. However, one who has not yet received his first Communion should not go to Communion after confession, even if the confessor by mistake should bid him go.

Q. 785. Which are the chief qualities of a good Confession?

A. The chief qualities of a good Confession are three: it must be humble, sincere, and entire.

Q. 786. When is our Confession humble?

A. Our Confession is humble when we accuse ourselves of our sins, with a deep sense of shame and sorrow for having offended God.

Q. 787. When is our Confession sincere?

A. Our Confession is sincere when we tell our sins honestly and truthfully, neither exaggerating nor excusing them.

Q. 788. Why is it wrong to accuse ourselves of sins we have not committed?

A. It is wrong to accuse ourselves of sins we have not committed, because, by our so doing, the priest cannot know the true state of our souls, as he must do before giving us absolution.

Q. 789. When is our Confession entire?

A. Our Confession is entire when we tell the number and kinds of our sins and the circumstances which change their nature.

Q. 790. What do you mean by the "kinds of sin?"

A. By the "kinds of sin," we mean the particular division or class to which the sins belong; that is, whether they be sins of blasphemy, disobedience, anger, impurity, dishonesty, etc. We can determine the kind of sin by discovering the commandment or precept of the Church we have broken or the virtue against which we have acted.

Q. 791. What do we mean by "circumstances which change the nature of sins?"

A. By "circumstances which change the nature of sins" we mean anything that makes it another kind of sin. Thus to steal is a sin, but to steal from the Church makes our theft sacrilegious. Again, impure actions are sins, but a person must say whether they were committed alone or with others, with relatives or strangers, with persons married or single, etc., because these circumstances change them from one kind of impurity to another.

Q. 792. What should we do if we cannot remember the number of our sins?

A. If we cannot remember the number of our sins, we should tell the number as nearly as possible, and say how often we may have sinned in a day, a week, or a month, and how long the habit or practice has lasted.

Q. 793. Is our Confession worthy if, without our fault, we forget to confess a mortal sin?

A. If without our fault we forget to confess a mortal sin, our Confession is worthy, and the sin is forgiven; but it must be told in Confession if it again comes to our mind.

Q. 794. May a person who has forgotten to tell a mortal sin in confession go to Holy Communion before going again to confession?

A. A person who has forgotten to tell a mortal sin in confession may go to communion before again going to confession, because the forgotten sin was forgiven with those confessed, and the confession was good and worthy.

Q. 795. Is it a grievous offense willfully to conceal a mortal sin in Confession?

A. It is a grievous offense willfully to conceal a mortal sin in Confession, because we thereby tell a lie to the Holy Ghost, and make our Confession worthless.

Q. 796. How is concealing a sin telling a lie to the Holy Ghost?

A. Concealing a sin is telling a lie to the Holy Ghost, because he who conceals the sin declares in confession to God and the priest that he committed no sins but what he has confessed, while the Holy Ghost, the Spirit of Truth, saw him committing the sin he now conceals and still sees it in his soul while he denies it.

Q. 797. Why is it foolish to conceal sins in confession?

A. It is foolish to conceal sins in confession:

1.(1) Because we thereby make our spiritual condition worse;

2.(2) We must tell the sin sometime if we ever hope to be saved;

3.(3) It will be made known on the day of judgment, before the world, whether we conceal it now or confess it.

Q. 798. What must he do who has willfully concealed a mortal sin in Confession?

A. He who has willfully concealed a mortal sin in Confession must not only confess it, but must also repeat all the sins he has committed since his last worthy Confession.

Q. 799. Must one who has willfully concealed a mortal sin in confession do more than repeat the sins committed since his last worthy confession?

A. One who has willfully concealed a mortal sin in confession must, besides repeating all the sins he has committed since his last worthy confession, tell also how often he has unworthily received absolution and Holy Communion during the same time.

Q. 800. Why does the priest give us a penance after Confession?

A. The priest gives us a penance after Confession, that we may satisfy God for the temporal punishment due to our sins.

Q. 801. Why should we have to satisfy for our sins if Christ has fully satisfied for them?

A. Christ has fully satisfied for our sins and after our baptism we were free from all guilt and had no satisfaction to make. But when we willfully sinned after baptism, it is but just that we should be obliged to make some satisfaction.

Q. 802. Is the slight penance the priest gives us sufficient to satisfy for all the sins confessed?

A. The slight penance the priest gives us is not sufficient to satisfy for all the sins confessed:

1.(1) Because there is no real equality between the slight penance given and the punishment deserved for sin;

2.(2) Because we are all obliged to do penance for sins committed, and this would not be necessary if the penance given in confession satisfied for all.

The penance is given and accepted in confession chiefly to show our willingness to do penance and make amends for our sins.

Q. 803. Does not the Sacrament of Penance remit all punishment due to sin?

A. The Sacrament of Penance remits the eternal punishment due to sin, but it does not always remit the temporal punishment which God requires as satisfaction for our sins.

Q. 804. Why does God require a temporal punishment as a satisfaction for sin?

A. God requires a temporal punishment as a satisfaction for sin to teach us the great evil of sin and to prevent us from falling again.

Q. 805. Which are the chief means by which we satisfy God for the temporal punishment due to sin?

A. The chief means by which we satisfy God for the temporal punishment due to sin are: Prayer, Fasting, Almsgiving; all spiritual and corporal works of mercy, and the patient suffering of the ills of life.

Q. 806. What fasting has the greatest merit?

A. The fasting imposed by the Church on certain days of the year, and particularly during Lent, has the greatest merit.

Q. 807. What is Lent?

A. Lent is the forty days before Easter Sunday, during which we do penance, fast and pray to prepare ourselves for the resurrection of Our Lord; and also to remind us of His own fast of forty days before His Passion.

Q. 808. What do we mean by "almsgiving"?

A. By almsgiving we mean money, goods, or assistance given to the poor or to charitable purposes. The law of God requires all persons to give alms in proportion to their means.

Q. 809. What "ills of life" help to satisfy God for sin?

A. The ills of life that help to satisfy God for sin are sickness, poverty, misfortune, trial, affliction, etc., especially, when we have not brought them upon ourselves by sin.

Q. 810. How did the Christians in the first ages of the Church do Penance?

A. The Christians in the first ages of the Church did public penance, especially for the sins of which they were publicly known to be guilty. Penitents were excluded for a certain time from Mass or the Sacrament, and some were obliged to stand at the door of the Church begging the prayers of those who entered.

Q. 811. What were these severe Penances of the First Ages of the Church called?

A. These severe penances of the first ages of the Church were called canonical penances, because their kind and duration were regulated by the Canons or laws of the Church.

Q. 812. How can we know spiritual from corporal works of mercy?

A. We can know spiritual from corporal works of mercy, for whatever we do for the soul is a spiritual work, and whatever we do for the body is a corporal work.

Q. 813. Which are the chief spiritual works of mercy?

A. The chief spiritual works of mercy are seven:

1.To admonish the sinner, to instruct the ignorant, to counsel the doubtful, to comfort the sorrowful, to bear wrongs patiently, to forgive all injuries, and to pray for the living and the dead.

Q. 814. When are we bound to admonish the sinner?

A. We are bound to admonish the sinner when the following conditions are fulfilled:

1.(1) When his fault is a mortal sin;

2.(2) When we have authority or influence over him, and

3.(3) When there is reason to believe that our warning will not make him worse instead of better.

Q. 815. Who are meant by the "ignorant" we are to instruct, and the "doubtful" we are to counsel?

A. By the ignorant we are to instruct and the doubtful we are to counsel, are meant those particularly who are ignorant of the truths of religion and those who are in doubt about matters of faith. We must aid such persons as far as we can to know and believe the truths necessary for salvation.

Q. 816. Why are we advised to bear wrong patiently and to forgive all injuries?

A. We are advised to bear wrongs patiently and to forgive all injuries, because, being Christians, we should imitate the example of Our Divine Lord, who endured wrongs patiently and who not only pardoned but prayed for those who injured Him.

Q. 817. If, then, it be a Christian virtue to forgive all injuries, why do Christians establish courts and prisons to punish wrongdoers?

A. Christians establish courts and prisons to punish wrongdoers, because the preservation of lawful authority, good order in society, the protection of others, and sometimes even the good of the guilty one himself, require that crimes be justly punished. As God Himself punishes crime and as lawful authority comes from Him, such authority has the right to punish, though individuals should forgive the injuries done to themselves personally.

Q. 818. Why is it a work of mercy to pray for the living and the dead?

A. It is a work of mercy to aid those who are unable to aid themselves. The living are exposed to temptations, and while in mortal sin they are deprived of the merit of their good works and need our prayers. The dead can in no way help themselves and depend on us for assistance.

Q. 819. Which are the chief corporal works of mercy?

A. The chief corporal works of mercy are seven:

1.To feed the hungry, to give drink to the thirsty, to clothe the naked, to ransom the captive, to harbor the harborless, to visit the sick, and to bury the dead.

Q. 820. How may we briefly state the corporal works of mercy?

A. We may briefly state the corporal works of mercy by saying that we are obliged to help the poor in all their forms of want.

Q. 821. How are Christians aided in the performance of works of mercy?

A. Christians are aided in the performance of works of mercy through the establishment of charitable institutions where religious communities of holy men or women perform these duties for us, provided we supply the necessary means by our almsgiving and good works.

Q. 822. Who are religious?

A. Religious are self-sacrificing men and women who, wishing to follow more closely the teachings of Our Lord, dedicate their lives to the service of God and religion. They live together in societies approved by the Church, under a rule and guidance of a superior. They keep the vows of chastity, poverty and obedience, and divide their time between prayer and good works. The houses in which they dwell are called convents or monasteries, and the societies in which they live are called religious orders, communities or congregations.

Q. 823. Are there any religious communities of priests?

A. There are many religious communities of priests, who, besides living according to the general laws of the Church, as all priests do, follow certain rules laid down for their community. Such priests are called the regular clergy, because living by rules to distinguish them from the secular clergy who live in their parishes under no special rule. The chief work of the regular clergy is to teach in colleges and give missions and retreats.

Q. 824. Why are there so many different religious communities?

A. There are many different religious communities:

1.(1) Because all religious are not fitted for the same work, and

2.(2) Because they desire to imitate Our Lord's life on earth as perfectly as possible; and when each community takes one of Christ's works and seeks to become perfect in it, the union of all their works continues as perfectly as we can the works He began upon earth.

Lesson Twentieth: On the Manner of Making a Good Confession

Q. 825. What should we do on entering the confessional?

A. On entering the confessional we should kneel, make the sign of the Cross, and say to the priest, "Bless me, father"; then add, "I confess to Almighty God and to you, father, that I have sinned."

Q. 826. Which are the first things we should tell the priest in Confession?

A. The first things we should tell the priest in Confession are the time of our last Confession, and whether we said the penance and went to Holy

Communion.

Q. 827. Should we tell anything else in connection with our last confession?

A. In connection with our last confession we should tell also what restrictions -- if any -- were placed upon us with regard to our occasions of sin, and what obligations with regard to the payment of debts, restitution, injuries done to others and the like, we were commanded to fulfill.

Q. 828. After telling the time of our last Confession and Communion what should we do?

A. After telling the time of our last Confession and Communion we should confess all the mortal sins we have since committed, and all the venial sins we may wish to mention.

Q. 829. What is a general confession?

A. A general confession is the telling of the sins of our whole life or a great part of it. It is made in the same manner as an ordinary confession, except that it requires more time and longer preparation.

Q. 830. When should a General Confession be made?

A. A general confession:

1.(1) Is necessary when we are certain that our past confessions were bad;

2.(2) It is useful on special occasions in our lives when some change in our way of living is about to take place;

3.(3) It is hurtful and must not be made when persons are scrupulous.

Q. 831. What are the signs of scruples and the remedy against them?

A. The signs of scruples are chiefly:

1.(1) To be always dissatisfied with our confessions;

2.(2) To be self-willed in deciding what is sinful and what is not.

The chief remedy against them is to follow exactly the advice of the confessor without questioning the reason or utility of his advice.

Q. 832. What must we do when the confessor asks us questions?

A. When the confessor asks us questions we must answer them truthfully and clearly.

Q. 833. What should we do after telling our sins?

A. After telling our sins we should listen with attention to the advice which the confessor may think proper to give.

Q. 834. What duties does the priest perform in the confessional?

A. In the confessional the priest performs the duties:

1.(1) Of a judge, by listening to our self-accusations and passing sentence upon our guilt or innocence;

2.(2) Of a father, by the good advice and encouragement he gives us;

3.(3) Of a teacher, by his instructions, and

4.(4) Of a physician, by discovering the afflictions of our soul and giving us the remedies to restore it to spiritual health.

Q. 835. Why is it beneficial to go always if possible to the same confessor?

A. It is beneficial to go always, if possible, to the same confessor, because our continued confessions enable him to see more clearly the true state of our soul and to understand better our occasions of sin.

Q. 836. Should we remain away from confession because we cannot go to our usual confessor?

A. We should not remain away from confession because we cannot go to our usual confessor, for though it is well to confess to the same priest, it is not necessary to do so. One should never become so attached to a confessor that his absence or the great inconvenience of going to him would become an excuse for neglecting the Sacraments.

Q. 837. How should we end our Confession?

A. We should end our Confession by saying, "I also accuse myself of all the sins of my past life," telling, if we choose, one or several of our past sins.

Q. 838. What should we do while the priest is giving us absolution?

A. While the priest is giving us absolution we should from our heart renew the Act of Contrition.

Lesson Twenty-First: On Indulgences

Q. 839. What is an Indulgence?

A. An Indulgence is the remission in whole or in part of the temporal punishment due to sin.

Q. 840. What does the word "indulgence" mean?

A. The word indulgence means a favor or concession. An indulgence obtains by a very slight penance the remission of penalties that would otherwise be severe.

Q. 841. Is an Indulgence a pardon of sin, or a license to commit sin?

A. An Indulgence is not a pardon of sin, nor a license to commit sin, and one who is in a state of mortal sin cannot gain an Indulgence.

Q. 842. How do good works done in mortal sin profit us?

A. Good works done in mortal sin profit us by obtaining for us the grace to repent and sometimes temporal blessings. Mortal sin deprives us of all our merit, nevertheless God will bestow gifts for every good deed as He will punish every evil deed.

Q. 843. How many kinds of Indulgences are there?

A. There are two kinds of Indulgences -- Plenary and Partial.

Q. 844. What is Plenary Indulgence?

A. A Plenary Indulgence is the full remission of the temporal punishment due to sin.

Q. 845. Is it easy to gain a Plenary Indulgence?

A. It is not easy to gain a Plenary Indulgence, as we may understand from its great privilege. To gain a Plenary Indulgence, we must hate sin, be heartily sorry for even our venial sins, and have no desire for even the slightest sin. Though we may not gain entirely each Plenary Indulgence we seek, we always gain a part of each; that is, a partial indulgence, greater or less in pro portion to our good dispositions.

Q. 846. Which are the most important Plenary Indulgences granted by the Church?

A. The most important Plenary Indulgences granted by the Church are:

1.(1) The Indulgences of a jubilee which the Pope grants every twenty-five years or on great occasions by which he gives special faculties to confessors for the absolution of reserved sins;

2.(2) The Indulgence granted to the dying in their last agony.

Q. 847. What is a Partial Indulgence?

A. A Partial Indulgence is the remission of part of the temporal punishment due to sin.

Q. 848. How long has the practice of granting Indulgences been in use in the Church, and what was its origin?

A. The practice of granting Indulgences has been in use in the Church since the time of the apostles. It had its origin in the earnest prayers of holy persons, and especially of the martyrs begging the Church for their sake to shorten the severe penances of sinners, or to change them into lighter penances. The request was frequently granted and the penance remitted, shortened or changed, and with the penance remitted the temporal punishment corresponding to it was blotted out.

Q. 849. How do we show that the Church has the power to grant Indulgences?

A. We show that the Church has the power to grant Indulgences, because Christ has given it power to remit all guilt without restriction, and if the Church has power, in the Sacrament of penance, to remit the eternal punishment -- which is the greatest -- it must have power to remit the temporal or lesser punishment, even outside the Sacrament of Penance.

Q. 850. How do we know that these Indulgences have their effect?

A. We know that these Indulgences have their effect, because the Church, through her councils, declares Indulgences useful, and if they have no effect they would be useless, and the Church would teach error in spite of Christ's promise to guide it.

Q. 851. Have there ever existed abuses among the faithful in the manner of using Indulgences?

A. There have existed, in past ages, some abuses among the faithful in the manner of using Indulgences, and the Church has always labored to correct such abuses as soon as possible. In the use of pious practices we must be always guided by our lawful superiors.

Q. 852. How have the enemies of the Church made use of the abuse of Indulgences?

A. The enemies of the Church have made use of the abuse of Indulgences to deny the doctrine of Indulgences, and to break down the teaching and limit the power of the Church. Not to be deceived in matters of faith, we must always distinguish very carefully between the abuses to which a devotion may lead and the truths upon which the devotion rests.

Q. 853. How does the Church by means of Indulgences remit the temporal punishment due to sin?

A. The Church, by means of Indulgences, remits the temporal punishment due to sin by applying to us the merits of Jesus Christ, and the superabundant satisfactions of the Blessed Virgin Mary and of the saints; which merits and satisfactions are its spiritual treasury.

Q. 854. What do we mean by the "superabundant satisfaction of the Blessed Virgin and the Saints"?

A. By the superabundant satisfaction of the Blessed Virgin and the saints, we mean all the satisfaction over and above what was necessary to satisfy for their own sins. As their good works were many and their sins few – the Blessed Virgin being sinless -- the satisfaction not needed for themselves is kept by the Church in a spiritual treasury to be used for our benefit.

Q. 855. Does the Church, by granting Indulgences, free us from doing Penance?

A. The Church, by granting Indulgences, does not free us from doing penance, but simply makes our penance lighter that we may more easily satisfy for our sins and escape the punishments they deserve.

Q. 856. Who has the power to grant Indulgences?

A. The Pope alone has the power to grant Indulgences for the whole Church; but the bishops have power to grant partial Indulgences in their own diocese. Cardinals and some others, by the special permission of the Pope, have the right to grant certain Indulgences.

Q. 857. Where shall we find the Indulgences granted by the Church?

A. We shall find the Indulgences granted by the Church in the declarations of the Pope and of the Sacred Congregation of Cardinals. These declarations are usually put into prayer books and books of devotion or instruction.

Q. 858. What must we do to gain an Indulgence?

A. To gain an Indulgence we must be in the state of grace and perform the works enjoined.

Q. 859. Besides being in a state of grace and performing the works enjoined, what else is necessary for the gaining of an Indulgence?

A. Besides being in a state of grace and performing the works enjoined, it is necessary for the gaining of an Indulgence to have at least the general intention of gaining it.

Q. 860. How and why should we make a general intention to gain all possible Indulgences each day?

A. We should make a general intention at our morning prayers to gain all possible Indulgences each day, because several of the prayers we say and good works we perform may have Indulgences attached to them, though we are not aware of it.

Q. 861. What works are generally enjoined for the gaining of Indulgences?

A. The works generally enjoined for the gaining of Indulgences are: The saying of certain prayers, fasting, and the use of certain articles of devotion;

visits to Churches or altars, and the giving of alms. For the gaining of Plenary Indulgences it is generally required to go to confession and Holy Communion and pray for the intention of the Pope.

Q. 862. What does praying for a person's intention mean?

A. Praying for a person's intention means praying for whatever he prays for or desires to obtain through prayer -- some spiritual or temporal favors.

Q. 863. What does an Indulgence of forty days mean?

A. An Indulgence of forty days means that for the prayer or work to which an Indulgence of forty days is attached, God remits as much of our temporal punishment as He remitted for forty days' canonical penance. We do not know just how much temporal punishment God remitted for forty days' public penance, but whatever it was, He remits the same now when we gain an Indulgence of forty days. The same rule applies to Indulgences of a year or any length of time.

Q. 864. Why did the Church moderate its severe penances?

A. The Church moderated its severe penances, because when Christians -- terrified by persecution – grew weaker in their faith, there was danger of some abandoning their religion rather than submit to the penances imposed. The Church, therefore, wishing to save as many as possible, made the sinner's penance as light as possible.

Q. 865. To what things may Indulgences be attached?

A. Plenary or Partial Indulgences may be attached to prayers and solid articles of devotion; to places such as churches, altars, shrines, etc., to be visited; and by a special privilege they are sometimes attached to the good works of certain persons.

Q. 866. When do things lose the Indulgences attached to them?

A. Things lose the Indulgences attached to them:

1.(1) When they are so changed at once as to be no longer what they were;

2.(2) When they are sold.

Rosaries and other indulgenced articles do not lose their indulgences, when they are loaned or given away, for the indulgence is not personal but attached to the article itself.

Q. 867. Will a weekly Confession suffice to gain during the week all Indulgences to which Confession is enjoined as one of the works?

A Weekly confession will suffice to gain during the week all Indulgences to which confession is enjoined as one of the works, provided we continue in a state of grace, perform the other works enjoined and have the intention of gaining these Indulgences.

Q. 868. How and when may we apply Indulgences for the benefit of the souls in Purgatory?

A. We may apply Indulgences for the benefit of the souls in Purgatory by way of intercession; whenever this application is mentioned and permitted by the Church in granting the Indulgence; that is, when the Church declares that the Indulgence granted is applicable to the souls of the living or the souls in Purgatory; so that we may gain it for the benefit of either.

Lesson Twenty-Second: On the Holy Eucharist

Q. 869. What does the word Eucharist strictly mean?

A. The word Eucharist strictly means pleasing, and this Sacrament is so called because it renders us most pleasing to God by the grace it imparts, and it gives us the best means of thanking Him for all His blessings.

Q. 870. What is the Holy Eucharist?

A. The Holy Eucharist is the Sacrament which contains the body and blood, soul and divinity, of our Lord Jesus Christ under the appearances of bread and wine.

Q. 871. What do we mean when we say the Sacrament which contains the Body and Blood?

A. When we say the Sacrament which contains the Body and Blood, we mean the Sacrament which is the Body and Blood, for after the Consecration there is no other substance present in the Eucharist.

Q. 872. When is the Holy Eucharist a Sacrament, and when is it a sacrifice?

A. The Holy Eucharist is a Sacrament when we receive it in Holy Communion and when it remains in the Tabernacle of the Altar. It is a sacrifice when it is offered up at Mass by the separate Consecration of the bread and wine, which signifies the separation of Our Lord's blood from His body when He died on the Cross.

Q. 873. When did Christ institute the Holy Eucharist?

A. Christ instituted the Holy Eucharist at the Last Supper, the night before He died.

Q. 874. Who were present when our Lord instituted the Holy Eucharist?

A. When Our Lord instituted the Holy Eucharist, the twelve Apostles were present.

Q. 875. How did our Lord institute the Holy Eucharist?

A. Our Lord instituted the Holy Eucharist by taking bread, blessing, breaking, and giving to His Apostles, saying:

"Take ye and eat. This is my body"; and then, by taking the cup of wine, blessing and giving it, saying to them:

"Drink ye all of this. This is my blood which shall be shed for the remission of sins. Do this for a commemoration of me."

Q. 876. What happened when our Lord said, "This is my body; this is my blood"?

A. When Our Lord said, "This is my body," the substance of the bread was changed into the substance of His body; when He said, "This is my blood," the substance of the wine was changed into the substance of His blood.

Q. 877. How do we prove the Real Presence, that is, that Our Lord is really and truly present in the Holy Eucharist?

A. We prove the Real Presence -- that is, that Our Lord is really and truly present in the Holy Eucharist:

1.(1) By showing that it is possible to change one substance into another;

2.(2) By showing that Christ did change the substance of bread and wine into the substance of His body and blood;

3.(3) By showing that He gave this power also to His Apostles and to the priests of His Church.

Q. 878. How do we know that it is possible to change one substance into another?

A. We know that it is possible to change one substance into another, because:

1.(1) God changed water into blood during the plagues of Egypt.

2.(2) Christ changed water into wine at the marriage of Cana.

3.(3) Our own food is daily changed into the substance of our flesh and blood; and what God does gradually, He can also do instantly by an act of His will.

Q. 879. Are these changes exactly the same as the changes that take place in the Holy Eucharist?

A. These changes are not exactly the same as the changes that take place in the Holy Eucharist, for in these changes the appearance also is changed, but in the Holy Eucharist only the substance is changed while the appearance remains the same.

Q. 880. How do we show that Christ did change bread and wine into the substance of His body and blood?

A. We show that Christ did change bread and wine into the substance of His body and blood:

1.(1) From the words by which He promised the Holy Eucharist;

2.(2) From the words by which He instituted the Holy Eucharist;

3.(3) From the constant use of the Holy Eucharist in the Church since the time of the Apostles;

4.(4) From the impossibility of denying the Real Presence in the Holy Eucharist, without likewise denying all that Christ has taught and done; for we have stronger proofs for the Holy Eucharist than for any other Christian truth.

Q. 881. Is Jesus Christ whole and entire both under the form of bread and under the form of wine?

A. Jesus Christ is whole and entire both under the form of bread and under the form of wine.

Q. 882. How do we know that under the appearance of bread we receive also Christ's blood; and under
the appearance of wine we receive also Christ's body?

A. We know that under the appearance of bread we receive also Christ's blood, and under the appearance of wine we receive also Christ's body; because in the Holy Eucharist we receive the living body of Our Lord, and a living body cannot exist without blood, nor can living blood exist without a body.

Q. 883. Is Jesus Christ present whole and entire in the smallest portion of the Holy Eucharist, under the form of either bread or wine?

A. Jesus Christ is present whole and entire in the smallest portion of the Holy Eucharist under the form of either bread or wine; for His body in the Eucharist is in a glorified state, and as it partakes of the character of a spiritual substance, it requires no definite size or shape.

Q. 884. Did anything remain of the bread and wine after their substance had been changed into the substance of the body and blood of our Lord?

A. After the substance of the bread and wine had been changed into the substance of the body and blood of Our Lord, there remained only the appearances of bread and wine.

Q. 885. What do you mean by the appearances of bread and wine?

A. By the appearances of bread and wine I mean the figure, the color, the taste, and whatever appears to the senses.

Q. 886. What is this change of the bread and wine into the body and blood of our Lord called?

A. This change of the bread and wine into the body and blood of Our Lord is called Transubstantiation.

Q. 887. What is the second great miracle in the Holy Eucharist?

A. The second great miracle in the Holy Eucharist is the multiplication of the presence of Our Lord's body in so many places at the same time, while the body itself is not multiplied -- for there is but one body of Christ.

Q. 888. Are there not, then, as many bodies of Christ as there are tabernacles in the world, or as there are Masses being said at the same time?

A. There are not as many bodies of Christ as there are tabernacles in the world, or as there are Masses being said at the same time; but only one body of Christ, which is everywhere present whole and entire in the Holy Eucharist, as God is everywhere present, while He is but one God.

Q. 889. How was the substance of the bread and wine changed into the substance of the body and blood of Christ?

A. The substance of the bread and wine was changed into the substance of the body and blood of Christ by His almighty power.

Q. 890. Does this change of bread and wine into the body and blood of Christ continue to be made in the Church?

A. This change of bread and wine into the body and blood of Christ continues to be made in the Church by Jesus Christ through the ministry of His priests.

Q. 891. When did Christ give His priests the power to change bread and wine into His body and blood?

A. Christ gave His priests the power to change bread and wine into His body and blood when He said to the Apostles, "Do this in commemoration of Me."

Q. 892. What do the words "Do this in commemoration of Me" mean?

A. The words "Do this in commemoration of Me" mean: Do what I, Christ, am doing at My last supper, namely, changing the substance of bread and wine into the substance of My body and blood; and do it in remembrance of Me.

Q. 893. How do the priests exercise this power of changing bread and wine into the body and blood of Christ?

A. The priests exercise this power of changing bread and wine into the body and blood of Christ through the words of consecration in the Mass, which are words of Christ: "This is my body; this is my blood."

Q. 894. At what part of the Mass does the Consecration take place?

A. The Consecration in the Mass takes place immediately before the elevation of the Host and Chalice, which are raised above the head of the priest that the people may adore Our Lord who has just come to the altar at the words of Consecration.

Lesson Twenty-Third: On the Ends for Which the Holy Eucharist Was Instituted

Q. 895. Why did Christ institute the Holy Eucharist?

A. Christ instituted the Holy Eucharist:

1. To unite us to Himself and to nourish our soul with His divine life.
2. To increase sanctifying grace and all virtues in our soul.
3. To lessen our evil inclinations.
4. To be a pledge of everlasting life.
5. To fit our bodies for a glorious resurrection.
6. To continue the sacrifice of the Cross in His Church.

Q. 896. Has the Holy Eucharist any other effect?

A. The Holy Eucharist remits venial sins by disposing us to perform acts of love and contrition. It preserves us from mortal sin by exciting us to greater fervor and strengthening us against temptation.

Q. 897. How are we united to Jesus Christ in the Holy Eucharist?

A. We are united to Jesus Christ in the Holy Eucharist by means of Holy Communion.

Q. 898. What is Holy Communion?

A. Holy Communion is the receiving of the body and blood of Christ.

Q. 899. Is it not beneath the dignity of Our Lord to enter our bodies under the appearance of ordinary food?

A. It is not beneath the dignity of Our Lord to enter our bodies under the appearance of ordinary food any more than it was beneath His dignity to enter the body of His Blessed Mother and remain there as an ordinary child for nine months. Christ's dignity, being infinite, can never be diminished by any act on His own or on our part.

Q. 900. Why does not the Church give Holy Communion to the people as it does to the priest under the appearance of wine also?

A. The Church does not give Holy Communion to the people as it does to the priest under the appearance of wine also, to avoid the danger of spilling the Precious Blood; to prevent the irreverence some might show if compelled to drink out of a chalice used by all, and lastly, to refute those who denied that Our Lord's blood is present under the appearance of bread also.

Q. 901. What is necessary to make a good Communion?

A. To make a good Communion it is necessary to be in the state of sanctifying grace and to fast according to the laws of the Church.

Q. 902. What should a person do who, through forgetfulness or any other cause, has broken the fast necessary for Holy Communion?

A. A person who through forgetfulness or any other cause has broken the fast necessary for Holy Communion, should again fast and receive Holy Communion the following morning if possible, without returning to confession. It is not a sin to break one's fast, but it would be a mortal sin to receive Holy Communion after knowingly breaking the fast necessary for it.

Q. 903. Does he who receives Communion in mortal sin receive the body and blood of Christ?

A. He who receives Communion in mortal sin receives the body and blood of Christ, but does not receive His grace, and he commits a great sacrilege.

Q. 904. Is it enough to be free from mortal sin to receive plentifully the graces of Holy Communion?

A. To receive plentifully the graces of Holy Communion it is not enough to be free from mortal sin, but we should be free from all affection to venial sin, and should make acts of lively faith, of firm hope, and ardent love.

Q. 905. What is the fast necessary for Holy Communion?

A. The fast necessary for Holy Communion is the abstaining from food, alcoholic drinks and non-alcoholic drinks for one hour before Holy Communion. Water does not break the fast.

Q. 906. Does medicine taken by necessity or food taken by accident break the fast for Holy Communion?

A. Medicine does not break the fast; food taken by accident within one hour before Communion breaks the fast.

Q. 907. Is any one ever allowed to receive Holy Communion when not fasting?

A. To protect the Blessed Sacrament from insult or injury, or when in danger of death, Holy Communion may be received without fasting.

Q. 908. Is the Holy Communion called by any other name when given to one in danger of death?

A. When the Holy Communion is given to one in danger of death, it is called Viaticum, and is given with its own form of prayer. In giving Holy Communion the priest says: "May the body of Our Lord Jesus Christ guard your soul to eternal life." In giving Holy Viaticum he says: "Receive, brother (or sister), the Viaticum of the body of Our Lord Jesus Christ, which will guard you from the wicked enemy and lead you into eternal life."

Q. 909. When are we bound to receive Holy Communion?

A. We are bound to receive Holy Communion, under pain of mortal sin, during the Easter time and when in danger of death.

Q. 910. Is it well to receive Holy Communion often?

A. It is well to receive Holy Communion often, as nothing is a greater aid to a holy life than often to receive the Author of all grace and the Source of all good.

Q. 911. How shall we know how often we should receive Holy Communion?

A. We shall know how often we shall receive Holy Communion only from the advice of our confessor, by whom we must be guided, and whom we must strictly obey in this as well as in all matters concerning the state of our soul.

Q. 912. What is a spiritual Communion?

A. A spiritual communion is an earnest desire to receive Communion in reality, by which desire we make all preparations and thanksgivings that we would make in case we really received the Holy Eucharist. Spiritual Communion is an act of devotion that must be pleasing to God and bring us blessings from Him.

Q. 913. What should we do after Holy Communion?

A. After Holy Communion we should spend some time in adoring Our Lord, in thanking Him for the grace we have received, and in asking Him for the blessings we need.

Q. 914. What length of time should we spend in thanksgiving after Holy Communion?

A. We should spend sufficient time in Thanksgiving after Holy Communion to show due reverence to the Blessed Sacrament; for Our Lord is personally with us as long as the appearance of bread and wine remains.

Q. 915. What should we be particular about when receiving Holy Communion?

A. When receiving Holy Communion we should be particular:

1.(1) About the respectful manner in which we approach and return from the altar;

2.(2) About our personal appearance, especially neatness and cleanliness;

3.(3) About raising our head, opening our mouth and putting forth the tongue in the proper manner;

4.(4) About swallowing the Sacred Host;

5.(5) About removing it carefully with the tongue, in case it should stick to the mouth, but never with the finger under any circumstances.

Lesson Twenty-Fourth: On the Sacrifice of the Mass

Q. 916. When and where are the bread and wine changed into the body and blood of Christ?

A. The bread and wine are changed into the body and blood of Christ at the Consecration in the Mass.

135

Q. 917. What is the Mass?

A. The Mass is the unbloody sacrifice of the body and blood of Christ.

Q. 918. Why is this Sacrifice called the Mass?

A. This Sacrifice is called the "Mass" very probably from the words "Ite Missa est," used by the priest as he tells the people to depart when the Holy Sacrifice is ended.

Q. 919. What is a sacrifice?

A. A sacrifice is the offering of an object by a priest to God alone, and the consuming of it to acknowledge that He is the Creator and Lord of all things.

Q. 920. Is the Mass the same sacrifice as that of the Cross?

A. The Mass is the same sacrifice as that of the Cross.

Q. 921. How is the Mass the same sacrifice as that of the Cross?

A. The Mass is the same sacrifice as that of the Cross because the offering and the priest are the same – Christ our Blessed Lord; and the ends for which the sacrifice of the Mass is offered are the same as those of the sacrifice of the Cross.

Q. 922. What were the ends for which the sacrifice of the Cross was offered?

A. The ends for which the sacrifice of the Cross was offered were:

1.1st. To honor and glorify God;

2.2nd. To thank Him for all the graces bestowed on the whole world;

3.3rd. To satisfy God's justice for the sins of men;

4.4th. To obtain all graces and blessings.

Q. 923. How are the fruits of the Mass distributed?

A. The fruits of the Mass are distributed thus:

1.The first benefit is bestowed on the priest who says the Mass;

2.The second on the person for whom the Mass is said, or for the intention for which it is said;

3.The third on those who are present at the Mass, and particularly on those who serve it, and

4.The fourth on all the faithful who are in communion with the Church.

Q. 924. Are all Masses of equal value in themselves or do they differ in worth?

A. All Masses are equal in value in themselves and do not differ in worth, but only in the solemnity with which they are celebrated or in the end for which they are offered.

Q. 925. How are Masses distinguished?

A. Masses are distinguished thus:

1.(1) When the Mass is sung by a bishop, assisted by a deacon and sub-deacon, it is called a Pontifical Mass;

2.(2) When it is sung by a priest, assisted by a deacon and sub-deacon, it is called a Solemn Mass;

3.(3) When sung by a priest without deacon and sub-deacon, it is called a Missa Cantata or High Mass;

4.(4) When the Mass is only read in a low tone it is called a low or private Mass.

Q. 926. For what end or intention may Mass be offered?

A. Mass may be offered for any end or intention that tends to the honor and glory of God, to the good of the Church or the welfare of man; but never for any object that is bad in itself, or in its aims; neither can it be offered publicly for persons who are not members of the true Church.

Q. 927. Explain what is meant by Requiem, Nuptial and Votive Masses.

A. A Requiem Mass is one said in black vestments and with special prayers for the dead. A Nuptial Mass is one said at the marriage of two Catholics, and it has special prayers for their benefit. A Votive Mass is one said in honor of some particular mystery or saint, on a day not set apart by the Church for the honor of that mystery or saint.

Q. 928. From what may we learn that we are to offer up the Holy Sacrifice with the priest?

A. We may learn that we are to offer up the Holy Sacrifice with the priest from the words used in the Mass itself; for the priest, after offering up the bread and wine for the Sacrifice, turns to the people and says: "Orate Fratres," etc., which means: "Pray, brethren, that my sacrifice and yours may be acceptable to God the Father Almighty,"
and the server answers in our name: "May the Lord receive the sacrifice from thy hands to the praise and glory of
His own name, and to our benefit and that of all His Holy Church."

Q. 929. From what did the custom of making an offering to the priest for saying Mass arise?

A. The custom of making an offering to the priest for saying Mass arose from the old custom of bringing to the
priest the bread and wine necessary for the celebration of Mass.

Q. 930. Is it not simony, or the buying of a sacred thing, to offer the priest money for saying Mass for your intention?

A. It is not simony, or the buying of a sacred thing, to offer the priest money for saying Mass for our intention, because the priest does not take the money for the Mass itself, but for the purpose of supplying the things necessary for Mass and for his own support.

Q. 931. Is there any difference between the sacrifice of the Cross and the sacrifice of the Mass?

A. Yes; the manner in which the sacrifice is offered is different. On the Cross Christ really shed His blood and was really slain; in the Mass there is no real shedding of blood nor real death, because Christ can die no more; but the sacrifice of the Mass, through the separate consecration of the bread and the wine, represents His death on the Cross.

Q. 932. What are the chief parts of the Mass?

A. The chief parts of the Mass are:

1.(1) The Offertory, at which the priests offers to God the bread and wine to be changed at the Consecration;

2.(2) The Consecration, at which the substance of the bread and wine are changed into the substance of Christ's body and blood;

3.(3) The Communion, at which the priest receives into his own body the Holy Eucharist under the appearance of both bread and wine.

Q. 933. At what part of the Mass does the Offertory take place, and what parts of the Mass are said before it?

A. The Offertory takes place immediately after the uncovering of the chalice. The parts of the Mass said before it are: The Introit, Kyrie, Gloria, Prayers, Epistle, Gospel and Creed. The Introit, Prayers, Epistle and Gospel change in each Mass to correspond with the feast celebrated.

Q. 934. What is the part of the Mass called in which the Words of Consecration are found?

A. The part of the Mass in which the words of Consecration are found is called the Canon. This is the most solemn part of the Mass, and is rarely and but slightly changed in any Mass.

Q. 935. What follows the Communion of the Mass?

A. Following the Communion of Mass, there are prayers of thanksgiving, the blessing of the people, and the saying of the last Gospel.

Q. 936. What things are necessary for Mass?

A. The things necessary for Mass are:

1.(1) An altar with linen covers, candles, crucifix, altar stone and Mass book;

2.(2) A Chalice with all needed in its use, and bread of flour from wheat and wine from the grape;

3.(3) Vestments for the priest, and

4.(4) An acolyte or server.

Q. 937. What is the altar stone, and of what does it remind us?

A. The altar stone is that part of the altar upon which the priest rests the Chalice during Mass. This stone contains some holy relics sealed up in it by the bishop, and if the altar is of wood this stone is inserted just in front of the Tabernacle. The altar stone reminds us of the early history of the Church, when the martyrs' tombs were used for altars by the persecuted Christians.

Q. 938. What lesson do we learn from the practice of using martyrs' tombs for altars?

A. From the practice of using martyrs' tombs for altars we learn the inconvenience, sufferings and dangers the early Christians willingly underwent for the sake of hearing Mass. Since the Mass is the same now as it was then, we should suffer every inconvenience rather than be absent from Mass on Sundays or holy days.

Q. 939. What things are used with the chalice during Mass?

A. The things used with the chalice during Mass are:

1.(1) The purificator or cloth for wiping the inside;

2.(2) The paten or small silver plate used in handling the host;

3.(3) The pall or white card used for covering the chalice at Mass;

4.(4) The corporal or linen cloth on which the chalice and host rest.

Q. 940. What is the host?

A. The host is the name given to the thin wafer of bread used at Mass. This name is generally applied before and after Consecration to the large particle of bread used by the priest, though the small particles given to the people are also called by the same name.

Q. 941. Are large and small hosts consecrated at every Mass?

A. A large host is consecrated at every Mass, but small hosts are consecrated only at some Masses at which they are to be given to the people or placed in the Tabernacle for the Holy Communion of the faithful.

Q. 942. What vestments does the priest use at Mass and what do they signify?

A. The vestments used by the priest at Mass are:

1.(1) The Amice, a white cloth around the shoulders to signify resistance to temptation;

2.(2) The Alb, a long white garment to signify innocence;

3.(3) The Cincture, a cord about the waist, to signify chastity;

4.(4) The Maniple or hanging vestment on the left arm, to signify penance;

5.(5) The Stole or long vestment about the neck, to signify immortality;

6.(6) The Chasuble or long vestment over all, to signify love and remind the priest, by its cross on front and back, of the Passion of Our Lord.

Q. 943. How many colors of vestments are used, and what do the colors signify?

A. Five colors of vestments are used, namely, white, red, green, violet or purple, and black. White signifies innocence and is used on the feasts of Our Blessed Lord, of the Blessed Virgin, and of some saints. Red signifies love, and is used on the feasts of the Holy Ghost, and of martyrs. Green signifies hope, and is generally used on Sundays from Epiphany to Pentecost. Violet signifies penance, and is used in Lent and Advent. Black signifies sorrow, and is used on Good Friday and at Masses for the dead. Gold is often used for white on great feasts.

Q. 944. What is the Tabernacle and what is the Ciborium?

A. The Tabernacle is the house-shaped part of the altar where the sacred vessels containing the Blessed Sacrament are kept. The Ciborium is the large silver or gold vessel which contains the Blessed Sacrament while in the Tabernacle, and from which the priest gives Holy Communion to the people.

Q. 945. What is the Ostensorium or Monstrance?

A. The Ostensorium or Monstrance is the beautiful wheel-like vessel in which the Blessed Sacrament is exposed and kept during the Benediction.

Q. 946. How should we assist at Mass?

A. We should assist at Mass with great interior recollection and piety and with every outward mark of respect and devotion.

Q. 947. Which is the best manner of hearing Mass?

A. The best manner of hearing Mass is to offer it to God with the priest for the same purpose for which it is said, to meditate on Christ's sufferings and death, and to go to Holy Communion.

Q. 948. What is important for the proper and respectful hearing of Mass?

A. For the proper and respectful hearing of Mass it is important to be in our place before the priest comes to the altar and not to leave it before the priest leaves the altar. Thus we prevent the confusion and distraction caused by late coming and too early leaving. Standing in the doorways, blocking up passages and disputing about places should, out of respect for the Holy Sacrifice, be most carefully avoided.

Q. 949. What is Benediction of the Blessed Sacrament, and what vestments are used at it?

A. Benediction of the Blessed Sacrament is an act of divine worship in which the Blessed Sacrament, placed in the ostensorium, is exposed for the adoration of the people and is lifted up to bless them. The vestments used at Benediction are: A cope or large silk cloak and a humeral or shoulder veil.

Q. 950. Why does the priest wear special vestments and use certain ceremonies while performing his sacred duties?

A. The priest wears special vestments and uses certain ceremonies while performing his sacred duties:

1.(1) To give greater solemnity and to command more attention and respect at divine worship;

2.(2) To instruct the people in the things that these vestments and ceremonies signify;

3.(3) To remind the priest himself of the importance and sacred character of the work in which he is the representative of Our Lord Himself.

Hence we should learn the meaning of the ceremonies of the Church.

Q. 951. How do we show that the ceremonies of the Church are reasonable and proper?

A. We show that the ceremonies of the Church are reasonable and proper from the fact that all persons in authority, rulers, judges and masters, require certain acts of respect from their subjects, and as we know Our Lord is present on the altar, the Church requires definite acts of reverence and respect at the services held in His honor and in His presence.

Q. 952. Are there other reasons for the use of ceremonies?

A. There are other reasons for the use of ceremonies:

1.(1) God commanded ceremonies to be used in the old law, and

2.(2) Our Blessed Lord Himself made use of ceremonies in performing some of His miracles.

Q. 953. How are the persons who take part in a Solemn Mass or Vespers named?

A. The persons who take part in a Solemn Mass or Vespers are named as follows: The priest who says or celebrates the Mass is called the celebrant; those who assist him as deacon and sub-deacon are called the ministers; those who serve are called acolytes, and the one who directs the ceremonies is called the master of ceremonies. If the celebrant be a bishop, the Mass or Vespers is called Pontifical Mass or Pontifical Vespers.

Q. 954. What is Vespers?

A. Vespers is a portion of the divine office or daily prayer of the Church. It is sung in Churches generally on Sunday afternoon or evening, and is usually followed by Benediction of the Blessed Sacrament.

Q. 955. Can one satisfy for neglecting Mass on Sunday by hearing Vespers on the same day?

A. One cannot satisfy for neglecting Mass on Sunday by hearing Vespers on the same day, because there is no law of the Church obliging us under pain of sin to attend Vespers, while there is a law obliging us under pain of mortal sin to hear Mass.

Lesson Twenty-Fifth: On Extreme Unction and Holy Orders

Q. 956. What is the Sacrament of Extreme Unction?

A. Extreme Unction is the Sacrament which, through the anointing and prayer of the priest, gives health and strength to the soul, and sometimes to the body, when we are in danger of death from sickness.

Q. 957. Why is this Sacrament called Extreme Unction?

A. Extreme means last, and Unction means an anointing or rubbing with oil, and because Catholics are anointed with oil at Baptism, Confirmation and Holy Orders, the last Sacrament in which oil is used is called Extreme Unction, or the last Unction or anointing.

Q. 958. Is this Sacrament called Extreme Unction if the person recovers after receiving it?

A. This Sacrament is always called Extreme Unction, even if it must be given several times to the same person, for Extreme Unction is the proper name of the Sacrament, and it may be given as often as a person recovering from one attack of sickness is in danger of death by another. In a lingering illness it may be repeated after a month or six weeks, if the person slightly recovers and again relapses into a dangerous condition.

Q. 959. To whom may Extreme Unction be given?

A. Extreme Unction may be given to all Christians dangerously ill, who have ever been capable of committing sin after baptism and who have the right dispositions for the Sacrament. Hence it is never given to children who have not reached the use of reason, nor to persons who have always been insane.

Q. 960. What are the right dispositions for Extreme Unction?

A. The right dispositions for Extreme Unction are:

1.(1) Resignation to the Will of God with regard to our recovery;
2.(2) A state of grace or at least contrition for sins committed, and
3.(3) A general intention or desire to receive the Sacrament.

This Sacrament is never given to heretics in danger of death, because they cannot be supposed to have the intention necessary for receiving it, nor the desire to make use of the Sacrament of Penance in putting themselves in a state of grace.

Q. 961. When and by whom was Extreme Unction instituted?

A. Extreme Unction was instituted at the time of the apostles, for James the Apostle exhorts the sick to receive it.

It was instituted by Our Lord Himself -- though we do not know at what particular time -- for He alone can make a visible act a means of grace, and the apostles and their successors could never have believed Extreme Unction a Sacrament and used it as such unless they had Our Lord's authority for so doing.

Q. 962. When should we receive Extreme Unction?

A. We should receive Extreme Unction when we are in danger of death from sickness, or from a wound or accident.

Q. 963. What parts of the body are anointed in Extreme Unction?

A. The parts of the body anointed in Extreme Unction are: The eyes, the ears, the nose or nostrils, the lips, the hands and the feet, because these represent our senses of sight, hearing, smell, taste and touch, which are the means through which we have committed most of our sins.

Q. 964. What things should be prepared in the sick-room when the priest is coming to give the last Sacraments?

A. When the priest is coming to give the last Sacraments, the following things should be prepared:

1.A table covered with a white cloth; a crucifix; two lighted candles in candlesticks; holy water in a small vessel, with a small piece of palm for a sprinkler; a glass of clean water; a tablespoon and a napkin or cloth, to be placed under the chin of the one receiving the Viaticum.

Besides these, if Extreme Unction also is to be given, there should be some cotton and a small piece of bread or lemon to purify the priest's fingers.

Q. 965. What seems most proper with regard to the things necessary for the last Sacraments?

A. It seems most proper that the things necessary for the last Sacraments should be carefully kept in every Catholic family, and should never, if possible, be used for any other purpose.

Q. 966. What else is to be observed about the preparation for the administration of the last Sacraments?

A. The further preparation for the administration of the last Sacraments requires that out of respect for the Sacraments, and in particular for the presence of Our Lord, everything about the sick-room, the sick person and even the attendants, should be made as neat and clean as possible. Especially should the face, hands and feet of the one to be anointed be thoroughly clean.

Q. 967. Should we wait until we are in extreme danger before we receive Extreme Unction?

A. We should not wait until we are in extreme danger before we receive Extreme Unction, but if possible we should receive it whilst we have the use of our senses.

Q. 968. What should we do in case of serious illness if the sick person will not consent or is afraid to receive the Sacraments, or, at least, wishes to put off their reception?

A. In case of serious illness, if the sick person will not consent, or is afraid to receive the Sacraments, or, at least, wishes to put off their reception, we should send for the priest at once and let him do what he thinks best in the case, and thus we will free ourselves from the responsibility of letting a Catholic die without the last Sacraments.

Q. 969. Which are the effects of the Sacrament of Extreme Unction?

A. The effects of Extreme Unction are:

1. 1st. To comfort us in the pains of sickness and to strengthen us against temptations;
2. 2nd. To remit venial sins and to cleanse our soul from the remains of sin;
3. 3rd. To restore us to health, when God sees fit.

Q. 970. Will Extreme Unction take away mortal sin if the dying person is no longer able to confess?

A. Extreme Unction will take away mortal sin if the dying person is no longer able to confess, provided he has the sorrow for his sins that would bee necessary for the worthy reception of the Sacrament of Penance.

Q. 971. How do we know that this Sacrament, more than any other, was instituted to benefit the body?

A. We know that this Sacrament more than any other was instituted to benefit the body:

1. (1) From the words of St. James exhorting us to receive it;
2. (2) It is given when the soul is already purified by the graces of Penance and Holy Viaticum;
3. (3) One of its chief objects is to restore us to health if it be for our spiritual good, as most of the prayers said in giving this Sacrament indicate.

Q. 972. Since Extreme Unction may restore us to health, should we not be glad to receive it?

A. Since Extreme Unction may restore us to health. we should be glad to receive it, and we should not delay its reception till we are so near death that God could restore us only by a miracle. Again, this Sacrament, like the others, gives sanctifying and sacramental grace, which we should be eager to obtain as soon as our sickness is sufficient to give us the privilege of receiving the last Sacraments.

Q. 973. What do you mean by the remains of sin?

A. By the remains of sin I mean the inclination to evil and the weakness of the will which are the result of our sins, and which remain after our sins have been forgiven.

Q. 974. How should we receive the Sacrament of Extreme Unction?

A. We should receive the Sacrament of Extreme Unction in the state of grace, and with lively faith and resignation to the will of God.

Q. 975. Who is the minister of the Sacrament of Extreme Unction?

A. The priest is the minister of the Sacrament of Extreme Unction.

Q. 976. What is the final preparation we should make for the reception of the last Sacraments?

A. The final preparation we should make for the reception of the last Sacraments consists in an earnest effort to be resigned to God's Holy Will, to excite ourselves to true sorrow for our sins, to profit by the graces given us, to keep worldly thoughts from the mind, and to dispose ourselves as best we can for the worthy reception of the Sacraments and the blessings of a good death.

Q. 977. At what time should persons dangerously ill attend to the final arrangement of their temporal or worldly affairs?

A. Persons dangerously ill should attend to the final arrangement of their temporal or worldly affairs at the very beginning of their illness, that these things may not distract them at the hour of death, and that they may give the last hours of their life entirely to the care of their soul.

Q. 978. What is the Sacrament of Holy Orders?

A. Holy Orders is a Sacrament by which bishops, priests, and other ministers of the Church are ordained and receive the power and grace to perform their sacred duties.

Q. 979. Besides bishops and priests, who are the other ministers of the Church?

A. Besides bishops and priests, the other ministers of the Church are deacons and subdeacons, who, while preparing for the priesthood, have received some of the Holy Orders, but who have not been ordained to the full powers of the priest.

Q. 980. Why is this Sacrament called Holy Orders?

A. This Sacrament is called Holy Orders because it is conferred by seven different grades or steps following one another in fixed order by which the sacred powers of the priesthood are gradually given to the one admitted to that holy state.

Q. 981. What are the grades by which one ascends to the priesthood?

A. The grades by which one ascends to the priesthood are:

1.(1) Tonsure, or the clipping of the hair by the bishop, by which the candidate for priesthood dedicates himself to the service of the altar;

2.(2) The four minor orders, Porter, Reader, Exorcist, and Acolyte, by which he is permitted to perform certain duties that laymen should not perform;

3.(3) Sub-deaconship, by which he takes upon himself the obligation of leading a life of perpetual chastity and of saying daily the divine office;

4.(4) Deaconship, by which be receives power to preach, baptize, and give Holy Communion.

The next step, priesthood, gives him power to offer the Holy Sacrifice of the Mass and forgive sins. These orders are not all given at once, but at times fixed by the laws of the Church.

Q. 982. Are not the different orders separate Sacraments?

A. These different orders are not separate Sacraments. Taken all together, some are a preparation for the Sacrament and the rest are but the one Sacrament of Holy Orders; as the roots, trunk and branches form but one tree.

Q. 983. What name is given to sub-deaconship, deaconship and priesthood?

A. Sub-deaconship, deaconship and priesthood are called major or greater orders, because those who receive them are bound for life to the service of the altar and they cannot return to the service of the world to live as ordinary laymen.

Q. 984. What double power does the Church possess and confer on her pastors?

A. The Church possesses and confers on her pastor, the power of orders and the power of jurisdiction; that is, the power to administer the Sacraments and sanctify the faithful, and the power to teach and make laws that direct the faithful to their spiritual good. A bishop has the full power of orders and the Pope alone has the full power of jurisdiction.

Q. 985. How do the pastors of the Church rank according to authority?

A. The pastors of the Church rank according to authority as follows:

1.(1) Priests, who govern parishes or congregations in the name of their bishop;

2.(2) Bishops, who rule over a number of parishes or a diocese;

3.(3) Archbishops, who have authority over a number of dioceses or a province;

4.(4) Primates, who have authority over the ecclesiastical or Church provinces of a nation;

5.(5) Patriarchs, who have authority over a whole country;

6. and last and highest, the Pope, who rules the Church throughout the world.

Q. 986. How do the prelates or higher officers of the Church rank in dignity?

A. The prelates or higher officers of the Church rank in dignity as they rank in authority, except that in dignity Cardinals are next to the Pope, and Vicars Apostolic, Monsignori, and others having titles follow bishops. Papal delegates and those specially appointed by the Pope rank according to the powers he has given them.

Q. 987. Who are Cardinals, what are their duties and how are they divided?

A. Cardinals are the members of the Supreme Council or Senate of the Church. Their duties are to advise and aid the Pope in the government of the Church, and to elect a new Pope when the reigning Pope dies. They are divided into committees called sacred congregations, each having, its special work to perform. All these congregations taken together are called the Sacred College of Cardinals, of which the whole number is seventy.

Q. 988. Who is a Monsignor?

A. A Monsignor is a worthy priest upon whom the Pope confers this title as a mark of esteem. It gives certain privileges and the right to wear purple like a bishop.

Q. 989. Who is a Vicar-General?

A. A Vicar-General is one who is appointed by the bishop to aid him in the government of his diocese. He shares the bishop's power and in the bishop's absence he acts for the bishop and with his authority.

Q. 990. Who is an Abbot?

A. An Abbot is one who exercises over a religious community of men authority similar in many things to that exercised by a bishop over his diocese. He has also certain privileges usually granted to bishops.

Q. 991. What is the pallium?

A. The pallium is a white woolen vestment worn by the Pope and sent by him to patriarchs, primates and archbishops. It is the symbol of the fullness of pastoral power, and reminds the wearer of the Good Shepherd, whose example he must follow.

Q. 992. What is necessary to receive Holy Orders worthily?

A. To receive Holy Orders worthily it is necessary to be in the state of grace, to have the necessary knowledge

and a divine call to this sacred office.

Q. 993. What name is given to this divine call and how can we discover this call?

A. This divine call is named a vocation to the priestly or religious life. We can discover it in our constant inclination to such a life from the pure and holy motive of serving God better in it, together with our fitness for it, or, at least, our ability to prepare for it, also in our true piety and mastery over our sinful passions and unlawful desires.

Q. 994. How should we finally determine our vocation?

A. We should finally determine our vocation:

1.(1) By leading a holy life that we may be more worthy of it;

2.(2) By praying to the Holy Ghost for light on the subject;

3.(3) By seeking the advice of holy and prudent persons and above all of our confessor.

Q. 995. What should parents and guardians bear in mind with regard to their children's vocations?

A. Parents and guardians should bear in mind with regard to their children's vocations:

1.(1) That it is their duty to aid their children to discover their vocation;

2.(2) That it is sinful for them to resist the Will of God by endeavoring to turn their children from their true vocation or to prevent them from following it by placing obstacles in their way, and, worst of all, to urge them to enter a state of life to which they have not been divinely called;

3.(3) That in giving their advice they should be guided only by the future good and happiness of their children and not by any selfish or worldly motive which may lead to the loss of souls.

Q. 996. How should Christians look upon the priests of the Church?

A. Christians should look upon the priests of the Church as the messengers of God and the dispensers of His mysteries.

Q. 997. How do we know that the priests of the Church are the messengers of God?

A. We know that the priests of the Church are the messengers of God, because Christ said to His apostles, and through them to their successors: "As the Father hath sent Me, I also send you"; that is to say, to preach the true religion, to administer the Sacraments, to offer Sacrifice, and to do all manner of good for the salvation of souls.

Q. 998. When did the priests of the Church receive this threefold power to preach, to forgive sins and to consecrate bread and wine?

A. The priests of the Church received this three-fold power to preach, to forgive sins and to consecrate bread and wine, when Christ said to them, through the apostles: "Go teach all nations"; "Whose sins you shall forgive they are forgiven," and "Do this for a commemoration of Me."

Q. 999. Why should we show great respect to the priests and bishops of the Church?

A. We should show great respect to the priests and bishops of the Church:

1. (1) Because they are the representatives of Christ upon earth, and

2. (2) Because they administer the Sacraments without which we cannot be saved.

Therefore, we should be most careful in what we do, say or think concerning God's ministers. To show our respect in proportion to their dignity, we address the priest as Reverend, the bishop as Right Reverend, the archbishop as Most Reverend, and the Pope as Holy Father.

Q. 1000. Should we do more than merely respect the ministers of God?

A. We should do more than merely respect the ministers of God. We should earnestly and frequently pray for them, that they may be enabled to perform the difficult and important duties of their holy state in a manner pleasing to God.

Q. 1001. Who can confer the Sacrament of Holy Orders?

A. Bishops can confer the Sacrament of Holy Orders.

Q. 1002. How do we know that there is a true priesthood in the Church?

A. We know that there is a true priesthood in the Church:

1.(1) Because in the Jewish religion, which was only a figure of the Christian religion, there was a true priesthood established by God;

2.(2) Because Christ conferred on His apostles and not on all the faithful the power to offer Sacrifice, distribute the Holy Eucharist and forgive sins.

Q. 1003. But is there need of a special Sacrament of Holy Orders to confer these powers?

A. There is need of a special Sacrament of Holy Orders to confer these powers:

1.(1) Because the priesthood which is to continue the work of the apostles must be visible in the Church, and it must therefore be conferred by some visible ceremony or outward sign;

2.(2) Because this outward sign called Holy Orders gives not only power but grace and was instituted by Christ, Holy Orders must be a Sacrament.

Q. 1004. Can bishops, priests and other ministers of the Church always exercise the power they have received in Holy Orders?

A. Bishops, priests and other ministers of the Church cannot exercise the power they have received in Holy Orders unless authorized and sent to do so by their lawful superiors. The power can never be taken from them, but the right to use it may be withdrawn for causes laid down in the laws of the Church, or for reasons that seem good to those in authority over them. Any use of sacred power without authority is sinful, and all who take part in such ceremonies are guilty of sin.

Lesson Twenty-Sixth: On Matrimony

Q. 1005. What is the Sacrament of Matrimony?

A. The Sacrament of Matrimony is the Sacrament which unites a Christian man and woman in lawful marriage.

Q. 1006. When are persons lawfully married?

A. Persons are lawfully married when they comply with all the laws of God and of the Church relating to marriage. To marry unlawfully is a mortal sin, and it deprives the souls of the grace of the Sacrament.

Q. 1007. When was marriage first instituted?

A. Marriage was first instituted in the Garden of Eden, when God created Adam and Eve and made them husband and wife, but it was not then a Sacrament, for their union did not confer any special grace.

Q. 1008. When was the contract of marriage raised to the dignity of a Sacrament?

A. The exact time at which the contract of marriages was raised to the dignity of a Sacrament is not known, but the fact that it was thus raised is certain from passages in the New Testament and from the constant teaching of the Church ever since the time of the apostles. Our Lord did not merely add grace to the contract, but He made the very contract a Sacrament, so that Christians cannot make this contract without receiving the Sacrament.

Q. 1009. What is the outward sign in the Sacrament of Matrimony, and in what does the whole essence of the marriage contract consist?

A. The outward sign in the Sacrament of matrimony is the mutual consent of the persons, expressed by words or signs in accordance with the laws of the Church. The whole essence of the marriage contract consists in the surrender by the persons of their bodies to each other and in declaring by word or sign that they make this surrender and take each other for husband and wife now and for life.

Q. 1010. What are the chief ends of the Sacrament of Matrimony?

A. The chief ends of the Sacrament of matrimony are:

1.(1) To enable the husband and wife to aid each other in securing the salvation of their souls; 2. (2) To propagate or keep up the existence of the human race by bringing children into the world to serve God; 3.(3) To prevent sins against the holy virtue of purity by faithfully obeying the laws of the marriage state.

Q. 1011. Can a Christian man and woman be united in lawful marriage in any other way than by the Sacrament of Matrimony?

A. A Christian man and woman cannot be united in lawful marriage in any other way than by the Sacrament of Matrimony, because Christ raised marriage to the dignity of a sacrament.

Q. 1012. Were, then, all marriages before the coming of Christ unlawful and invalid?

A. All marriages before the coming of Christ were not unlawful and invalid. They were both lawful and valid when the persons contracting them followed the dictates of their conscience and the laws of God as they knew them; but such marriages were only contracts. Through their evil inclinations many forgot or neglected the true character of marriage till Our Lord restored it to its former unity and purity.

Q. 1013. What do we mean by impediments to marriage?

A. By impediments to marriage we mean certain restrictions, imposed by the law of God or of the Church, that render the marriage invalid or unlawful when they are violated in entering into it. These restrictions regard age, health, relationship, intention, religion and other matters affecting the good of the Sacrament.

Q. 1014. Can the Church dispense from or remove these impediments to marriage?

A. The Church can dispense from or remove the impediments to marriage that arise from its own laws; but it cannot dispense from impediments that arise from the laws of God and nature. Every lawmaker can change or excuse from the laws made by himself or his equals, but he cannot, of his own authority, change or excuse from laws made by a higher power.

Q. 1015. What is required that the Church may grant, when it is able, dispensations from the impediments to marriage or from other laws?

A. That the Church may grant dispensations from the impediments to marriage or from other laws, there must be a good and urgent reason for granting such dispensations. The Church does not grant dispensations without cause and merely to satisfy the wishes of those who ask for them.

Q. 1016. Why does the Church sometimes require the persons to whom dispensations are granted to pay a tax or fee for the privilege?

A. The Church sometimes requires the persons to whom dispensations are granted to pay a tax or fee for the privilege:

1.(1) That persons on account of this tax be restrained from asking for dispensations and may comply with the general laws; 2.(2) That the Church may not have to bear the expense of supporting an office for granting privileges to a few.

Q. 1017. What should persons who are about to get married do?

A. Persons who are about to get married should give their pastor timely notice of their intention, make known to him privately whatever they suspect might be an impediment to the marriage, and make sure of all arrangements before inviting their friends.

Q. 1018. What timely notice of marriage should be given to the priest, and why?

A. At least three weeks notice of marriage should be given to the priest, because, according to the laws of the Church, the names of the persons about to get married must be announced and their intended marriage published at the principal Mass in their parish for three successive Sundays.

Q. 1019. Why are the banns of matrimony published in the Church?

A. The banns of matrimony are published in the Church that any person who might know of any impediment to the marriage may have an opportunity to declare it privately to the priest before the marriage takes place and thus prevent an invalid or unlawful marriage. Persons who know of such impediments and fail to declare them in due time are guilty of sin

Q. 1020. What things in particular should persons arranging for their marriage make known to the priest?

A. Persons arranging for their marriage should make known to the priest whether both are Christians and Catholics; whether either has been solemnly engaged to another person; whether they have ever made any vow to God with regard to chastity or the like; whether they are related and in what degree; whether either was ever married to any member of the other's family and whether either was ever godparent in baptism for the other.

Q. 1021. What else must they make known?

A. They must also make known whether either was married before and what proof can be given of the death of the former husband or wife; whether they really intend to get married, and do so of their own will; whether they are of lawful age; whether they are sound in body or suffering from any deformity that might prevent their marriage, and lastly, whether they live in the parish in which they ask to be married, and if so, how long they have lived in it.

Q. 1022. What is particularly necessary that persons may do their duty in the marriage state?

A. That persons may do their duty in the marriage state, it is particularly necessary that they should be well instructed, before entering it, in the truths and duties of their religion for how will they teach their children these things if they are ignorant of them themselves?

Q. 1023. Can the bond of Christian marriage be dissolved by any human power?

A. The bond of Christian marriage cannot be dissolved by any human power.

Q. 1024. Does not a divorce granted by courts of justice break the bond of marriage?

A. Divorce granted by courts of justice or by any human power does not break the bond of marriage, and one who makes use of such a divorce to marry again while the former husband or wife lives commits a sacrilege and lives in the sin of adultery. A civil divorce may give a sufficient reason for the persons to live apart and it may determine their rights with regard to support, the control of the children and other temporal things, but it has no effect whatever upon the bond and spiritual nature of the Sacrament.

Q. 1025. Does not the Church sometimes allow husband and wife to separate and live apart?

A. The Church sometimes, for very good reasons, does allow husband and wife to separate and live apart; but that is not dissolving the bond of marriage, or divorce as it is called, for though separated they are still husband and wife, and neither can marry again till the other dies.

Q. 1026. Has not the Church sometimes allowed Catholics once married to separate and marry again?

A. The Church has never allowed Catholics once really married to separate and marry again, but it has sometimes declared persons apparently married free to marry again, because their first marriage was null; that is, no marriage on account of some impediment not discovered till after the ceremony.

Q. 1027. What evils follow divorce so commonly claimed by those outside the true Church and granted by civil authority?

A. The evils that follow divorce so commonly claimed by those outside the true Church and granted by civil authority are very many; but chiefly:

1.(1) A disregard for the sacred character of the Sacrament and for the spiritual welfare of the children; 2. (2) The loss of the true idea of home and family followed by bad morals and sinful living.

Q. 1028. Which are the effects of the Sacrament of Matrimony?

A. The effects of the Sacrament of Matrimony are:

1.1st. To sanctify the love of husband and wife; 2. 2nd. To give them grace to bear with each other's weaknesses; 3. 3rd. To enable them to bring up their children in the fear and love of God.

Q. 1029. What do we mean by bearing with each other's weaknesses?

A. By bearing with each other's weaknesses we mean that the husband and wife must be patient with each other's faults, bad habits or dispositions, pardon them easily, and aid each other in overcoming them.

Q. 1030. How are parents specially fitted to bring up their children in the fear and love of God?

A. Parents are specially fitted to bring up their children in the fear and love of God:

1.(1) By the special grace they receive to advise and direct their children and to warn them against evil; 2. (2) By the experience they have acquired in passing through life from childhood to the position of parents.

Children should, therefore, conscientiously seek and accept the direction of good parents.

Q. 1031. To receive the Sacrament of Matrimony worthily is it necessary to be in the state of grace?

A. To receive the Sacrament of Matrimony worthily it is necessary to be in the state of grace, and it is necessary also to comply with the laws of the Church.

Q. 1032. With what laws of the Church are we bound to comply in receiving the Sacrament of Matrimony?

A. In receiving the Sacrament of matrimony we are bound to comply with whatever laws of the Church concern Matrimony; such as laws forbidding solemn marriage in Lent and Advent; or marriage with relatives or with persons of a different religion, and in general all laws that refer to any impediment to marriage.

Q. 1033. In how many ways may persons be related?

A. Persons may be related in four ways. When they are related by blood their relationship is called consanguinity; when they are related by marriage it is called affinity; when they are related by being god-parents in Baptism or Confirmation, it is called spiritual affinity; when they are related by adoption, it is called legal affinity.

Q. 1034. Who has the right to make laws concerning the Sacrament of marriage?

A. The Church alone has the right to make laws concerning the Sacrament of marriage, though the state also has the right to make laws concerning the civil effects of the marriage contract.

Q. 1035. What do we mean by laws concerning the civil effects of the marriage contract?

A. By laws concerning the civil effects of the marriage contract we mean laws with regard to the property or debts of the husband and wife, the inheritance of their children, or whatever pertains to their temporal affairs. All persons are bound to obey the laws of their country when these laws are not opposed to the laws of God.

Q. 1036. Does the Church forbid the marriage of Catholics with persons who have a different religion or no religion at all?

A. The Church does forbid the marriage of Catholics with persons who have a different religion or no religion at all.

Q. 1037. Why does the Church forbid the marriage of Catholics with persons who have a different religion or no religion at all?

A. The Church forbids the marriage of Catholics with persons who have a different religion, or no religion at all, because such marriages generally lead to indifference, loss of faith, and to the neglect of the religious education of the children.

Q. 1038. What are the marriages of Catholics with persons of a different religion called, and when does the Church permit them by dispensation?

A. The marriages of Catholics with persons of a different religion are called mixed marriages. The Church permits them by dispensation only under certain conditions and for urgent reasons; chiefly to prevent a greater evil.

Q. 1039. What are the conditions upon which the Church will permit a Catholic to marry one who is not a Catholic?

A. The conditions upon which the Church will permit a Catholic to marry one who is not a Catholic are:

1. (1) That the Catholic be allowed the free exercise of his or her religion ;
2. (2) That the Catholic shall try by teaching and good example to lead the one who is not a Catholic to embrace the true faith; 3. (3) That all the children born of the marriage shall be brought up in the Catholic religion.

The marriage ceremony must not be repeated before a heretical minister. Without these promises, the Church will not consent to a mixed marriage, and if the Church does not consent the marriage is unlawful.

Q. 1040. What penalty does the Church impose on Catholics who marry before a Protestant minister?

A. Catholics who marry before a Protestant minister incur excommunication; that is, a censure of the Church or spiritual penalty which prevents them from receiving the Sacrament of Penance till the priest who hears their confession gets special faculties or permission from the bishop; because by such a marriage they make profession of a false religion in acknowledging as a priest one who has neither sacred power nor authority.

Q. 1041. How does the Church show its displeasure at mixed marriages?

A. The Church shows its displeasure at mixed marriages by the coldness with which it sanctions them, prohibiting all religious ceremony at them by forbidding the priest to use any sacred vestments, holy water or blessing of the ring at such marriages; by prohibiting them also from taking place in the Church or even in the sacristy. On the other hand, the Church shows its joy and approval at a true Catholic marriage by the Nuptial Mass and solemn ceremonies.

Q. 1042. Why should Catholics avoid mixed marriages?

A. Catholics should avoid mixed marriages:

1.(1) Because they are displeasing to the Church and cannot bring with them the full measure of God's grace and blessing; 2.(2) Because the children should have the good example of both parents in the practice of their religion; 3.(3) Because such marriages give rise to frequent disputes on religious questions between husband and wife and between their relatives; 4.(4) Because the one not a Catholic, disregarding the sacred character of the Sacrament, may claim a divorce and marry again, leaving the Catholic married and abandoned.

Q. 1043. Does the Church seek to make converts by its laws concerning mixed marriages?

A. The Church does not seek to make converts by its laws concerning mixed marriages, but seeks only to keep its children from losing their faith

153

and becoming perverts by constant company with persons not Catholics. The Church does not wish persons to become Catholics merely for the sake of marrying Catholics. Such conversions are, as a rule, not sincere, do no good, but rather make such converts hypocrites and guilty of greater sins, especially sins of sacrilege.

Q. 1044. Why do many marriages prove unhappy?

A. Many marriages prove unhappy because they are entered into hastily and without worthy motives.

Q. 1045. When are marriages entered into hastily?

A. Marriages are entered into hastily when persons do not sufficiently consider and investigate the character, habits and dispositions of the one they intend to marry. It is wise to look for lasting qualities and solid virtues in a life-long companion and not to be carried away with characteristics that please only for a time.

Q. 1046. When are motives for marriage worthy?

A. Motives for marriage are worthy when persons enter it for the sake of doing God's will and fulfilling the end for which He instituted the Sacrament. Whatever is opposed to the true object of the Sacrament and the sanctification of the husband and wife must be an unworthy motive.

Q. 1047. How should Christians prepare for a holy and happy marriage?

A. Christians should prepare for a holy and happy marriage by receiving the Sacraments of Penance and Holy Eucharist; by begging God to grant them a pure intention and to direct their choice; and by seeking the advice of their parents and the blessing of their pastors.

Q. 1048. How may parents be guilty of great injustice to their children in case of marriage?

A. Parents may be guilty of great injustice to their children in case of marriage by seeking the gratification of their own aims and desires, rather than the good of their children, and thus for selfish and unreasonable motives forcing their children to marry persons they dislike or preventing them from marrying the persons chosen by the dictates of their conscience, or compelling them to marry when they have no vocation for such a life or no true knowledge of its obligations.

Q. 1049. May persons receive the Sacrament of Matrimony more than once?

A. Persons may receive the sacrament of Matrimony more than once, provided they are certain of the death of the former husband or wife and comply with the laws of the Church.

Q. 1050. Where and at what time of the day should Catholics be married?

A. Catholics should be married before the altar in the Church. They should be married in the morning, and with a Nuptial Mass if possible.

Q. 1051. What must never be forgotten by those who attend a marriage ceremony in the Church?

A. They who attend a marriage ceremony in the Church must never forget the presence of the Blessed Sacrament, and that all laughing, talking, or irreverence is forbidden then as at other times. Women must never enter into the presence of the Blessed Sacrament with uncovered heads, and their dress must be in keeping with the strict modesty that Our Lord's presence demands, no matter what worldly vanity or social manners may require.

Lesson Twenty-Seventh: On the Sacramentals

Q. 1052. What is a sacramental?
A. A sacramental is anything set apart or blessed by the Church to excite good thoughts and to increase devotion, and through these movements of the heart to remit venial sin.

Q. 1053. How do the Sacramentals excite good thoughts and increase devotion?
A. The Sacramentals excite good thoughts by recalling to our minds some special reason for doing good and avoiding evil; especially by reminding us of some holy person, event or thing through which blessings have come to us. They increase devotion by fixing our minds on particular virtues and by helping us to understand and desire them.

Q. 1054. Do the Sacramentals of themselves remit venial sins?
A. The Sacramentals of themselves do not remit venial sins, but they move us to truer devotion, to greater love for God and greater sorrow for our sins, and this devotion, love and sorrow bring us grace, and the grace remits venial sins.

Q. 1055. Why does the Church use Sacramentals?
A. The Church uses Sacramentals to teach the faithful of every class the truths of religion, which they may learn as well by their sight as by their hearing; for God wishes us to learn His laws by every possible means, by every power of soul and body.

Q. 1056. Show by an example how Sacramentals aid the ignorant in learning the truths of faith.
A. Sacramentals aid the ignorant in learning the truths of faith as children learn from pictures before they are able to read. Thus one who cannot read the account of Our Lord's passion may learn it from the Stations of the Cross, and one who kneels before a crucifix and looks on the bleeding head, pierced hands and wounded side, is better able to understand Christ's sufferings

Q. 1057. What are the Stations or Way of the Cross?
A. The Stations or Way of the Cross is a devotion instituted by the Church to aid us in meditating on Christ's passion and death. Fourteen crosses or stations, each with a picture of some scene in the passion, are arranged at distances apart. By passing from one station to another and praying before each while we meditate upon the scene it represents, we make the Way of the Cross in memory of Christ's painful journey during His passion, and we gain the indulgence granted for this pious exercise.

Q. 1058. Are prayers and ceremonies of the Church also Sacramentals?

A. Prayers and ceremonies of the Church are also Sacramentals because they excite good thoughts and increase devotion. Whatever the Church dedicates to a pious use or devotes to the worship of God may be called a Sacramental.

Q. 1059. On what ground does the Church make use of ceremonies?

A. The Church makes use of ceremonies:

1. (1) After the example of the Old Law, in which God described and commanded ceremonies; 2. (2) After the example of Our Lord, who rubbed clay on the eyes of the blind to whom He wished to restore sight, though He might have performed the miracle without any external act; 3. (3) On the authority of the Church itself, to whom Christ gave power to do whatever was necessary for the instruction of all men; 4. (4) To add solemnity to religious acts.

Q. 1060. How may persons sin in using Sacramentals?

A. Persons may sin in using Sacramentals by using them in a way or for a purpose prohibited by the Church; also by believing that the use of Sacramentals will save us in spite of our sinful lives. We must remember that Sacramentals can aid us only through the blessing the Church gives them and through the good dispositions they excite in us. They have, therefore, no power in themselves, and to put too much confidence in their use leads to superstition.

Q. 1061. What is the difference between the Sacraments and the sacramentals?

A. The difference between the Sacraments and the sacramentals is:

1.1st. The Sacraments were instituted by Jesus Christ and the sacramentals were instituted by the Church; 2.2nd. The Sacraments give grace of themselves when we place no obstacle in the way; 3.3rd. The sacramentals excite in us pious dispositions, by means of which we may obtain grace.

Q. 1062. May the Church increase or diminish the number of Sacraments and Sacramentals?

A. The Church can never increase nor diminish the number of Sacraments, for as Christ Himself instituted them, He alone has power to change their number; but the Church may increase or diminish the number of the Sacramentals as the devotion of its people or the circumstances of the time and place require, for since the Church instituted them they must depend entirely upon its laws.

Q. 1063. Which is the chief sacramental used in the Church?

A. The chief sacramental used in the Church is the sign of the cross.

Q. 1064. How do we make the sign of the cross?

A. We make the sign of the cross by putting the right hand to the forehead, then on the breast, and then to the left and right shoulders, saying, "In the name of the Father, and of the Son, and of the Holy Ghost, Amen."

Q. 1065. What is a common fault with many in blessing themselves?

A. A common fault with many in blessing themselves is to make a hurried motion with the hand which is in no way a sign of the cross. They perform this act of devotion without thought or intention, forgetting that the Church grants an indulgence to all who bless themselves properly while they have sorrow for their sins.

Q. 1066. Why do we make the sign of the cross?

A. We make the sign of the cross to show that we are Christians and to profess our belief in the chief mysteries of our religion.

Q. 1067. How is the sign of the cross a profession of faith in the chief mysteries of our religion?

A. The sign of the cross is a profession of faith in the chief mysteries of our religion because it expresses the mysteries of the Unity and Trinity of God and of the Incarnation and death of our Lord.

Q. 1068. How does the sign of the cross express the mystery of the Unity and Trinity of God?

A. The words, "In the name," express the Unity of God; the words that follow, "of the Father, and of the Son, and of the Holy Ghost," express the mystery of the Trinity.

Q. 1069. How does the sign of the cross express the mystery of the Incarnation and death of our Lord?

A. The sign of the cross expresses the mystery of the Incarnation by reminding us that the Son of God, having become man, suffered death on the cross.

Q. 1070. What other sacramental is in very frequent use?

A. Another sacramental in very frequent use is holy water.

Q. 1071. What is holy water?

A. Holy water is water blessed by the priest with solemn prayer to beg God's blessing on those who use it, and protection from the powers of darkness.

Q. 1072. How does the water blessed on Holy Saturday, or Easter Water, as it is called, differ from the holy water blessed at other times?

A. The water blessed on Holy Saturday, or Easter Water, as it is called, differs from the holy water blessed at other times in this, that the Easter water is blessed with greater solemnity, the paschal candle, which represents Our Lord risen from the dead, having been dipped into it with a special prayer.

Q. 1073. Is water ever blessed in honor of certain saints?

A. Water is sometimes blessed in honor of certain saints and for special purposes. The form of prayer to be used in such blessings is found in the Roman Ritual -- the book containing prayers and ceremonies for the administration of the Sacraments and of blessings authorized by the Church.

Q. 1074. Are there other sacramentals besides the sign of the cross and holy water?

A. Beside the sign of the cross and holy water there are many other sacramentals, such as blessed candles, ashes, palms, crucifixes, images of the Blessed Virgin and of the saints, rosaries, and scapulars.

Q. 1075. When are candles blessed in the Church and why are they used?

A. Candles are blessed in the Church on the feast of the Purification of the Blessed Virgin -- February 2nd. They are used chiefly to illuminate and ornament our altars, as a mark of reverence for the presence of Our Lord and of joy at His coming.

Q. 1076. What praiseworthy custom is now in use in many places?

A. A praiseworthy custom now in use in many places is the offering by the faithful on the feast of the Purification of candles for the use of the altar during the year. It is pleasing to think we have candles burning in our name on the altar of God, and if the Jewish people yearly made offerings to their temple, faithful Christians should not neglect their altars and churches where God Himself dwells.

Q. 1077. When are ashes blessed in the Church and why are they used?

A. Ashes are blessed in the Church on Ash Wednesday. They are used to keep us in mind of our humble origin, and of how the body of Adam, our forefather, was formed out of the slime or clay of the earth; also to remind us of death, when our bodies will return to dust, and of the necessity of doing penance for our sins. These ashes are obtained by burning the blessed palms of the previous year.

Q. 1078. When are palms blessed and of what do they remind us?

A. Palms are blessed on Palm Sunday. They remind us of Our Lord's triumphal entry into Jerusalem, when the people, wishing to honor Him and make Him king, strewed palm branches and even their own garments in His path, singing: Hosanna to the Son of David.

Q. 1079. What is the difference between a cross and a crucifix?

A. A cross has no figure on it and a crucifix has a figure of Our Lord. The word crucifix means fixed or nailed to the cross.

Q. 1080. What is the Rosary?

A. The Rosary is a form of prayer in which we say a certain number of Our Fathers and Hail Marys, meditating or thinking for a short time before each decade; that is, before each Our Father and ten Hail Marys, on some particular event in the life of Our Lord. These events are called mysteries of the Rosary. The string of beads on which these prayers are said is also called a Rosary. The ordinary beads are of five decades, or one-third of the whole Rosary.

Q. 1081. Who taught the use of the Rosary in its present form?

A. St. Dominic taught the use of the Rosary in its present form. By it he instructed his hearers in the chief truths of our holy religion and converted many to the true faith.

Q. 1082. How do we say the Rosary, or beads?

A. To say the Rosary or beads we bless ourselves with the cross, then say the Apostles' Creed and the Our Father on the first large bead, then the Hail Mary on each of the three small beads, and then Glory be to the Father, etc.

Then we mention or think of the first mystery we wish to honor, and say an Our Father on the large bead and a Hail Mary on each small bead of the ten that follow. At the end of every decade, or ten Hail Marys, we say "Glory be to the Father;" etc. Then we mention the next mystery and do as before, and so on to the end.

Q. 1083. How many mysteries of the Rosary are there?

A. There are fifteen mysteries of the Rosary arranged in the order in which these events occurred in the life of Our Lord, and divided into five joyful, five sorrowful, and five glorious mysteries.

Q. 1084. Say the five joyful mysteries of the Rosary.

A. The five joyful mysteries of the Rosary are:

1.(1) The Annunciation -- the Angel Gabriel telling the Blessed Virgin that she is to be the Mother of God; 2.(2) The Visitation -- the Blessed Virgin goes to visit her cousin, St. Elizabeth, the mother of St. John the Baptist; 3.(3) The Nativity, or birth, of Our Lord; 4.(4) The Presentation of the Child Jesus in the temple -- His parents offered Him to God; 5.(5) The finding of the Child Jesus in the temple -- His parents had lost Him in Jerusalem for three days.

Q. 1085. Say the five sorrowful mysteries of the Rosary.

A. The five sorrowful mysteries of the Rosary are:

1. (1) The Agony in the Garden -- Our Lord was in dreadful anguish and bathed in a bloody sweat; 2. (2) The Scourging at the Pillar -- Christ was stripped of His garments and lashed in a cruel manner; 3. (3) The Crowning with Thorns -- He was mocked as a king by heartless men; 4. (4) The Carriage of the Cross -- from the place He was condemned to Calvary, the place of Crucifixion; 5. (5) The Crucifixion -- He was nailed to the cross amid the jeers and blasphemies of His enemies.

Q. 1086. Say the five glorious mysteries of the Rosary.

A. The five glorious mysteries of the Rosary are:

1.(1) The Resurrection of Our Lord; 2. (2) The Ascension of Our Lord; 3. (3) The Coming of the Holy Ghost upon the Apostles; 4. (4) The Assumption of the Blessed Virgin -- after death she was taken body and soul into heaven; 5. (5) The Coronation of the Blessed Virgin -- on entering heaven she was made queen of all the Angels and Saints and placed in dignity next to her Divine Son, Our Blessed Lord.

Q. 1087. On what days, according to the pious custom of the faithful, are the different mysteries of the Rosary usually said?

A. According to the pious custom of the faithful, the different mysteries of the Rosary are usually said on the following days, namely: the joyful on Mondays and Thursdays, the sorrowful on Tuesdays and Fridays, and the glorious on Sundays, Wednesdays and Saturdays.

Q. 1088. What do the letters I. N. R. I. over the crucifix mean?

A. The letters I. N. R. I. over the crucifix are the first letters of four Latin words that mean Jesus of Nazareth, King of the Jews. Our Lord did say He was king of the Jews, but He also said that He was not their temporal or earthly king, but their spiritual and heavenly king.

Q. 1089. To what may we attribute the desire of the Jews to put Christ to death?

A. We may attribute the desire of the Jews to put Christ to death to the jealously, hatred and ill-will of their priests and the Pharisees, whose faults He rebuked and whose hypocrisy He exposed. By their slanders and lies they induced the people to follow them in demanding Our Lord's crucifixion.

Q. 1090. With whom did the Blessed Virgin live after the death of Our Lord?

A. After the death of Our Lord the Blessed Virgin lived for about eleven years with the Apostle St. John the Evangelist, called also the Beloved Disciple. He wrote one of the four Gospels, three Epistles, and the Apocalypse, or Book of Revelations -- the last book of the Bible. He lived to the age of a hundred years or more and died last of all the apostles.

Q. 1091. What do we mean by the Assumption of the Blessed Virgin, and why do we believe in it?

A. By the Assumption of the Blessed Virgin we mean that her body was taken up into heaven after her death. We believe in it:

1.(1) Because the Church cannot teach error, and yet from an early age the Church has celebrated the Feast of the Assumption; 2. (2) Because no one ever claimed to have a relic of our Blessed Mother's body, and surely the apostles, who knew and loved her, would have secured some relic had her body remained upon earth.

Q. 1092. What do the letters I. H. S. on an altar or sacred things mean?

A. The letters I. H. S. on an altar or sacred things means the name Jesus; for it is in that way the Holy Name is written in the Greek language when some of the letters are left out.

Q. 1093. What is the scapular, and why is it worn?

A. The scapular is a long, broad piece of woolen cloth forming a part of the religious dress of monks, priests and sisters of some religious orders. It is worn over the shoulders and extends from the shoulders to the feet. The small scapular made in imitation of it, and consisting of two small pieces of cloth fastened together by strings, is worn by the faithful as a promise or proof of their willingness to practice some particular devotion, indicated by the kind of scapular they wear.

Q. 1094. How many kinds of scapulars are there in use among the faithful?

A. Among the faithful there are many kinds of scapulars in use, such as the brown scapular or scapular of Mount Carmel worn in honor of Our Lord's passion; the white, in honor of the Holy Trinity; the blue, in honor of the Immaculate Conception; and the black, in honor of the seven dolors of the Blessed Virgin. When these are joined together and worn as one they are called the five scapulars. The brown scapular is best known and entitles its wearer to the greatest privileges and indulgences.

Q. 1095. What are the seven dolors of the Blessed Virgin?

A. The seven dolors of the Blessed Virgin are the chief sorrowful events in the life of Our Blessed Lady. They are:

1.(1) The circumcision of our Lord -- when she saw his blood shed for the first time; 2.(2) Her flight into Egypt -- to save the life of the Infant Jesus, when Herod sought to kill Him; 3.(3) The three days she lost her Son in Jerusalem; 4.(4) When she saw him carrying the cross; 5.(5) When she saw him die; 6.(6) When His dead body was taken down from the cross; 7.(7) When it was laid in the sepulchre or tomb.

Q. 1096. What are the seven dolor beads, and how do we say them?

A. Seven dolor beads are beads constructed with seven medals, each bearing a representation of one of the seven dolors, and seven beads between each medal and the next. At each medal we meditate on the proper dolor and the say a Hail Mary on each of the bead following it.

Q. 1097. What is an Agnus Dei?

A. An Agnus Dei is a small piece of beeswax stamped with the image of a lamb and cross. It is solemnly blessed by the Pope with special prayers for those who carry it about their person in honor of Our Blessed Redeemer, whom we call the Lamb of God, Who taketh away the sins of the world. The wax is usually covered with silk or some fine material.

Lesson Twenty-Eighth: On Prayer

Q. 1098. Is there any other means of obtaining God's grace than the Sacraments?

A. There is another means of obtaining God's grace, and it is prayer.

Q. 1099. What is prayer?

A. Prayer is the lifting up of our minds and hearts to God, to adore Him, to thank Him for His benefits, to ask His forgiveness, and to beg of Him all the graces we need whether for soul or body.

Q. 1100. How many kinds of prayer are there?

A. There are two kinds of prayer:

1. Mental prayer, called meditation, in which we spend the time thinking of God or of one or more of the truths He has revealed, that by these thoughts we may be persuaded to lead holier lives;

2. Vocal prayer, in which we express these pious thoughts in words.

Q. 1101. Why is mental prayer most useful to us?

A. Mental prayer is most useful to us because it compels us, while we are engaged in it, to keep our attention fixed on God and His holy laws and to keep our hearts and minds lifted up to Him.

Q. 1102. How can we make a meditation?

A. We can make a meditation:

1. By remembering that we are in the presence of God;

2. By asking the Holy Ghost to give us grace to benefit by the meditation;

3. By reflecting seriously on some sacred truth regarding our salvation;

4. By drawing some good resolution from the thoughts we have had; and

5. By thanking God for the knowledge and grace bestowed on us through the meditation.

Q. 1103. Where may we find subjects or points for meditation?

A. We may find the subjects or points for meditation in the words of the Our Father, Hail Mary or Apostles' Creed; also in the questions and answers of our Catechism, in the Holy Bible, and in books of meditation.

Q. 1104. Is prayer necessary to salvation?

A. Prayer is necessary to salvation, and without it no one having the use of reason can be saved.

Q. 1105. At what particular times should we pray?

A. We should pray particularly on Sundays and holy days, every morning and night, in all dangers, temptations, and afflictions.

Q. 1106. How should we pray?

A. We should pray:

1. With attention;

2. With a sense of our own helplessness and dependence upon God;

3. With a great desire for the graces we beg of God;

4. With trust in God's goodness;

5. With perseverance.

Q. 1107. What should our attention at prayer be?

A. Our attention at prayer should be threefold, namely, attention to the words, that we may say them correctly and distinctly; attention to their meaning, if we understand it, and attention to God, to whom the words are addressed.

Q. 1108. What should be the position of the body when we pray?

A. At prayer the most becoming position of the body is kneeling upright, but whether we pray kneeling, standing or sitting, the position of the body should always be one indicating reverence, respect and devotion. We may pray even lying down or walking, for Our Lord Himself says we should pray at all times.

Q. 1109. What should we do that we may pray well?

A. That we may pray well we should make a preparation before prayer:

1. By calling to mind the dignity of God, to whom we are about to speak, and our own unworthiness to appear in His presence;

2. By fixing upon the precise grace or blessing for which we intend to ask;

3. By remembering God's power and willingness to give if we truly need and earnestly, humbly and confidently ask.

Q. 1110. Why does God not always grant our prayers?

A. God does not always grant our prayers for these and other reasons:

1. Because we may not pray in the proper manner;

2. That we may learn our dependence on Him, prove our confidence in Him, and merit rewards by our patience and perseverance in prayer.

Prudent persons do not grant every request; why, then, should God do so?

Q. 1111. What assurance have we that God always hears and rewards our prayers, though He may not grant what we ask?

A. We have the assurance of Our Lord Himself that God always hears and rewards our prayers, though He may not grant what we ask; for Christ said: "Ask and it shall be given you," and "if you ask the Father anything in My name, He will give it to you."

Q. 1112. Which are the prayers most recommended to us?

A. The prayers most recommended to us are the Lord's Prayer, the Hail Mary, the Apostles' Creed, the Confiteor, and the Acts of Faith, Hope, Love, and Contrition.

Q. 1113. Are prayers said with distractions of any avail?

A. Prayers said with willful distraction are of no avail.

Q. 1114. Why are prayers said with willful distraction of no avail?

A. Prayers said with willful distraction are of no avail because they are mere words, such as a machine might utter, and since there is no lifting up of the mind or heart with them they cannot be prayer.

Q. 1115. Do, then, the distractions which we often have at prayer deprive our prayers of all merit?

A. The distractions which we often have at prayer do not deprive our prayers of all merit, because they are not willful when we try to keep them away, for God rewards our good intentions and the efforts we make to pray well.

Q. 1116. What, then, is a distraction?

A. A distraction is any thought that, during prayer, enters our mind to turn our thoughts and hearts from God and from the sacred duty we are performing.

Q. 1117. What are the fruits of prayer?

A. The fruits of prayer are:
1. It strengthens our faith,
2. nourishes our hope,
3. increases our love for God,
4. keeps us humble,
5. merits grace and atones for sin.

Q. 1118. Why should we pray when God knows our needs?

A. We pray not to remind God or tell Him of what we need, but to acknowledge that He is the Supreme Giver, to adore and worship Him by showing our entire dependence upon Him for every gift to soul or body.

Q. 1119. What little prayers may we say even at work?

A. Even at work we may say little aspirations such as "My God, pardon my sins; Blessed be the Holy Name of Jesus; Holy Spirit, enlighten me; Holy Mary, pray for me," etc.

Q. 1120. Did Our Lord Himself pray, and why?

A. Our Lord Himself very frequently prayed, often spending the whole night in prayer. He prayed before every important action, not that He needed to pray, but to set us an example of how and when we should pray.

Q. 1121. Why does the Church conclude most of its prayers with the words "through Jesus Christ Our Lord"?

A. The Church concludes most of its prayers with the words "through Jesus Christ Our Lord" because it is only through His merits that we can obtain grace, and because "there is no other name given to men whereby we must be saved."

Q. 1122. Was any special promise made in favor of the united prayers of two or more persons?

A. A special promise was made in favor of the united prayers of two or more persons when Our Lord said: "Where there are two or three gathered together in My name, there am I in the midst of them." Therefore, the united prayers of a congregation, sodality or family, and, above all, the public prayers of the whole Church, have great influence with God. We should join in public prayers out of true devotion, and not from habit, or, worse, to display our piety.

Q. 1123. What is the most suitable place for prayer?

A. The most suitable place for prayer is in the Church -- the house of prayer -- made holy by special blessings and, above all, by the Real Presence of Jesus dwelling in the Tabernacle. Still, Our Lord exhorts us to pray also in secret, for His Father, who seeth in secret, will repay us.

Q. 1124. For what should we pray?

A. We should pray:

1. For ourselves, for the blessings of soul and body that we may be devoted servants of God;

2. For the Church, for all spiritual and temporal wants, that the true faith may be everywhere known and professed;

3. For our relatives, friends and benefactors, particularly for those we may in any way have injured;

4. For all men, for the protection of the good and conversion of the wicked, that virtue may flourish and vice disappear;

5. For our spiritual rulers, the Pope, our bishops, priests and religious communities, that they may faithfully perform their sacred duties;

6. For our country and temporal rulers, that they may use their power for the good of their subjects and for the honor and glory of God.

Lesson Twenty-Ninth: On the Commandments of God

Q. 1125. Is it enough to belong to God's Church in order to be saved?

A. It is not enough to belong to the Church in order to be saved, but we must also keep the Commandments of God and of the Church.

Q. 1126. Are not the commandments of the Church also commandments of God?

A. The commandments of the Church are also commandments of God, for they are made by His authority and under the guidance of the Holy Ghost; nevertheless, the Church can change or abolish its own commandments, while it cannot change or abolish the commandments given directly by God Himself.

Q. 1127. Which are the Commandments that contain the whole law of God?

A. The Commandments which contain the whole law of God are these two: 1.1st. Thou shalt love the Lord thy God with thy whole heart, with thy whole soul, with thy whole strength, and with thy whole mind; 2.2nd. Thou shalt love thy neighbor as thyself.

Q. 1128. Why do these two Commandments of the love of God and of our neighbor contain the whole law of God?

A. These two Commandments of the love of God and of our neighbor contain the whole law of God because all the other Commandments are given either to help us to keep these two, or to direct us how to shun what is opposed to them.

Q. 1129. Explain further how the two commandments of the love of God and of our neighbor contain the teaching of the whole ten commandments.

A. The two commandments of the love of God and of our neighbor contain the teaching of the whole ten commandments because the first three of the ten commandments refer to God and oblige us to worship Him alone, respect His name and serve Him as He wills, and these things we will do if we love Him; secondly, the last seven of the ten commandments refer to our neighbor and forbid us to injure him in body, soul, goods or reputation, and if we love him we will do him no injury in any of these, but, on the contrary, aid him as far as we can.

Q. 1130. Which are the Commandments of God?

A. The Commandments of God are these ten:

1.1. I am the Lord thy God, who brought thee out of the land of Egypt, out of the house of bondage. Thou shalt not have strange gods before me. Thou shalt not make to thyself a graven thing, nor the likeness of any thing that is in heaven above, or in the earth beneath, nor of those things that are in the waters under the earth. Thou shalt not adore them, nor serve them. 2.2. Thou shalt not take the name of the Lord thy God in vain. 3.3. Remember thou keep holy the Sabbath day. 4.4. Honor thy father and thy mother. 5.5. Thou shalt not kill. 6.6. Thou shalt not commit adultery. 7.7. Thou shalt not steal. 8.8. Thou shalt not bear false witness against thy neighbor. 9.9. Thou shalt not covet thy neighbor's wife. 10.10. Thou shalt not covet thy neighbor's goods.

Q. 1131. What does the first commandment mean by a "graven thing" or "the likeness of anything" in heaven, in the earth or in the waters?

A. The first commandment means by a "graven thing" or "the likeness of anything" in heaven, in the earth or in the waters, the statue, picture or image of any creature in heaven or of any animal on land or in water intended for an idol and to be worshipped as a god.

Q. 1132. Who gave the Ten Commandments?

A. God Himself gave the Ten Commandments to Moses on Mount Sinai, and Christ our Lord confirmed them.

Q. 1133. How and when were the Commandments give to Moses?

A. The Commandments, written on two tables of stone, were given to Moses in the midst of fire and smoke, thunder and lightning, from which God spoke to him on the mountain, about fifty days after the Israelites were delivered from the bondage of Egypt and while they were on their journey through the desert to the Promised Land.

Q. 1134. What do we mean when we say Christ confirmed the Commandments?

A. When we say Christ confirmed the Commandments we mean that He strongly approved them, and gave us by His teaching a fuller and clearer knowledge of their meaning and importance.

Q. 1135. Was anyone obliged to keep the Commandments before they were given to Moses?

A. All persons, from the beginning of the world, were obliged to keep the Commandments, for it was always sinful to blaspheme God, murder, steal or violate any of the Commandments, though they were not written till the time of Moses.

Q. 1136. How many kinds of laws had the Jews before the coming of Our Lord?

A. Before the coming of Our Lord the Jews had three kinds of laws: 1.(1) Civil laws, regulating the affairs of their nation; 2. (2) Ceremonial laws, governing their worship in the temple; 3.(3) Moral laws, guiding their religious belief and actions.

Q. 1137. To which of these laws did the Ten Commandments belong?

A. The Ten Commandments belong to the moral law, because they are a compendium or short account of what we must do in order to save our souls; just as the Apostles' Creed is a compendium of what we must believe.

Q. 1138. When did the civil and ceremonial laws of the Jews cease to exist?

A. The civil laws of the Jews ceased to exist when the Jewish people, shortly before the coming of Christ, ceased to be an independent nation. The ceremonial laws ceased to exist when the Jewish religion ceased to be the true religion; that is, when Christ established the Christian religion, of which the Jewish religion was only a figure or promise.

Q. 1139. Why were not also the moral laws of the Jews abolished when the Christian religion was established?

A. The moral laws of the Jews could not be abolished by the establishment of the Christian religion because they regard truth and virtue and have been revealed by God, and whatever God has revealed as true must be always true, and whatever He has condemned as bad in itself must be always bad.

Lesson Thirtieth: On the First Commandment

Q. 1140. What is the first Commandment?

A. The first Commandment is: I am the Lord thy God: thou shalt not have strange gods before me.

Q. 1141. What does the commandment mean by "strange gods"?

A. By strange gods the commandment means idols or false gods, which the Israelites frequently worshipped when, through their sins, they had abandoned the true God.

Q. 1142. How may we, in a sense, worship strange gods?

A. We, in a sense, may worship strange gods by giving up the salvation of our souls for wealth, honors, society, worldly pleasures, etc., so that we would offend God, renounce our faith or give up the practice of our religion for their sake.

Q. 1143. How does the first Commandment help us to keep the great Commandment of the love of God?

A. The first Commandment helps us to keep the great Commandment of the love of God because it commands us to adore God alone.

Q. 1144. How do we adore God?

A. We adore God by faith, hope, and charity, by prayer and sacrifice.

Q. 1145. By what prayers do we adore God?

A. We adore God by all our prayers, but in particular by the public prayers of the Church, and, above all, by the Holy Sacrifice of the Mass.

Q. 1146. How may the first Commandment be broken?

A. The first Commandment make be broken by giving to a creature the honor which belongs to God alone; by false worship; and by attributing to a creature a perfection which belongs to God alone.

Q. 1147. What is the honor which belongs to God alone?

A. The honor which belongs to God alone is a divine honor, in which we offer Him sacrifice, incense or prayer, solely for His own sake and for His own glory. To give such honor to any creature, however holy, would be idolatry.

Q. 1148. How do we offer God false worship?

A. We offer God false worship by rejecting the religion He has instituted and following one pleasing to ourselves, with a form of worship He has never authorized, approved or sanctioned.

Q. 1149. Why must we serve God in the form of religion He has instituted and in no other?

A. We must serve God in the form of religion He has instituted and in no other, because heaven is not a right, but a promised reward, a free gift of God, which we must merit in the manner He directs and pleases.

Q. 1150. When do we attribute to a creature a perfection which belongs to God alone?

A. We attribute to a creature a perfection which belongs to God alone when we believe it possesses knowledge or power independently of God, so that it may, without His aid, make known the future or perform miracles.

Q. 1151. Do those who make use of spells and charms, or who believe in dreams, in mediums, spiritists, fortune-tellers, and the like, sin against the first Commandment?

A. Those who make use of spells and charms, or who believe in dreams, in mediums, spiritists, fortune-tellers, and the like, sin against the first Commandment, because they attribute to creatures perfections which belong to God alone.

Q. 1152. What are spells and charms?

A. Spells and charms are certain words, by the saying of which superstitious persons believe they can avert evil, bring good fortune or produce some supernatural or wonderful effect. They may be also objects or articles worn about the body for the same purpose.

Q. 1153. Are not Agnus Deis, medals, scapulars, etc., which we wear about our bodies also charms?

A. Agnus Deis, medals, scapulars, etc., which we wear about our bodies, are not charms, for we do not expect any help from these things themselves, but, through the blessing they have received from the Church, we expect help from God, the Blessed Mother, or the Saint in whose honor we wear them. On the contrary, they who wear charms expect help from the charms themselves, or from some evil spirit.

Q. 1154. What must we carefully guard against in all our devotions and religious practices?

A. In all our devotions and religious practices we must carefully guard against expecting God to perform miracles when natural causes may bring about what we hope for. God will sometimes miraculously help us, but, as a rule, only when all natural means have failed.

Q. 1155. What are dreams and why is it forbidden to believe in them?

A. Dreams are the thoughts we have in sleep, when our will is unable to guide them. It is forbidden to believe in them, because they are often ridiculous, unreasonable, or wicked, and are not governed by either reason or faith.

Q. 1156. Are bad dreams sinful in themselves?

A. Bad dreams are not sinful in themselves, because we cannot prevent them, but we may make them sinful:

1. (1) By taking pleasure in them when we awake, and 2. (2) By bad reading or immodest looks, thoughts, word or actions before going to sleep;

for by any of these things we may make ourselves responsible for the bad dreams.

Q. 1157. Did not God frequently in the Old Law make use of dreams as a means of making known His will?

A. God did frequently in the Old Law make use of dreams as a means of making known His Will; but on such occasions He always gave proof that what He made known was not a mere dream, but rather a revelation or inspiration. He no longer makes use of such means, for He now makes known His will through the inspiration of His Church.

Q. 1158. What are mediums and spiritists?

A. Mediums and spiritists are persons who pretend to converse with the dead or with spirits of the other world. They pretend also to give this power to others, that they may know what is going on in heaven, purgatory or hell.

Q. 1159. What other practice is very dangerous to faith and morals?

A. Another practice very dangerous to faith and morals is the use of mesmerism or hypnotism, because it is liable to sinful abuses, for it deprives a person for a time of the control of his reason and will and places his body and mind entirely in the power of another.

Q. 1160. What are fortune tellers?

A. Fortune tellers are imposters who, learning the past, or guessing at it, pretend to know also the future and to be able to reveal it to anyone who pays for the knowledge. They pretend also to know whatever concerns things lost or stolen, and the secret thoughts, actions or intentions of others.

Q. 1161. How do we, by believing in spells, charms, mediums, spiritists and fortune tellers, attribute to creatures the perfections of God?

A. By believing in spells, charms, mediums, spiritists and fortune tellers we attribute to creatures the perfections of God because we expect these creatures to perform miracles, reveal the hidden judgments of God, and make known His designs for the future with regard to His creatures, things that only God Himself may do.

Q. 1162. Is it sinful to consult mediums, spiritists, fortune tellers and the like when we do not believe in them, but through mere curiosity to hear what they may say?

A. It is sinful to consult mediums, spiritists, fortune tellers and the like even when we do not believe in them, but through mere curiosity, to hear what they may say:

1.(1) Because it is wrong to expose ourselves to the danger of sinning even though we do not sin; 2. (2) Because we may give scandal to others who are not certain that we go through mere curiosity; 3. (3) Because by our pretended belief we encourage these impostors to continue their wicked practices.

Q. 1163. Are sins against faith, hope, and charity also sins against the first Commandment?

A. Sins against faith, hope and charity are also sins against the first Commandment.

Q. 1164. How does a person sin against faith?

A. A person sins against faith:

1.1st. By not trying to know what God has taught; 2.2nd. By refusing to believe all that God has taught; 3.3rd. By neglecting to profess his belief in what God has taught.

Q. 1165. How do we fail to try to know what God has taught?

A. We fail to try to know what God has taught by neglecting to learn the Christian doctrine.

Q. 1166. What means have we of learning the Christian doctrine?

A. We have many means of learning the Christian doctrine: In youth we have Catechism and special instructions suited to our age; later we have sermons, missions, retreats, religious sodalities and societies through which we may learn. At all times, we have books of instruction, and, above all, the priests of the Church, ever ready to teach us. God will not excuse our ignorance if we neglect to learn our religion when He has given us the means.

Q. 1167. Should we learn the Christian doctrine merely for our own sake?

A. We should learn the Christian doctrine not merely for our own sake, but for the sake also of others who may sincerely wish to learn from us the truths of our holy faith.

Q. 1168. How should such instruction be given to those who ask it of us?

A. Such instruction should be given to those who ask it of us in a kind and Christian spirit, without dispute or bitterness. We should never attempt to explain the truths of our religion unless we are certain of what we say. When we are unable to answer what is asked we should send those who inquire to the priest or to others better instructed than ourselves.

Q. 1169. Who are they who do not believe all that God has taught?

A. They who do not believe all that God has taught are the heretics and infidels.

Q. 1170. Name the different classes of unbelievers and tell what they are.

A. The different classes of unbelievers are:

1. (1) Atheists, who deny there is a God; 2. (2) Deists, who admit there is a God, but deny that He revealed a religion; 3. (3) Agnostics, who will neither admit nor deny the existence of God; 4. (4) Infidels, who have never been baptized, and who, through want of faith, refuse to be baptized; 5. (5) Heretics, who have been baptized Christians, but do not believe all the articles of faith; 6. (6) Schismatics, who have been baptized and believe all the articles of faith, but do not submit to the authority of the Pope; 7. (7) Apostates, who have rejected the true religion, in which they formerly believed, to join a false religion; 8. (8) Rationalists and Materialists, who believe only in material things.

Q. 1171. Will the denial of only one article of faith make a person a heretic?

A. The denial of only one article of faith will make a person a heretic and guilty of mortal sin, because the Holy Scripture says: "Whosoever shall keep the whole law but offend in one point is become guilty of all."

Q. 1172. What is an article of faith?

A. An article of faith is a revealed truth so important and so certain that no one can deny or doubt it without rejecting the testimony of God. The Church very clearly points out what truths are articles of faith that we may distinguish them from pious beliefs and traditions, so that no one can be guilty of the sin of heresy without knowing it.

Q. 1173. Who are they who neglect to profess their belief in what God has taught?

A. They who neglect to profess their belief in what God has taught are all those who fail to acknowledge the true Church in which they really believe.

Q. 1174. How do persons who are members of the Church neglect to profess their belief?

A. Persons who are members of the Church neglect to profess their belief by living contrary to the teachings of the Church: that is, by neglecting Mass or the Sacraments, doing injury to their neighbor, and disgracing their religion by sinful and scandalous lives.

Q. 1175. What chiefly prevents persons who believe in the Church from becoming members of it?

A. A want of Christian courage chiefly prevents persons who believe in the Church from becoming members of it. They fear too much the opinion or displeasure of others, the loss of position or wealth, and, in general, the trials they may have to suffer for the sake of the true faith.

Q. 1176. What does Our Lord say of those who neglect the true religion for the sake of relatives or friends, or from fear of suffering?

A. Our Lord says of those who neglect the true religion for the sake of relatives or friends, or from fear of suffering: "He that loveth father or mother more than Me, is not worthy of Me; and he that loveth son or daughter more than Me, is not worthy of Me"; also: "And whosoever does not carry his cross and come after Me cannot be My disciple."

Q. 1177. What excuse do some give for neglecting to seek and embrace the true religion?

A. Some give as an excuse for neglecting to seek and embrace the true religion that we should live in the religion in which we were born, and that one religion is as good as another if we believe we are serving God.

Q. 1178. How do we show that such an excuse is false and absurd?

A. We show that such an excuse is false and absurd because:

1.(1) It is false and absurd to say that we should remain in error after we have discovered it; 2. (2) Because if one religion is as good as another, Our Lord would not have abolished the Jewish religion, nor the apostles have preached against heresy.

Q. 1179. Can they who fail to profess their faith in the true Church in which they believe expect to be saved while in that state?

A. They who fail to profess their faith in the true Church in which they believe cannot expect to be saved while in that state, for Christ has said: "Whosoever shall deny me before men, I will also deny him before my Father who is in heaven."

Q. 1180. Are we obliged to make open profession of our faith?

171

A. We are obliged to make open profession of our faith as often as God's honor, our neighbor's spiritual good or our own requires it. "Whosoever," says Christ, "shall confess me before men, I will also confess him before my Father who is in heaven."

Q. 1181. When does God's honor, our neighbor's spiritual good, or our own good require us to make an open profession of our faith?

A. God's honor, our neighbor's spiritual good, or our own good requires us to make an open profession of our faith as often as we cannot conceal our religion without violating some law of God or of His Church, or without giving scandal to others or exposing ourselves to the danger of sinning. Pious practices not commanded may often be omitted without any denial of faith.

Q. 1182. Which are the sins against hope?

A. The sins against hope are presumption and despair.

Q. 1183. What is presumption?

A. Presumption is a rash expectation of salvation without making proper use of the necessary means to obtain it.

Q. 1184. How may we be guilty of presumption?

A. We may be guilty of presumption:

1. (1) By putting off confession when in a state of mortal sin; 2. (2) By delaying the amendment of our lives and repentance for past sins; 3. (3) By being indifferent about the number of times we yield to any temptation after we have once yielded and broken our resolution to resist it; 4. (4) By thinking we can avoid sin without avoiding its near occasion; 5. (5) By relying too much on ourselves and neglecting to follow the advice of our confessor in regard to the sins we confess.

Q. 1185. What is despair?

A. Despair is the loss of hope in God's mercy.

Q. 1186. How may we be guilty of despair?

A. We may be guilty of despair by believing that we cannot resist certain temptations, overcome certain sins or amend our lives so as to be pleasing to God.

Q. 1187. Are all sins of presumption and despair equally great?

A. All sins of presumption and despair are not equally great. They may be very slight or very great in proportion to the degree in which we deny the justice or mercy of God.

Q. 1188. How do we sin against the love of God?

A. We sin against the love of God by all sin, but particularly by mortal sin.

Lesson Thirty-First: The First Commandment -- On the Honor and Invocation of the Saints

Q. 1189. Does the first Commandment forbid the honoring of the saints?

A. The first Commandment does not forbid the honoring of the saints, but rather approves of it; because by honoring the saints, who are the chosen friends of God, we honor God Himself.

Q. 1190. What does "invocation" mean?

A. Invocation means calling upon another for help or protection, particularly when we are in need or danger. It is used specially with regard to calling upon God or the saints, and hence it means prayer.

Q. 1191. How do we show that by honoring the Saints we honor God Himself?

A. We honor the Saints because they honor God. Therefore, it is for His sake that we honor them, and hence by honoring them we honor Him.

Q. 1192. Give another reason why we honor God by honoring the Saints.

A. Another reason why we honor God by honoring the Saints is this: As we honor our country by honoring its heroes, so do we honor our religion by honoring its Saints. By honoring our religion we honor God, who taught it. Therefore, by honoring the Saints we honor God, for love of whom they became religious heroes in their faith.

Q. 1193. Does the first Commandment forbid us to pray to the saints?

A. The first Commandment does not forbid us to pray to the saints.

Q. 1194. Why does the first commandment not forbid us to pray to the Saints?

A. The first commandment does not forbid us to pray to the Saints, because if we are allowed to ask the prayers of our fellow-creatures upon earth we should be allowed also to ask the prayers of our fellow-creatures in heaven. Moreover, the Saints must have an interest in our welfare, because whatever tends to make us good, tends also to the glory of God.

Q. 1195. What do we mean by praying to the saints?

A. By praying to the saints we mean the asking of their help and prayers.

Q. 1196. Do we not slight God Himself by addressing our prayers to saints?

A. We do not slight God Himself by addressing our prayers to saints, but, on the contrary, show a greater respect for His majesty and sanctity, acknowledging, by our prayers to the saints, that we are unworthy to address Him for ourselves, and that we, therefore, ask His holy friends to obtain for us what we ourselves are not worthy to ask.

Q. 1197. How do we know that the saints hear us?

A. We know that the saints hear us, because they are with God, who makes our prayers known to them.

Q. 1198. Why do we believe that the saints will help us?

A. We believe that the saints will help us because both they and we are members of the same Church, and they love us as their brethren.

Q. 1199. How are the saints and we members of the same Church?

A. The saints and we are members of the same Church, because the Church in heaven and the Church on earth are one and the same Church, and all its members are in communion with one another.

Q. 1200. What is the communion of the members of the Church called?

A. The Communion of the members of the Church is called the Communion of Saints.

Q. 1201. What does the communion of saints mean?

A. The communion of saints means the union which exists between the members of the Church on earth with one another, and with the blessed in Heaven, and with the suffering souls in Purgatory.

Q. 1202. What benefits are derived from the communion of saints?

A. The following benefits are derived from the communion of saints: the faithful on earth assist one another by their prayers and good works, and they are aided by the intercession of the saints in Heaven, while both the saints in Heaven and the faithful on earth help the souls in Purgatory.

Q. 1203. How can we best honor the Saints, and where shall we learn their virtues?

A. We can best honor the saints by imitating their virtues, and we shall learn their virtues from the written accounts of their lives. Among the Saints we shall find models for every age, condition or state of life.

Q. 1204. Does the first Commandment forbid us to honor relics?

A. The first Commandment does not forbid us to honor relics, because relics are the bodies of the saints or objects directly connected with them or with our Lord.

Q. 1205. How many kinds or classes of relics are there?

A. There are three kinds or classes of relics:

1.(1) The body or part of the body of a saint; 2. (2) Articles, such as clothing or books, used by the saint; 3. (3) Articles that have touched a relic of the body or other relic.

Q. 1206. What is there special about a relic of the true cross on which Our Lord Died, and also about the instruments of His Passion?

A. The relics of the true Cross and relics of the thorns, nails, etc., used in the Passion are entitled to a very special veneration, and they have certain privileges with regard to their use and the manner of keeping them that other relics have not. A relic of the true Cross is never kept or carried with other relics.

Q. 1207. What veneration does the Church permit us to give to relics?

A. The Church permits us to give relics a veneration similar to that we give images. We do not venerate the relics for their own sake, but for the sake of the persons they represent. The souls of canonized saints are certainly in heaven, and we are certain that their bodies also will be there. Therefore, we may honor their bodies because they are to be glorified in heaven and were sanctified upon earth.

Q. 1208. What care does the Church take in the examination and distribution of relics?

A. The Church takes the greatest care in the examination and distribution of relics.

1. (1) The canonization or beatification of the person whose relic we receive must be certain. 2. (2) The relics are sent in sealed packets, that must be opened only by the bishop of the diocese to which the relics are sent, and each relic or packet must be accompanied by a document or written paper proving its genuineness. 3. (3) The relics cannot be exposed for public veneration until the bishop examines them and pronounces them authentic; that is, that they are what they are claimed to be.

Q. 1209. What should we be certain of before using any relic or giving it to another?

A. Before using any relic or giving it to another we should be certain that all the requirements of the Church concerning it have been fulfilled, and that the relic really is, as far as it is possible for any one to know, what we believe it to be.

Q. 1210. Has God Himself honored relics?

A. God Himself has frequently honored relics by permitting miracles to be wrought through them. There is an example given in the Bible, in the IV Book of Kings, where it is related that a dead man was restored to life when his body touched the bones, that is, the relics of the holy prophet Eliseus.

Q. 1211. Does the first Commandment forbid the making of images?

A. The first Commandment does forbid the making of images if they are made to be adored as gods, but it does not forbid the making of them to put us in mind of Jesus Christ, His Blessed Mother, and the saints.

Q. 1212 How do we show that it is only the worship and not the making of images that is forbidden by the first commandment?

A. We show that it is only the worship and not the making of images that is forbidden by the first commandment:

1. (1) Because no one thinks it sinful to carve statues or make photographs or paintings of relatives or friends; 2. (2) Because God Himself commanded the making of images for the temple after He had given the first commandment, and God never contradicts Himself.

Q. 1213. Is it right to show respect to the pictures and images of Christ and His saints?

A. It is right to show respect to the pictures and images of Christ and His saints, because they are the representations and memorials of them.

Q. 1214. Have we in this country any civil custom similar to that of honoring the pictures and images of saints?

A. We have, in this country, a civil custom similar to that of honoring pictures and images of saints, for, on Decoration or Memorial Day, patriotic citizens place flowers, flags, or emblems about the statues of our deceased civil heroes, to honor the persons these statues represent; for just as we can dishonor a man by abusing his image, so we can honor him by treating it with respect and reverence.

Q. 1215. Is it allowed to pray to the crucifix or to the images and relics of the saints?

175

A. It is not allowed to pray to the crucifix or images and relics of the saints, for they have no life, nor power to help us, nor sense to hear us.

Q. 1216. Why do we pray before the crucifix and the images and relics of the saints?

A. We pray before the crucifix and the images and relics of the saints because they enliven our devotion by exciting pious affections and desires, and by reminding us of Christ and of the saints, that we may imitate their virtues.

Lesson Thirty-Second: From the Second to the Fourth Commandment

Q. 1217. What is the second Commandment?

A. The second Commandment is: Thou shalt not take the name of the Lord thy God in vain.

Q. 1218. What do you mean by taking God's name in vain?

A. By taking God's name in vain I mean taking it without reverence, as in cursing or using in a light and careless manner, as in exclamation.

Q. 1219. What are we commanded by the second Commandment?

A. We are commanded by the second Commandment to speak with reverence of God and of the saints, and of all holy things, and to keep our lawful oaths and vows.

Q. 1220. Is it sinful to use the words of Holy Scripture in a bad or worldly sense?

A. It is sinful to use the words of Holy Scripture in a bad or worldly sense, to joke in them or ridicule their sacred meaning, or in general to give them any meaning but the one we believe God has intended them to convey.

Q. 1221. What is an oath?

A. An oath is the calling upon God to witness the truth of what we say.

Q. 1222. How is an oath usually taken?

A. An oath is usually taken by laying the hand on the Bible or by lifting the hand towards heaven as a sign that we call God to witness that what we are saying is under oath and to the best of our knowledge really true.

Q. 1223. What is perjury?

A. Perjury is the sin one commits who knowingly takes a false oath; that is, swears to the truth of what he knows to be false. Perjury is a crime against the law of our country and a mortal sin before God.

Q. 1224. Who have the right to make us take an oath?

A. All persons to whom the law of our country has given such authority have the right to make us take an oath. They are chiefly judges, magistrates and public officials, whose duty it is to enforce the laws. In religious matters bishops and others to whom authority is given have also the right to make us take an oath.

Q. 1225. When may we take an oath?

A. We may take an oath when it is ordered by lawful authority or required for God's honor or for our own or our neighbor's good.

Q. 1226. When may an oath be required for God's honor or for our own or our neighbor's good?

A. An oath may be required for God's honor or for our own or our neighbor's good when we are called upon to defend our religion against false charges; or to protect our own or our neighbor's property or good name; or when we are required to give testimony that will enable the lawful authorities to discover the guilt or innocence of a person accused.

Q. 1227. Is it ever allowed to promise under oath, in secret societies or elsewhere, to obey another in whatever good or evil he commands?

A. It is never allowed to promise under oath, in secret societies or elsewhere, to obey another in whatever good or evil he commands, for by such an oath we would declare ourselves ready and willing to commit sin, if ordered to do so, while God commands us to avoid even the danger of sinning. Hence the Church forbids us to join any society in which such oaths are taken by its members.

Q. 1228. What societies in general are we forbidden to join?

A. In general we are forbidden to join:

1. (1) All societies condemned by the Church; 2. (2) All societies of which the object is unlawful and the means used sinful; 3. (3) Societies in which the rights and freedom of our conscience are violated by rash or dangerous oaths; 4. (4) Societies in which any false religious ceremony or form of worship is used.

Q. 1229. Are trades unions and benefit societies forbidden?

A. Trades unions and benefit societies are not in themselves forbidden because they have lawful ends, which they can secure by lawful means. The Church encourages every society that lawfully aids its members spiritually or temporally, and censures or disowns every society that uses sinful or unlawful means to secure even a good end; for the Church can never permit anyone to do evil that good may come of it.

Q. 1230. Is it lawful to vow or promise strict obedience to a religious superior?

A. It is lawful to vow or promise strict obedience to a religious superior, because such superior can exact obedience only in things that have the sanction of God or of His Church.

Q. 1231. What is necessary to make an oath lawful?

A. To make an oath lawful it is necessary that what we swear to be true, and that there be a sufficient cause for taking an oath.

Q. 1232. What is a vow?

A. A vow is a deliberate promise made to God to do something that is pleasing to Him.

Q. 1233. Which are the vows most frequently made?

A. The vows most frequently made are the three vows of poverty, chastity and obedience, taken by persons living in religious communities or consecrated to God. Persons living in the world are sometimes permitted to make such vows privately, but this should never be done without the advice and consent of their confessor.

Q. 1234. What do the vows of poverty, chastity and obedience require?

A. The vows of poverty, chastity and obedience require that those who make them shall not possess or keep any property or goods for themselves alone; that they shall not marry or be guilty of any immodest acts, and that they shall strictly obey their lawful superiors.

Q. 1235. Has it always been a custom with pious Christians to make vows and promises to God?

A. It has always been a custom with pious Christians to make vows and promises to God; to beg His help for some special end, or to thank Him for some benefit received. They have promised pilgrimages, good works or alms and they have vowed to erect churches, convents, hospitals or schools.

Q. 1236. What is a pilgrimage?

A. A pilgrimage is a journey to a holy place made in a religious manner and for a religious purpose.

Q. 1237. Is it a sin not to fulfill our vows?

A. Not to fulfill our vows is a sin, mortal or venial, according to the nature of the vow and the intention we had in making it.

Q. 1238. Are we bound to keep an unlawful oath or vow?

A. We are not bound, but, on the contrary, positively forbidden to keep an unlawful oath or vow. We are guilty of sin in taking such an oath or making such a vow, and we would be guilty of still greater sin by keeping them.

Q. 1239. What is forbidden by the second Commandment?

A. The second Commandment forbids all false, rash, unjust, and unnecessary oaths, blasphemy, cursing, and profane words.

Q. 1240. When is an oath rash, unjust or unnecessary?

A. An oath is rash when we are not sure of the truth of what we swear; it is unjust when it injures another unlawfully; and it is unnecessary when there is no good reason for taking it.

Q. 1241. What is blasphemy, and what are profane words?

A. Blasphemy is any word or action intended as an insult to God. To say He is cruel or find fault with His works is blasphemy. It is a much greater sin than cursing or taking God's name in vain. Profane words mean here bad, irreverent or irreligious words.

Q. 1242. What is the third Commandment?

A. The third Commandment is: Remember thou keep holy the Sabbath day.

Q. 1243. What are we commanded by the third Commandment?

A. By the third Commandment we are commanded to keep holy the Lord's day and the holydays of obligation, on which we are to give our time to the service and worship of God.

Q. 1244. What are holydays of obligation?

A. Holydays of obligation are special feasts of the Church on which we are bound, under pain of mortal sin, to hear Mass and to keep from servile or bodily labors when it can be done without great loss or inconvenience. Whoever, on account of their circumstances, cannot give up work on holydays of obligation should make every effort to hear Mass and should also explain in confession the necessity of working on holydays.

Q. 1245. How are we to worship God on Sundays and holydays of obligation?

A. We are to worship God on Sundays and holydays of obligation by hearing Mass, by prayer, and by other good works.

Q. 1246. Name some of the good works recommended for Sunday.

A. Some of the good works recommended for Sunday are: The reading of religious books or papers, teaching Catechism, bringing relief to the poor or sick, visiting the Blessed Sacrament, attending Vespers, Rosary or other devotions in the Church; also attending the meetings of religious sodalities or societies. It is not necessary to spend the whole Sunday in such good works, but we should give some time to them, that for the love of God we may do a little more than what is strictly commanded.

Q. 1247. Is it forbidden, then, to seek any pleasure or enjoyment on Sunday?

A. It is not forbidden to seek lawful pleasure or enjoyment on Sunday, especially to those who are occupied during the week, for God did not intend the keeping of the Sunday to be a punishment, but a benefit to us. Therefore, after hearing Mass we may take such recreation as is necessary or useful for us; but we should avoid any vulgar, noisy or disgraceful amusements that turn the day of rest and prayer into a day of scandal and sin.

Q. 1248. Are the Sabbath day and the Sunday the same?

A. The Sabbath day and the Sunday are not the same. The Sabbath is the seventh day of the week, and is the day which was kept holy in the old law; the Sunday is the first day of the week, and is the day which is kept holy in the new law.

Q. 1249. What is meant by the Old and New Law?

A. The Old Law means the law or religion given to the Jews; the New Law means the law or religion given to Christians.

Q. 1250. Why does the Church command us to keep the Sunday holy instead of the Sabbath?

A. The Church commands us to keep the Sunday holy instead of the Sabbath because on Sunday Christ rose from the dead, and on Sunday He sent the Holy Ghost upon the Apostles.

Q. 1251. Do we keep Sunday instead of Saturday holy for any other reason?

A. We keep Sunday instead of Saturday holy also to teach that the Old Law is not now binding upon us, but that we must keep the New Law, which takes its place.

Q. 1252. What is forbidden by the third Commandment?

A. The third Commandment forbids all unnecessary servile work and whatever else may hinder the due observance of the Lord's day.

Q. 1253. What are servile works?

A. Servile works are those which require labor rather of body than of mind.

Q. 1254. From what do servile works derive their name?

A. Servile works derive their name from the fact that such works were formerly done by slaves. Therefore, reading, writing, studying and, in general, all works that slaves did not perform are not considered servile works.

Q. 1255. Are servile works on Sunday ever lawful?

A. Servile works are lawful on Sundays when the honor of God, the good of our neighbor, or necessity requires them.

Q. 1256. Give some examples of when the honor of God, the good of our neighbor or necessity may require servile works on Sunday.

A. The honor of God, the good of our neighbor or necessity may require servile works on Sunday, in such cases as the preparation of a place for Holy Mass, the saving of property in storms or accidents, the cooking of meals and similar works.

Lesson Thirty-Third: From the Fourth to the Seventh Commandment

Q. 1257. What is the fourth Commandment?

A. The fourth Commandment is: Honor thy father and thy mother.

Q. 1258. What does the word "honor" in this commandment include?

A. The word "honor" in this commandment includes the doing of everything necessary for our parents' spiritual and temporal welfare, the showing of proper respect, and the fulfillment of all our duties to them.

Q. 1259. What are we commanded by the fourth Commandment?

A. We are commanded by the fourth Commandment to honor, love and obey our parents in all that is not sin.

Q. 1260. Why should we refuse to obey parents or superiors who command us to sin?

A. We should refuse to obey parents or superiors who command us to sin because they are not then acting with God's authority, but contrary to it and in violation of His laws.

Q. 1261. Are we bound to honor and obey others than our parents?

A. We are also bound to honor and obey our bishops, pastors, magistrates, teachers, and other lawful superiors.

Q. 1262. Who are meant by magistrates?

A. By magistrates are meant all officials of whatever rank who have a lawful right to rule over us and our temporal possessions or affairs.

Q. 1263. Who are meant by lawful superiors?

A. By lawful superiors are meant all persons to whom we are in any way subject, such as employers or others under whose authority we live or work.

Q. 1264. What is the duty of servants or workmen to their employers?

A. The duty of servants or workmen to their employers is to serve them faithfully and honestly, according to their agreement, and to guard against injuring their property or reputation.

Q. 1265. Have parents and superiors any duties toward those who are under their charge?

A. It is the duty of parents and superiors to take good care of all under their charge and give them proper direction and example.

Q. 1266. If parents or superiors neglect their duty or abuse their authority in any particular, should we follow their direction and example in that particular?

A. If parents or superiors neglect their duty or abuse their authority in any particular we should not follow their direction or example in that particular, but follow the dictates of our conscience in the performance of our duty.

Q. 1267. What is the duty of employers to their servants or workmen?

A. The duty of employers to their servants or workmen is to see that they are kindly and fairly treated and provided for, according to their agreement, and that they are justly paid their wages at the proper time.

Q. 1268. What is forbidden by the fourth Commandment?

A. The fourth Commandment forbids all disobedience, contempt, and stubbornness towards our parents or lawful superiors.

Q. 1269. What is meant by contempt and stubbornness?

A. By contempt is meant willful disrespect for lawful authority, and by stubbornness is meant willful determination not to yield to lawful authority.

Q. 1270. What is the fifth Commandment?

A. The fifth Commandment is: Thou shalt not kill.

Q. 1271. What killing does this commandment forbid?

A. This commandment forbids the killing only of human beings.

Q. 1272. How do we know that this commandment forbids the killing only of human beings?

A. We know that this commandment forbids the killing only of human beings because, after giving this commandment, God commanded that animals be killed for sacrifice in the temple of Jerusalem, and God never contradicts Himself.

Q. 1273. What are we commanded by the fifth Commandment?

A. We are commanded by the fifth Commandment to live in peace and union with our neighbor, to respect his rights, to seek his spiritual and bodily welfare, and to take proper care of our own life and health.

Q. 1274. What sin is it to destroy one's own life, or commit suicide, as this act is called?

A. It is a mortal sin to destroy one's own life or commit suicide, as this act is called, and persons who willfully and knowingly commit such an act die in a state of mortal sin and are deprived of Christian burial. It is also wrong to expose one's self unnecessarily to the danger of death by rash or foolhardy feats of daring.

Q. 1275. Is it ever lawful for any cause to deliberately and intentionally take away the life of an innocent person?

A. It is never lawful for any cause to deliberately and intentionally take away the life of an innocent person. Such deeds are always murder, and can never be excused for any reason, however important or necessary.

Q. 1276. Under what circumstances may human life be lawfully taken?

A. Human life may be lawfully taken:

1. (1) In self-defense, when we are unjustly attacked and have no other means of saving our own lives; 2. (2) In a just war, when the safety or rights of the nation require it; 3. (3) By the lawful execution of a criminal, fairly tried and found guilty of a crime punishable by death when the preservation of law and order and the good of the community require such execution.

Q. 1277. What is forbidden by the fifth Commandment?

A. The fifth Commandment forbids all willful murder, fighting, anger, hatred, revenge, and bad example.

Q. 1278. Can the fifth commandment be broken by giving scandal or bad example and by inducing others to sin?

A. The fifth commandment can be broken by giving scandal or bad example and inducing others to sin, because such acts may destroy the life of the soul by leading it into mortal sin.

Q. 1279. What is scandal?

A. Scandal is any sinful word, deed or omission that disposes others to sin, or lessens their respect for God and holy religion.

Q. 1280. Why are fighting, anger, hatred and revenge forbidden by the fifth commandment?

A. Fighting, anger, hatred and revenge are forbidden by the fifth commandment because they are sinful in themselves and may lead to murder. The commandments forbid not only whatever violates them, but also whatever may lead to their violation.

Q. 1281. What is the sixth Commandment?

A. The sixth Commandment is: Thou shalt not commit adultery.

Q. 1282. What are we commanded by the sixth Commandment?

A. We are commanded by the sixth Commandment to be pure in thought and modest in all our looks, words, and actions.

Q. 1283. It is a sin to listen to immodest conversation, songs or jokes?

A. It is a sin to listen to immodest conversation, songs or jokes when we can avoid it, or to show in any way that we take pleasure in such things.

Q. 1284. What is forbidden by the sixth Commandment?

A. The sixth Commandment forbids all unchaste freedom with another's wife or husband; also all immodesty with ourselves or others in looks, dress, words, and actions.

Q. 1285. Why are sins of impurity the most dangerous?

A. Sins of impurity are the most dangerous:

1. (1) Because they have the most numerous temptations; 2. (2) Because, if deliberate, they are always mortal, and 3. (3) Because, more than other sins, they lead to the loss of faith.

Q. 1286. Does the sixth Commandment forbid the reading of bad and immodest books and newspapers?

A. The sixth Commandment does forbid the reading of bad and immodest books and newspapers.

Q. 1287. What should be done with immodest book and newspapers?

A. Immodest books and newspapers should be destroyed as soon as possible, and if we cannot destroy them ourselves we should induce their owners to do so.

Q. 1288. What books does the Church consider bad?

A. The Church considers bad all books containing teaching contrary to faith or morals, or that willfully misrepresent Catholic doctrine and practice.

Q. 1289. What places are dangerous to the virtue of purity?

A. Indecent theaters and similar places of amusement are dangerous to the virtue of purity, because their entertainments are frequently intended to suggest immodest things.

Lesson Thirty-Fourth: From the Seventh to the End of the Tenth Commandment

Q. 1290. What is the seventh Commandment?

A. The seventh Commandment is: Thou shalt not steal.

Q. 1291. What sin is it to steal?

A. To steal is a mortal or venial sin, according to the amount stolen either at once or at different times. Circumstances may make the sin greater or less, and they should be explained in confession.

Q. 1292. Is stealing ever a sacrilege?

A. Stealing is a sacrilege when the thing stolen belongs to the Church and when the stealing takes place in the Church.

Q. 1293. What sins are equivalent to stealing?

A. All sins of cheating, defrauding or wronging others of their property; also all sins of borrowing or buying with the intention of never repaying are equivalent to stealing.

Q. 1294. In what other ways may persons sin against honesty?

A. Persons may sin against honesty also by knowingly receiving, buying or sharing in stolen goods; likewise by giving or taking bribes for dishonest purposes.

Q. 1295. What are we commanded by the seventh Commandment?

A. By the seventh Commandment we are commanded to give to all men what belongs to them and to respect their property.

Q. 1296. How may persons working for others be guilty of dishonesty?

A. Persons working for others may be guilty of dishonesty by idling the time for which they are paid; also by doing bad work or supplying bad material without their employer's knowledge.

Q. 1297. In what other way may a person be guilty of dishonesty?

A. A person may be guilty of dishonesty in getting money or goods by false pretenses and by using either for purposes for which they were not given.

Q. 1298. What is forbidden by the seventh Commandment?

A. The seventh Commandment forbids all unjust taking or keeping what belongs to another.

Q. 1299. What must we do with things found?

A. We must return things found to their lawful owners as soon as possible, and we must also use reasonable means to find the owners if they are unknown to us.

Q. 1300. What must we do if we discover we have bought stolen goods?

A. If we discover we have bought stolen goods and know their lawful owners we must return the goods to them as soon as possible without demanding compensation from the owner for what we paid for the goods.

Q. 1301. Are we bound to restore ill-gotten goods?

A. We are bound to restore ill-gotten goods, or the value of them, as far as we are able; otherwise we cannot be forgiven.

Q. 1302. What must we do if we cannot restore all we owe, or if the person to whom we should restore be dead?

A. If we cannot restore all we owe, we must restore as much as we can, and if the person to whom we should restore be dead we must restore to his children or heirs, and if these cannot be found we may give alms to the poor.

Q. 1303. What must one do who cannot pay his debts and yet wishes to receive the Sacraments?

A. One who cannot pay his debts and yet wishes to receive the Sacraments must sincerely promise and intend to pay them as soon as possible, and must without delay make every effort to do so.

Q. 1304. Are we obliged to repair the damage we have unjustly caused?

A. We are bound to repair the damage we have unjustly caused.

Q. 1305. What is the eighth Commandment?

A. The eighth Commandment is: Thou shalt not bear false witness against thy neighbor.

Q. 1306. What are we commanded by the eighth Commandment?

A. We are commanded by the eighth Commandment to speak the truth in all things, and to be careful of the honor and reputation of every one.

Q. 1307. What is a lie?

A. A lie is a sin committed by knowingly saying what is untrue with the intention of deceiving. To swear to a lie makes the sin greater, and such swearing is called perjury. Pretense, hypocrisy, false praise, boasting, etc., are similar to lies.

Q. 1308. How can we know the degree of sinfulness in a lie?

A. We can know the degree of sinfulness in a lie by the amount of harm it does and from the intention we had in telling it.

Q. 1309. Will a good reason for telling a lie excuse it?

A. No reason, however good, will excuse the telling of a lie, because a lie is always bad in itself. It is never allowed, even for a good intention to do a thing that is bad in itself.

Q. 1310. What is forbidden by the eighth Commandment?

A. The eighth Commandment forbids all rash judgments, backbiting, slanders, and lies.

Q. 1311. What are rash judgment, backbiting, slander and detraction?

A. Rash judgment is believing a person guilty of sin without a sufficient cause. Backbiting is saying evil things of another in his absence. Slander is telling lies about another with the intention of injuring him. Detraction is revealing the sins of another without necessity.

Q. 1312. Is it ever allowed to tell the faults of another?

A. It is allowed to tell the faults of another when it is necessary to make them known to his parents or superiors, that the faults may be corrected and the wrong doer prevented from greater sin.

Q. 1313. What is tale-bearing, and why is it wrong?

A. Tale-bearing is the act of telling persons what others have said about them, especially if the things said be evil. It is wrong, because it gives rise to anger, hatred and ill-will, and is often the cause of greater sins.

Q. 1314. What must they do who have lied about their neighbor and seriously injured his character?

A. They who have lied about their neighbor and seriously injured his character must repair the injury done as far as they are able, otherwise they will not be forgiven.

Q. 1315. What is the ninth Commandment?

A. The ninth Commandment is: Thou shalt not covet thy neighbor's wife.

Q. 1316. What are we commanded by the ninth Commandment?

A. We are commanded by the ninth Commandment to keep ourselves pure in thought and desire.

Q. 1317. What is forbidden by the ninth Commandment?

A. The ninth Commandment forbids unchaste thoughts, desires of another's wife or husband, and all other unlawful impure thoughts and desires.

Q. 1318. Are impure thoughts and desires always sins?

A. Impure thoughts and desires are always sins, unless they displease us and we try to banish them.

Q. 1319. What is the tenth Commandment?

A. The tenth Commandment is: Thou shalt not covet thy neighbor's goods.

Q. 1320. What does covet mean?

A. Covet means to wish to get wrongfully what another possesses or to begrudge his own to him.

Q. 1321. What are we commanded by the tenth Commandment?

A. By the tenth Commandment we are commanded to be content with what we have, and to rejoice in our neighbor's welfare.

Q. 1322. Should we not, then, try to improve our position in the world?

A. We should try to improve our position in the world, provided we can do so honestly and without exposing ourselves to greater temptation or sin.

Q. 1323. What is forbidden by the tenth Commandment?

A. The tenth Commandment forbids all desires to take or keep wrongfully what belongs to another.

Q. 1324. In what does the sixth commandment differ from the ninth, and the seventh differ from the tenth?

A. The sixth commandment differs from the ninth in this, that the sixth refers chiefly to external acts of impurity, while the ninth refers more to sins of thought against purity. The seventh commandment refers chiefly to external acts of dishonesty, while the tenth refers more to thoughts against honesty.

Lesson Thirty-Fifth: On the First and Second Commandments of the Church

Q. 1325. Are not the commandments of the Church also commandments of God?

A. The commandments of the Church are also commandments of God, because they are made by His authority, and we are bound under pain of sin to observe them.

Q. 1326. What is the difference between the commandments of God and the Commandments of the Church?

A. The commandments of God were given by God Himself to Moses on Mount Sinai; the commandments of the Church were given on different occasions by the lawful authorities of the Church. The Commandments given by God Himself cannot be changed by the Church; but the commandments made by the Church itself may be changed by its authority as necessity requires.

Q. 1327. Which are the chief commandments of the Church?

A. The chief commandments of the Church are six:

1. To hear Mass on Sundays and holydays of obligation. 2. To fast and abstain on the days appointed. 3. To confess at least once a year. 4. To receive the Holy Eucharist during the Easter time. 5. To contribute to the support of our pastors. 6. Not to marry persons who are not Catholics, or who are related to us within the third degree of kindred, nor privately without witnesses, nor to solemnize marriage at forbidden times.

Q. 1328. Why has the Church made commandments?

A. The Church has made commandments to teach the faithful how to worship God and to guard them from the neglect of their religious duties.

Q. 1329. Is it a mortal sin not to hear Mass on a Sunday or a holyday of obligation?

A. It is a mortal sin not to hear Mass on a Sunday or a holyday of obligation, unless we are excused for a serious reason. They also commit a mortal sin who, having others under their charge, hinder them from hearing Mass, without a sufficient reason.

Q. 1330. What is a "serious reason" excusing one from the obligation of hearing Mass?

A. A "serious reason" excusing one from the obligation of hearing Mass is any reason that makes it impossible or very difficult to attend Mass, such as severe illness, great distance from the Church, or the need of certain works that cannot be neglected or postponed.

Q. 1331. Are children obliged, under pain of mortal sin, the same as grown persons, to hear Mass on Sundays and holydays of obligation?

A. Children who have reached the use of reason are obliged under pain of mortal sin, the same as grown persons, to hear Mass on Sundays and holydays of obligation; but if they are prevented from so doing by parents, or others, then the sin falls on those who prevent them.

Q. 1332. Why were holydays instituted by the church?

A. Holydays were instituted by the Church to recall to our minds the great mysteries of religion and the virtues and rewards of the saints.

Q. 1333. How many holydays of obligation are there in this country?

A. In this country there are six holydays of obligation, namely:

1. (1) Feast of the Immaculate Conception (Dec. 8th);
2. (2) Christmas (Dec. 25th);
3. (3) Feast of the Circumcision of Our Lord (Jan. 1st);
4. (4) Feast of the Ascension of Our Lord (forty days after Easter);
5. (5) Feast of the Assumption of the Blessed Virgin (Aug. 15th); and
6. (6) Feast of All Saints (Nov. 1st).

Q. 1334. How should we keep the holydays of obligation?

A. We should keep the holydays of obligation as we should keep the Sunday.

Q. 1335. Why are certain holydays called holydays of obligation?

A. Certain holydays are called holydays of obligation because on such days we are obliged under pain of mortal sin to hear Mass and keep from servile works as we do on Sundays.

Q. 1336. What should one do who is obliged to work on a holyday of obligation?

A. One who is obliged to work on a holyday of obligation should, if possible, hear Mass before going to work, and should also explain this necessity in confession, so as to obtain the confessor's advice on the subject.

Q. 1337. What do you mean by fast-days?

A. By fast-days I mean days on which we are allowed but one full meal.

Q. 1338. Is it permitted on fast days to take any food besides the one full meal?

A. It is permitted on fast days, besides the one full meal, to take two other meatless meals, to maintain strength, according to each one's needs. But together these two meatless meals should not equal another full meal.

Q. 1339. Who are obliged to fast?

A. All persons over 21 and under 59 years of age, and whose health and occupation will permit them to fast.

Q. 1340. Does the Church excuse any classes of persons from the obligation of fasting?

A. The Church does excuse certain classes of persons from the obligation of fasting on account of their age, the condition of their health, the nature of their work, or the circumstances in which they live. These things are explained in the Regulations for Lent, read publicly in the Churches each year.

Q. 1341. What should one do who doubts whether or not he is obliged to fast?

A. In doubt concerning fast, a parish priest or confessor should be consulted.

Q. 1342. When do fast days chiefly occur in the year?

A. Fast days chiefly occur in the year during Lent and Advent, on the Ember days and on the vigils or eves of some great feasts. A vigil falling on a Sunday is not observed.

Q. 1343. What do you mean by Lent, Advent, Ember days and the vigils of great feasts?

A. Lent is the seven weeks of penance preceding Easter. Advent is the four weeks of preparation preceding Christmas. Ember days are three days set apart in each of the four seasons of the year as special days of prayer and thanksgiving. Vigils are the days immediately preceding great feasts and spent in spiritual preparation for them.

Q. 1344. What do you mean by days of abstinence?

A. By days of abstinence I mean days on which no meat at all may be taken (complete abstinence) or on which meat may be taken only once a day (partial abstinence). This is explained in the regulations for Lent. All the Fridays of the year are days of abstinence except when a Holyday of obligation falls on a Friday outside of Lent.

Q. 1345. Are children and persons unable to fast bound to abstain on days of abstinence?

A. Children, from the age of seven years, and persons who are unable to fast are bound to abstain on days of abstinence, unless they are excused for sufficient reason.

Q. 1346. Why does the Church command us to fast and abstain?

A. The Church commands us to fast and abstain, in order that we may mortify our passions and satisfy for our sins.

Q. 1347. What is meant by our passions and what by mortifying them?

A. By our passions are meant our sinful desires and inclinations. Mortifying them means restraining them and overcoming them so that they have less power to lead us into sin.

Q. 1348. Why does the Church command us to abstain from flesh-meat on Fridays?

A. The Church commands us to abstain from flesh-meat on Fridays in honor of the day on which our Saviour died.

Lesson Thirty-Sixth: On the Third, Fourth, Fifth, and Sixth Commandments of the Church

Q. 1349. What is meant by the command of confessing at least once a year?

A. By the command of confessing at least once a year is meant that we are obliged, under pain of mortal sin, to go to confession within the year.

Q. 1350. Should we confess only once a year?

A. We should confess frequently, if we wish to lead a good life.

Q. 1351. Should we go to confession at our usual time even if we think we have not committed sin since our last confession?

A. We should go to confession at our usual time even if we think we have not committed sin since our last confession, because the Sacrament of Penance has for its object not only to forgive sins, but also to bestow grace and strengthen the soul against temptation.

Q. 1352. Should children go to confession?

A. Children should go to confession when they are old enough to commit sin, which is commonly about the age of seven years.

Q. 1353. What sin does he commit who neglects to receive Communion during the Easter time?

A. He who neglects to receive Communion during the Easter time commits a mortal sin.

Q. 1354. What is the Easter time?

A. The Easter time is, in this country, the time between the first Sunday of Lent and Trinity Sunday.

Q. 1355. When is Trinity Sunday?

A. Trinity Sunday is the Sunday after Pentecost, or eight weeks after Easter Sunday; so that there are fourteen weeks in which one may comply with the command of the Church to receive Holy Communion between the first Sunday of Lent and Trinity Sunday.

Q. 1356. Are we obliged to contribute to the support of our pastors?

A. We are obliged to contribute to the support of our pastors, and to bear our share in the expense of the Church and school.

Q. 1357. Where did the duty of contributing to the support of the Church and clergy originate?

A. The duty of contributing to the support of the Church and clergy originated in the Old Law, when God commanded all the people to contribute to the support of the temple and of its priests.

Q. 1358. What does the obligation of supporting the Church and school imply?

A. The obligation of supporting the Church and school implies the duty of making use of the Church and school by attending religious worship in the one and by giving Catholic education in the other; because if the Church and school were not necessary for our spiritual welfare we would not be commanded to support them.

Q. 1359. Does the fifth commandment of the Church include the support only of our pastors and the Church and school?

A. The fifth commandment of the Church includes the support also of our holy father, the Pope, bishops, priests, missions, religious institutions and religion in general.

Q. 1360. What is the meaning of the commandment not to marry within the third degree of kindred?

A. The meaning of the commandment not to marry within the third degree of kindred is that no one is allowed to marry another within the third degree of blood relationship.

Q. 1361. Who are in the third degree of blood relationship?

A. Second cousins are in the third degree of blood relationship, and persons whose relationship is nearer than second cousins are in closer degrees of kindred. It is unlawful for persons thus related to marry without a dispensation or special permission of the Church.

Q. 1362. Are there other relationships besides blood relationship that render marriage unlawful without a dispensation?

A. There are other relationships besides blood relationship that render marriage unlawful without a dispensation, namely, the relationships contracted by marriage, which are called degrees of affinity, and the relationship contracted by being sponsors at Baptism, which is called spiritual affinity.

Q. 1363. What should persons about to marry do, if they suspect they are related to each other?

A. Persons about to marry, if they suspect they are related to each other, should make known the facts to the priest, that he may examine the degree of relationship and procure a dispensation if necessary.

Q. 1364. What is the meaning of the command not to marry privately?

A. The command not to marry privately means that none should marry without the blessing of God's priests or without witnesses.

Q. 1365. What sin is it for Catholics to be married before the minister of another religion?

A. It is a mortal sin for Catholics to be married before the minister of another religion, and they who attempt to do so incur excommunication, and absolution from their sin is reserved to the bishop.

Q. 1366. What is the meaning of the precept not to solemnize marriage at forbidden times?

A. The meaning of the precept not to solemnize marriage at forbidden times is that during Lent and Advent the marriage ceremony should not be performed with pomp or a nuptial Mass.

Q. 1367. What is the nuptial Mass?

A. The nuptial Mass is a Mass appointed by the Church to invoke a special blessing upon the married couple.

Q. 1368. Should Catholics be married at a nuptial Mass?

A. Catholics should be married at a nuptial Mass, because they thereby show greater reverence for the holy Sacrament and bring richer blessings upon their wedded life.

Q. 1369. What restrictions does the Church place on the ceremonies of marriage when one of the persons is not a Catholic?

A. The Church places several restrictions on the ceremonies of marriage when one of the persons is not a Catholic. The marriage cannot take place in the church; the priest cannot wear his sacred vestments nor use holy water nor bless the ring nor the marriage itself. The Church places these restrictions to show her dislike for such marriages, commonly called mixed marriages.

Q. 1370. Why does the Church dislike mixed marriages?

A. The Church dislikes mixed marriages because such marriages are frequently unhappy, give rise to many disputes, endanger the faith of the Catholic member of the family, and prevent the religious education of the children.

Lesson Thirty-Seventh: On the Last Judgment and the Resurrection, Hell, Purgatory, and Heaven

Q. 1371. When will Christ judge us?

A. Christ will judge us immediately after our death, and on the last day.

Q. 1372. What is the judgment called which we have to undergo immediately after death?

A. The judgment we have to undergo immediately after death is called the Particular Judgment.

Q. 1373. Where will the particular judgment be held?

A. The particular judgment will be held in the place where each person dies, and the soul will go immediately to its reward or punishment.

Q. 1374. What is the judgment called which all men have to undergo on the last day?

A. The judgment which all men have to undergo on the last day is called the General Judgment.

Q. 1375. Will the sentence given at the particular judgment be changed at the general judgment?

A. The sentence given at the particular judgment will not be changed at the general judgment, but it will be repeated and made public to all.

Q. 1376. Why does Christ judge men immediately after death?

A. Christ judges men immediately after death to reward or punish them according to their deeds.

Q. 1377. How may we daily prepare for our judgment?

A. We may daily prepare for our judgment by a good examination of conscience, in which we will discover our sins and learn to fear the punishment they deserve.

Q. 1378. What are the rewards or punishments appointed for men's souls after the Particular Judgment?

A. The rewards or punishments appointed for men's souls after the Particular Judgment are Heaven, Purgatory, and Hell.

Q. 1379. What is Hell?

A. Hell is a state to which the wicked are condemned, and in which they are deprived of the sight of God for all eternity, and are in dreadful torments.

Q. 1380. Will the damned suffer in both mind and body?

A. The damned will suffer in both mind and body, because both mind and body had a share in their sins. The mind suffers the "pain of loss" in which it is tortured by the thought of having lost God forever, and the body suffers the "pain of sense" by which it is tortured in all its members and senses.

Q. 1381. What is Purgatory?

A. Purgatory is the state in which those suffer for a time who die guilty of venial sins, or without having satisfied for the punishment due to their sins.

Q. 1382. Why is this state called Purgatory?

A. This state is called Purgatory because in it the souls are purged or purified from all their stains; and it is not, therefore, a permanent or lasting state for the soul.

Q. 1383. Are the souls in Purgatory sure of their salvation?

A. The souls in Purgatory are sure of their salvation, and they will enter heaven as soon as they are completely purified and made worthy to enjoy that presence of God which is called the Beatific Vision.

Q. 1384. Do we know what souls are in Purgatory, and how long they have to remain there?

A. We do not know what souls are in Purgatory nor how long they have to remain there; hence we continue to pray for all persons who have died apparently in the true faith and free from mortal sin. They are called the faithful departed.

Q. 1385. Can the faithful on earth help the souls in Purgatory?

A. The faithful on earth can help the souls in Purgatory by their prayers, fasts, alms, deeds; by indulgences, and by having Masses said for them.

Q. 1386. Since God loves the souls in Purgatory, why does He punish them?

A. Though God loves the souls in Purgatory, He punishes them because His holiness requires that nothing defiled may enter heaven and His justice requires that everyone be punished or rewarded according to what he deserves.

Q. 1387. If every one is judged immediately after death, what need is there of a general judgment?

A. There is need of a general judgment, though every one is judged immediately after death, that the providence of God, which, on earth, often permits
the good to suffer and the wicked to prosper, may in the end appear just before all men.

Q. 1388. What is meant by "the Providence of God"?

A. By "the Providence of God" is meant the manner in which He preserves,
provides for, rules and governs the world and directs all things by His infinite Will.

Q. 1389. Are there other reasons for the general judgment?

A. There are other reasons for the general judgment, and especially that
Christ Our Lord may receive from the whole world the honor denied Him at
His first coming, and that all may be forced to acknowledge Him their God
and Redeemer.

**Q. 1390. Will our bodies share in the reward or punishment of our
souls?**

A. Our bodies will share in the reward or punishment of our souls, because
through the resurrection they will again be united to them.

**Q. 1391. When will the general resurrection or rising of all the dead
take place?**

A. The general resurrection or rising of all the dead will take place at the
general judgment, when the same bodies in which we lived on earth will
come forth from the grave and be united to our souls and remain united with
them forever either in heaven or in hell.

Q. 1392. In what state will the bodies of the just rise?

A. The bodies of the just will rise glorious and immortal.

Q. 1393. Will the bodies of the damned also rise?

A. The bodies of the damned will also rise, but they will be condemned to
eternal punishment.

Q. 1394. Why do we show respect for the bodies of the dead?

A. We show respect for the bodies of the dead because they were the
dwelling-place of the soul, the medium through which it received the Sacraments, and because they were created to occupy a place in heaven.

Q. 1395. What is Heaven?

A. Heaven is the state of everlasting life in which we see God face to face,
are made like unto Him in glory, and enjoy eternal happiness.

Q. 1396. In what does the happiness in heaven consist?

A. The happiness in heaven consists in seeing the beauty of God, in knowing Him as He is, and in having every desire fully satisfied.

Q. 1397. What does St. Paul say of heaven?

A. St. Paul says of heaven, "That eye hath not seen. nor ear heard, neither
hath it entered into the heart of man what things God hath prepared for them
that love Him." (I. Cor. ii., 9.)

**Q. 1398. Are the rewards in heaven and the punishments in hell the
same for all who enter into either of these states?**

A. The rewards of heaven and the punishments in hell are not the same for all who enter into either of these states, because each one's reward or punishment is in proportion to the amount of good or evil he has done in this world. But as heaven and hell are everlasting, each one will enjoy his reward or suffer his punishment forever.

Q. 1399. What words should we bear always in mind?

A. We should bear always in mind these words of our Lord and Saviour Jesus Christ: "What doth it profit a man if he gain the whole world and suffer the loss of his own soul, or what exchange shall a man give for his soul? For the Son of man shall come in the glory of His Father with His angels; and then will He render to every man according to his works."

Q. 1400. Name some of the more essential religious truths we must know and believe.

A. Some of the more essential religious truths we must know and believe are:

1. (1) That there is but one God, and He will reward the good and punish the wicked.

2. (2) That in God there are three Divine Persons: the Father, the Son, and the Holy Ghost, and these Divine Persons are called the Blessed Trinity.

3. (3) That Jesus Christ, the Second Person of the Blessed Trinity, became man and died for our redemption.

4. (4) That the grace of God is necessary for our salvation.

5. (5) That the human soul is immortal.

Printed in the USA
CPSIA information can be obtained
at www.ICGtesting.com
LVHW091524151223
766290LV00003B/38